C000146998

Money from Nothing

Indebtedness and Aspiration in South Africa

Deborah James

Stanford University Press
Stanford, California

Stanford University Press
Stanford, California

© 2015 by the Board of Trustees of the Leland Stanford Junior University. All rights reserved.

No part of this book may be reproduced or transmitted in any form or by any means, electronic or mechanical, including photocopying and recording, or in any information storage or retrieval system without the prior written permission of Stanford University Press.

Printed in the United States of America on acid-free, archival-quality paper

Library of Congress Cataloging-in-Publication Data

James, Deborah, Dr., author.
  Money from nothing : indebtedness and aspiration in South Africa / Deborah James.
    pages cm
  Includes bibliographical references and index.
    ISBN 978-0-8047-9111-3 (cloth : alk. paper)—ISBN 978-0-8047-9267-7 (pbk. : alk. paper)
    1. Debt—South Africa.   2. Consumer credit—South Africa.   3. Social mobility—South
Africa.   4. Social status—South Africa.   5. Consumption (Economics)—South Africa.
6. Blacks—South Africa—Economic conditions.   7. Blacks—South Africa—Social
conditions.   8. South Africa—Social conditions—1994-   I. Title.
  HG3756.S6J36 2015
  332.70968—dc23
                                                                              2014025920

    ISBN 978-0-8047-9315-5 (electronic)

Published in southern African countries (Angola, Botswana, Democratic Republic of Congo, Lesotho, Madagascar, Malawi, Mauritius, Mozambique, Namibia, Seychelles, South Africa, Swaziland, United Republic of Tanzania, Zambia, and Zimbabwe) by WITS UNIVERSITY PRESS.

Typeset by Newgen in 10/14 Minion

Money from Nothing

To my parents, David and Jenepher James

And in memory of Colin Murray, mentor
and friend since my student days

Contents

Illustrations

Tables

Acknowledgments

THE FIELD RESEARCH for this book, conducted during 2007 and 2008, involved the incurring of many debts. Getting myself into the field involved particular challenges, given that I was engaged in the tough and unforgiving administrative task of chairing my department at the time. I am grateful to all who helped and held discussions with me and helped me navigate my way around how to investigate this difficult topic: Belinda Bozzoli, Mareesa Erasmus, Nickle Felgate, Frans Haupt, Isabel Hofmeyr, Sekibakiba Lekgoathi, Abigail Mlate, Khumisho Moguerane, Christopher Mulaudzi, Isak Niehaus, Geoffrey Nkadimeng, Charles van Onselen, Nokuthula Skhosana, and Glenda Webster. Xolela May and Elroy Paulus, both then in the Black Sash, also gave invaluable assistance. Others who generously gave their time to talk to me were Vangile Bingma, Livia Chiloane, Lesedi Dibakwane, Marlene Heymans, Mduduzi Hlabangane, Dawn Jackson, Daisy Mohlala, Cynthia Makgobane, Phoebe Mashile, Lindiwe Malinga, Nosa Mashile, Bongi Mhlanga, Richard Mutshekwane, Chutie Namane, Koti Ngobeni, Modiegi Nong, Sisinyane Pholo, Daphney Shiba, Paul Slot, Daphney Smith, Carolyn Stauffer, Thomas Thale, Mpho Thekiso, Dudu Thobela, Mavis Thobela, Johannes Tshoeu, Carel Van Aardt, and Garth Whitford. The list goes on, and it would take pages to name everybody. If I have omitted anyone, I apologize: but those not listed here are named in the book. I also owe a lot to those who assisted me in the field: Sputla Thobela, Eliazaar Mohlala, Daphney Shiba, Rosemary Ngunyula. Jens Andersson and Judith Wolf generously accommodated me when I was in the Lowveld. Thanks to Annie de Sa, who transcribed numerous interviews, Caitlin Pearson, who did the index, and Wendy Phillips, who drew the maps.

The research was part of a team effort, funded by Grant RES-062-23-1290 by the Economic and Social Research Council of the United Kingdom for the project "Investing, Engaging in Enterprise, Gambling and Getting into Debt: Popular Economies and Citizen Expectations in South Africa," which I gratefully acknowledge. Opinions expressed in this book are my own.

Although the book is not a joint effort but is based largely on the research I did as my part of the project, it has been informed by the many discussions, formal and informal, which I had with the research team members and by their own writings, both published and unpublished, that resulted. Those wishing to know more are invited to look at the joint publishing effort that came out of the project—a special issue of the journal *Africa*, vol. 82, no. 1: "Popular Economies in South Africa"—as well as the project website (http://www2.lse.ac.uk/anthro pology/research/popular_economies/). My grateful thanks to Erik Bähre, Max Bolt, Lizzy Hull, Detlev Krige, Fraser McNeill, David Neves, and Ilana van Wyk for their inspiring academic companionship over the two years of the project. All have gone on to do great things, fully justifying the faith I had in their abilities from the beginning.

If one measures academic influence and collegiality like ripples spreading out from the center of a pool, the next ring of people to thank are the participants in the workshops that were run as part of the project. Particular gratitude to Keith Hart, who has been both academic mentor and guiding light from early in the project's conception. Catherine Alexander, Max Bolt, Sophie Chevalier, and Robert Ross all made valuable comments and gave excellent insights. For his inspiring mentorship in the longer term, I am—as ever—grateful to Adam Kuper.

For help in planning and carrying out the final workshop, the intention of which was dissemination to the wider public, the ripples of gratitude spread yet further. Thanks to Belinda Bozzoli and Liz Gunner, then both at the Wits Institute for Social and Economic Research (WISER), Witwatersrand University, who made it possible to hold the 2010 event on their premises; to Najibha Deshmukh, for her excellent administrative skills; and to Linda Mabin, for acting as an able assistant. I am extremely grateful to Nic Dawes, then editor of the *Mail and Guardian* newspaper, for agreeing to give the keynote address at that workshop; and to Andreas Dafinger, Penny Hawkins, Marlene Heymans, Sam Masinga, Krishen Sukdev, Stuart Theobald, and Louise Whittaker, for their contributions to it.

Many colleagues offered valuable insights when I presented versions of the material in this book at various departmental seminars during the period 2010–12. My gratitude to Laura Bear and my colleagues in the Anthropology Department at the London School of Economics (LSE); Mukulika Banerjee and those attending the department's staff research seminar at LSE; Tom Boylston and members of the Africa seminar at LSE; Kate Meagher and the Department of International Development at LSE; Sophie Day and the Anthropology Department at Goldsmiths College; Andreas Dafinger and faculty members at Central European University in Budapest; Gerhard Anders and faculty members at University of Zurich; Elizabeth Ewart and the Anthropology Department at Oxford University; John Bowen and those attending the Department of Anthropology's seminar at Washington University in St. Louis; Astrid Ludin and members of the of the Max Planck Institute, Halle; Brinkley Messick and members of the anthropology faculty at Columbia University; Keith Breckenridge and Catherine Burns and those attending the seminar at WISER, Witwatersrand University; Kees van der Waal and the Department of Sociology and Anthropology, Stellenbosch University.

I also presented material at a number of conferences during the same period: thanks to Gerhard Anders and those attending the CAS@50 conference, University of Edinburgh; Keith Hart and Sophie Chevalier and those attending the European Association of Social Anthropologists conference, Nanterre; Holly High and those attending the conference "Debt: Interdisciplinary Considerations of an Enduring Human Passion," Centre for Research in the Arts, Social Sciences and Humanities, Cambridge University; Karen Sykes and those attending the conference "The Value Question Today: Interdisciplinary Perspectives on the Moral Economy," University of Manchester; Susana Narotzky and those attending the workshop on moral economies at Universitat Barcelona; and (again) Susana Narotzky and Nico Besnier and those attending the Wenner-Gren conference "Crisis, Value, and Hope: Rethinking the Economy," Sintra, Portugal.

Heartfelt gratitude to Professor Hendrik Geyer, Maria Mouton, Goldi van Heerden, Nel-Mari Loock, the other staff members, and all my co-fellows at the Stellenbosch Institute for Advanced Study, Wallenberg Research Centre, at Stellenbosch University, South Africa, for giving me a wonderfully conducive and quiet place to think and write while I was finishing this book. I am indebted to the Mellon Foundation for a generous grant that made it possible for me to spend time at Witwatersrand University while I was attending to the book's final details; to Peter Delius and Hylton White, who invited me and to all who showed me warmth and hospitality during my visit; and to Geoff Stacey and Annie Smythe, for accommodating me.

I am also grateful to those who kindly read the manuscript and offered valuable comments: Ruben Andersson, Tom Boylston, Lizzy Hull, and Patrick Pearson. Thanks to the Black Sash for permission to use the front cover of the handbook *Debt and Credit* and to the Johannesburg Housing Company for permission to use its budget form.

Finally, as usual, warm and heartfelt expressions of gratitude to my family for various forms of hospitality, nurture, and support. To my parents, David and Jenepher James, and my parents-in-law, Norman and Lynne Pearson, for extending a warm welcome whenever I was visiting South Africa on fieldwork, and especially to Nicholas James and Jennifer Daniels for putting me up in Johannesburg. To my stepson Nickle and his wife, Nicky (and later the beautiful Juliet), and my stepson Oskar and his wife, Siobhan; thanks for warm companionship in Johannesburg and help with some details of the research. To my children, Ben and Caitlin; and my husband, Patrick, thanks for putting up with my absences and for rallying around to support one another during them. Particular thanks to Patrick, who was there every night on the other end of Skype to do the *Guardian* crossword. I am, as always, more than grateful, and then some.

Abbreviations

ABIL	African Bank Investments Limited
ANC	African National Congress
ASCRA	Accumulated Savings and Credit Associations
BEE	Black Economic Empowerment
COSATU	Congress of South African Trade Unions
DFID	Department for International Development
DTI	Department of Trade and Industry
FNB	First National Bank
GTZ	Deutsche Gesellschaft für Technische Zusammenarbeit
LSM	Living Standards Measure
NCA	National Credit Act
NDM	National Democratic Movement
SACP	South African Communist Party
SANNC	South African Native National Congress
SASOL	South African Coal, Oil, and Gas Corporation
STD	Standard Bank
TRC	Truth and Reconciliation Commission

Non-English Words and Phrases

bohlabela	those of the East (seSotho)
e a lekana	it is equal (seSotho)
bangane	friends (xiTsonga)
geld	money (Afrikaans)
go balabala	to emphasize (seSotho)
go bea	to lay down or save (seSotho)
go bêrêka	to work (seSotho)
go hlôkômêla lapa	to care for the household (seSotho)
go ja	to eat (seSotho)
go ja tšhêlêtê	to waste money (seSotho)
go tšintšala	to exchange
ilobolo/lobola	bridewealth (isiZulu)
induna	headman, farm foreman (isiZulu)
ka kgwêdi	on account, lit. by the month (seSotho)
kapolô	removing mourning clothes, lit. unveiling
leoto	wheel (seSotho)
mashonisa	informal moneylender, loan shark (isiZulu)
modulasetulô	chairperson, leader
mošatê	chief's place (seSotho)

nama, e a fella	flesh, from the head to the legs (seSotho)
patêla	to pay (seSotho, from the Afrikaans, *betaal*)
samp	dried corn kernels that have been stamped until broken (native American origin)
sekôlôtô	debt (seSotho), from the Afrikaans, *skuld*, to owe; to have guilt.
skuld	debt, guilt (Afrikaans)
spaza	small informal retailer
setokofela	*stokvel*, savings club (seSotho)
stokvel	savings club (township vernacular, from "stock fair")
thiakene machaka	build yourselves, relatives (xiTonga)
thušanang	help each other
toyi-toyi	a protest dance (township vernacular)
tšhêlêtê	money (seSotho), from the Afrikaans, *geld*
unamêla kamêla	ride the camel (seSotho)

A Note on Currency

DURING 2008 AND 2009, the period of research, the South African rand fluctuated: on average it was equal to £0.07 GBP and US$0.12.

That is, R10 = 0.70 pence or US$1.20; R100 = £7 or US$12.00.

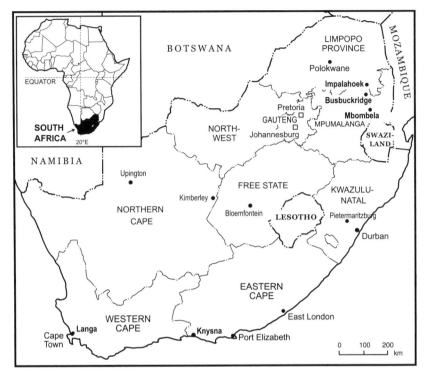

Map 1 Map of South Africa showing field sites and places mentioned in the text
Source: Drawn by Wendy Phillips.

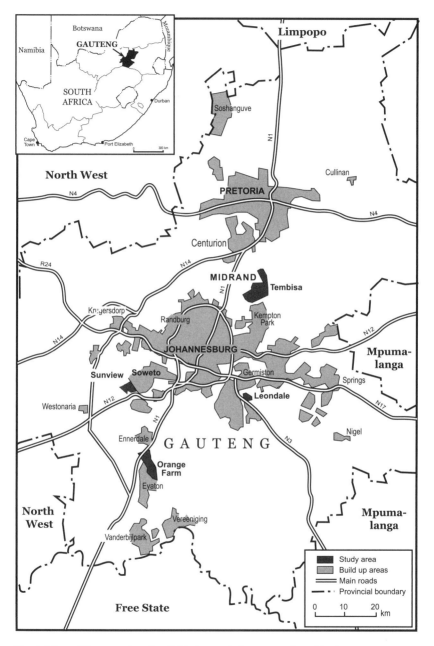

Map 2 Map of Gauteng showing field sites and places mentioned in the text
Source: Drawn by Wendy Phillips.

Introduction

The Wellsprings of Consumption and Debt in South Africa

AS APARTHEID CAME to an end in 1994, the world watched and rejoiced at the dramatic death of a brutal regime. Work had already begun to reverse its worst effects. The Truth and Reconciliation Commission sought to uncover the horrors and brutality wrought by the security forces, and the land reform program aimed to restore the ownership rights of the black majority. At the same time, a surprise in the eyes of many, a neoliberal-style economy was being created. This was unexpected given the Marxist orientation of the African National Congress (ANC) and its Moscow-aligned emphasis on the nationalization of assets, but it was deemed important in order to secure investor confidence and to smooth the transition. The novel economic policy, however, had unforeseen consequences, one of which was what appeared to be significant rates of indebtedness in the population. Statistics showed that many people were getting in over their heads. This had its roots not only in the changes that had taken place—the creation of a new black middle class seemed difficult to achieve without recourse to credit—but also in the historical legacy of apartheid itself. Policy makers soon recognized that issues of credit and indebtedness, in turn, would require new legislation: "consumer" rights had never seemed as pressing as the "human" ones denied during apartheid, but they were now in need of urgent attention.

As consumers' new aspirations were unleashed, it began to appear that the freedom to exercise political choice was being paralleled—even outstripped—by the freedom to engage in conspicuous consumption. "I didn't join the revolution to be poor," said one prominent government spokesperson. The media reported that he and his ilk were consuming glitzy and even kitschy goods and

1

branded products, and they criticized the allegedly shallow values of the newly upwardly mobile. The superficiality of consumerism did not seem to fit with the seriousness of the egalitarian aspirations that originally motivated South Africa's transition.

Particularly worrying to those in the policy world was the fact that the pursuit of such new forms of consumption often seemed to be attended by stress and suffering. The moment of freedom was accompanied, and made possible, by something with the appearance of its opposite: that is, indebtedness, often described as the modern equivalent of slavery or peonage. The offering and taking up of credit was expanded and "democratized" in an unprecedented way in South Africa after 1994, and there has been much decrying of the unsustainable levels of consumer borrowing that have resulted.

Seen from one perspective, this simply sounds like the local version of a worldwide story: the expansion of credit to the "subprime" parts of society and the resulting global financial crisis. But the angry criticisms in the South African press of the banking and credit sector did not echo the clamor of those being leveled at the global financial system. They *preceded* them by several years, as this book will clarify. The content of the criticisms chimes, though, with remarkable resonance. Graeber's coruscating analysis of the way the newly financialized credit system acted with impunity to create money from nothing, all the while confident that victims would be forced to bail the system out when it collapsed like a giant Ponzi scheme (2011, 373), might well have been written about South Africa in the 1990s rather than the United States in the 2000s.

Besides the time lag, there are other differences that mark off the South African case. In South Africa, it is the borrowers rather than the lenders upon whom the spotlight, in the end, has fallen. And within that borrower community, those upon whom concern is mainly focused, and those who are the intended object of state regulatory measures, are blacks rather than whites.[1] They are also earners rather than the under- or unemployed. Concerning the first of these criteria: surveys and statistics do not reveal race to be an important correlative of indebtedness. Analyses that give attention to racial categories show, on the contrary, that white consumers have owed more than black ones through the postdemocracy period. But those whose borrowing has been of greatest concern are the people mostly previously excluded, by a "dual economy of credit" or "credit apartheid,"[2] from borrowing of any kind.

Concerning the second criterion, surveys reveal that those with the greatest levels of debt after 1994 were not the unemployed or the poorest of the poor but were salary and wage earners in the middle of the scale. Echoing what happens in many other settings where stable pay packets are subjected to less-than-stable pressures (see Parry 2012), the fact that people earn a regular salary means that they qualify for credit, but the obligations and expenditures they incur by virtue of their position in the workforce "places pressure on them to borrow at a level that is unsustainable" (Daniels 2004, 842).

It was, then, largely borrowers, and those belonging to the burgeoning new and aspirant black middle class, who were put under the microscope. This group in its present guise was largely brought into being, or substantially expanded, as a result of processes set in motion after the dawn of the new democracy, especially under President Thabo Mbeki's government, and their cares and concerns carried considerable weight. They continued to do so during the period of office of his successor, Jacob Zuma, although his populist "man of the people" stance gave the middle class less overt prominence.

Whatever the president and whatever his approach, the political clout of the black middle class since the advent of democracy in South Africa has thus been of great significance. One reason for this is the key role of the trade union federation Congress of South African Trade Unions (COSATU) in the governing tripartite alliance. This federation traditionally represented workers in the commercial sector, but workers in the public service now outnumber them. And the public service too has changed: it is now largely staffed by black employees, whereas whites formerly predominated. The ranks of salaried workers, especially recipients of state salaries (e.g., nurses, teachers, police officers), alongside lower- to middle-level employees in councils, municipalities, and parastatals (enterprises in which the state, if no longer an owner, is a majority shareholder), are admittedly smaller in number and thus electorally less influential than the vast majority of poorer people and the unemployed.[3] But it is this group whose spending and borrowing habits have been a cause of particular concern to the government.

The words used here—*plight, problem, stress, suffering*—indicate a negative view of debt and indebtedness. This view has been highlighted, and questioned, by Gustav Peebles, in a 2010 review of anthropological writings on debt. The idea that "debt is bad" is widespread. It is often accompanied by the assumption that "credit is good" (Peebles 2010, 226), without much thought about the way the two are intrinsically connected. His point prompts one to question whether the new consumerism of South Africa's post-1994 social order might be viewed from a vantage point that celebrates the benefits rather than condemns the disadvantages of borrowing, thus viewing debt "in the 'positive' light of an en-abling condition" (Shneiderman 2011, 9).[4] Attending to this kind of perspec-tive, the way new opportunities for credit were suddenly made available after 1994 to those who had been denied them beforehand, arguably offered con-siderable advantage. Having access to loans helped to unleash the inventively hybrid novelty and creativity of a new generation of consumers, thus facilitat-ing that generation's "transformative social potentials" (Nuttall 2004, 451; see also Mbembe 2004). The things people bought, less easily quantifiable than the money they borrowed, were believed to be necessary: debt was thus justified. Such ideas of worth contested the assumption that one single measure—that is, money—be used to measure value and demand repayment.

Furthermore, credit could be seen as having enabled the expansion of that very same middle class, laying the grounds for its present and future politi-cal and economic role. That expansion in turn made possible South Africa's negotiated settlement, postponing (though perhaps not indefinitely) whatever more populist and revolutionary tendencies might be waiting in the wings. The money householders were able to borrow was thus of crucial importance in the story of South Africa's transition, perhaps much more than what anyone expected or realized.[5]

Whether we take the negative or the positive view, whether we focus on the repayment obligations incurred later or the material possibilities afforded in the here and now, two anecdotal examples give us an idea of the character and wide spread of the phenomenon. Both were reported in newspapers in December 2012. One, carried by the national weekly *Mail and Guardian*, is a story about the ruling elite: the other, in the *Wall Street Journal*, focuses on an earner with a humbler income. The first concerns President Jacob Zuma, a man loyally supported by poorer sectors of the electorate but often derided by the more cosmopolitan for his tendency to live beyond his means. Respond-ing to heated speculation about whether state resources were used to fund the rebuilding of his luxury home, Zuma initially maintained that he had paid for it himself by taking out a mortgage. But the newspaper leaked a secret auditors' report, revealing that he had received money from a variety of sources. These ranged from businesspeople wishing to buy influence or seeking government contracts to large commercial banks that had "bent over backwards to accom-modate Zuma because of his political position ... despite the fact that [he] had a terrible credit profile and defaulted regularly."[6]

The second story concerns the insurance salesman Gerald Mopelong, described as a "working class South African." Up to a third of his salary, he says, goes toward paying for "basics like gas and food as well as relative luxuries like new clothes for his teenage children." Although he is "always squeezed" to repay his bills, "lenders ranging from curbside loan sharks to South Africa's biggest banks want him to borrow even more." The article goes on to describe the extent of unsecured lending—personal loans, unsecured debt, and overdrafts that are not backed by assets such as houses—that "has allowed many . . . to bridge their earnings and the lifestyles they aspire to have."[7]

These examples demonstrate the wide spectrum of earners affected by the indebtedness epidemic (or enabled by the credit bonanza). They also point to the fact that, for people at either end of the spectrum, loans from commercial banks coexist with those that come from beyond the official financial sector. In the first newspaper report, on Jacob Zuma, the nonbank providers were businesspeople seeking political influence; in the second, they were loan sharks charging high rates of interest. The big banks and other formal financial institutions have certainly been more dominant in the South African economy than they are in the economies of other African countries. Adding to its influence, the financial sector "deepened" considerably between 1995 and 2000, when efforts were made to "bank the unbanked" and when a number of new and smaller lenders joined those banks in offering loans.[8] But this deepening did not displace the unofficial counterpart of the banks. Rather, that counterpart—sometimes dubbed "informal"—grew larger, deepened, and became more financialized in turn.

How did this curious interweaving of economic formality and informality come into being? To answer this question, it is necessary to say something about the setting in which attempts to control credit apartheid took root, as well as the nature of the regime that originally allowed lending to flourish and later tried to curb it. While some have characterized postapartheid South Africa as "neoliberal" (Marais 2011, 139), others have debated the usefulness of that term. Ideologies privileging free-market capitalism were certainly widespread, and aspects of "millennial" capitalism became prevalent after the rapid liberalization of the 1990s (Comaroff and Comaroff 2000), but the actual extent and influence of market models was limited. The attempted privileging of the market as a harbinger of change was, indeed, made possible only through state-initiated planning and regulatory frameworks, such as black economic empowerment. Government intervention was also necessary to effect redistribution. Many have become dependent on pensions, disability, or child support grants, further evidence of the role of the state in what at first appears a thoroughgoing market economy. Although some maintain that state regulation—especially since the financial crisis—has become increasingly integral to the neoliberal project,[9] others claim that the existence of considerable state spending means that South Africa cannot easily be described as a classic case in which market models have free reign; the country, rather, has been characterized as possessing a "distributional regime" (Seekings and Nattrass 2005, 314). Or, as I have written elsewhere, "neoliberal means serve to ensure the ever wider spread of redistribution" (James 2012, 37).[10]

At the same time that the economy was rapidly liberalizing, it was also, in the late 1990s and early 2000s, becoming extensively financialized: something that, in the absence of investment in manufacturing and production, has been seen as accounting for South Africa's "jobless growth" during that period.[11] Black consumers of all kinds began to take advantage of the credit opportunities they had previously been denied, and particular sectors of the white community started microlending businesses to cater to and exploit this new market. This was accompanied by, and often necessitated, the opening of bank accounts and the associated registering of clients' personal details by retailers (i.e., "banking the unbanked"), often with ready access to earlier records as captured during the apartheid regime (Breckenridge 2005, 2010). Shortly thereafter, demonstrating what was to become its characteristic combination of market-driven and regulatory tendencies, the state—whose policies, during the 1990s, had initially enabled such developments by opening up the economy and the provision of credit in one fell swoop—then sought, during the 2000s, to regulate the negative effects of this borrowing by passing new legislation to outlaw "reckless lending."[12]

Resulting from these impulses that followed each other in short order, and exhibiting varying degrees of legal formality, three distinct lending sectors were in evidence by the late 2000s. Each one, supplementing or plugging gaps left by the other two, supplied this new market in its own way. Reflecting the ethnic and racial divisions of South Africa's past and of its new dispensation, each has a linguistic-ethnic specificity. First, and by far the biggest, is the mainstream or formal financial sector, historically dominated by an "oligopoly" of British-owned banks and rooted in the English-speaking capitalist sector (Verhoef 2009, 157, 181). Here, the "big four" banks—Absa, First National, Nedbank,

Standard—have been predominant. Alongside the credit cards, housing loans, and vehicle finance it offers, the sector also provides store cards for clothing and food, loans for furniture and appliances, and the like. Blacks, having had very restricted access to such loans before the 1990s under credit apartheid, were offered them in profusion thereafter. Second is the new microlending sector, which offers mostly smaller and short-term loans. It grew exponentially in the 1990s and was mostly run by Afrikaans-speaking former civil servants who invested their redundancy (severance) packages in these businesses. They did so after leaving state employ when the ANC became the ruling party. Initially free to charge "uncapped" interest rates, and engaging in practices that were later prohibited—such as the confiscation and use of borrowers' ATM cards by way of loan security—many of these subsequently registered as microlenders under the National Credit Act, which obliged them to charge monthly interest of no more than 44 percent. Third, more difficult to quantify, are the *mashonisas*, or neighborhood moneylenders.[13] The sector, growing proportionately to its formal microlending counterpart, came to be defined by its difference to that counterpart: its protagonists were defined as loan sharks because they remained unregistered under the act. (Since borrowers are often ignorant of the regulations, some use the term *mashonisa*, however, to refer to both registered and unregistered lenders). The biggest operators among them use customers' ATM cards to withdraw the money owed to them at month's end before returning the cards to their owners, and they typically charge monthly interest of 50 percent, in excess of the new cap on the interest rate imposed by the act. In this classically financialized manner, taking advantage of efforts that had been made to bank the unbanked, some community moneylenders were ensuring repayment by continuing to use the techniques earlier deployed, but now outlawed for use, by those who were now registered (and hence considered "formal" and "regulated").

There will be more about the close relationships between formal and informal arrangements (Guyer 2004; Hart 1973, 2010) as the book progresses. For the moment, let us return to the "revolution" that the government spokesperson cited earlier "didn't join to be poor." South Africa did not, in fact, have a revolution as many expected it would. Instead, it experienced what radical critics have called an "elite transition," or at least one with "limits," leaving the power of capitalism largely intact but under a novel guise.[14] The terms established by that negotiated settlement meant that whatever revolution South Africa did experience was one of a different kind. It was one that opened up the possibility of borrowing to many who were formerly denied it, who aimed—like both President Zuma and Gerald Mopelong at opposite ends of the scale—to be able to bridge the gap between their earnings and the lifestyles to which they aspired. There was, though, something specific about South Africa's credit-debt revolution. Coming on top of the credit apartheid that preceded this period of reckless lending, the sudden unleashing of loans was bound to have effects that were racially skewed. This book explores how the long-term obligations entailed in debt are connected to the long-term expectations (and hoped-for consequences) of upward mobility. If the repayments are left to be made in the future, the lifestyles they are intended to procure likewise remain, in many cases, looked forward to rather than achieved in the here and now.

As it turns out, the precipitous onset of borrowing possibilities that were unleashed by this credit-debt revolution did not—as might have been thought inevitable—uniformly intensify the character of South African capitalism. Instead, it mediated that capitalism in a number of ways. The book aims to illuminate some of the underpinnings and contradictory aspects of this situation. It illustrates how difficult it is to separate "bad" from "good" protagonists; "perpetrators" from "victims," and "benefactors" from "beneficiaries." Many of those who lend money borrow it as well; conversely, borrowers are also lenders. Challenging the idea that we are in the presence of a total change, the book also shows how householders, savings club members, intermediaries, repossession agents, debt collectors, and debt counselors all play roles premised on older arrangements.

Seen over the long term, the situation resulting from these interrelated roles, positions, and interests may turn out to be transitional, but for the time being it seems entrenched. Whether the situation is of long or short duration, the book shows how forces of state and market intertwine to create a redistributive neoliberalism in which people at all levels attempt to make "money from nothing." As the banks did with the poor housing purchasers in the subprime mortgage market in the United States, so a far wider spectrum of lenders does to a wider spectrum of borrowers in South Africa. In both cases, gaining access to the money—however small the amount—of the widest possible range of people is essential to generate profit in a system based more on consumption than production.

Researching Debt and Credit

My awareness that this was a topic demanding attention was prompted during a field trip to South Africa in 2006, well before issues of debt had hit the headlines elsewhere. At that point, critical attention was being directed at the creditors rather than the debtors. Reports in the newspapers, and discussion and phone-in shows on the radio, were resonant with talk of a crisis of indebtedness, largely caused, it was claimed, by reckless lending. There was talk, too, of the effects—hoped for, if not yet experienced—of the National Credit Act that had recently been passed. Interested in investigating the realities of indebtedness, but convinced that this needed to be done in context, a team of researchers of which I was part proposed to explore a range of "popular economies," in which getting into debt would be considered alongside a series of related activities such as investing, saving, owning property, and engaging in enterprise. My own research, conducted during 2007 and 2008, took debt as its particular focus in this broader field.

Debt was a topic that posed particular challenges. The reluctance of people to discuss their personal finances, especially where these showed them up as owing money they were ashamed of being unable to repay, was a key problem. A second concerned people's unwillingness to discuss illegal moneylending (or borrowing), especially given that this had just been legislated against by the government. Even registered or formal lenders and retailers, wary of being found responsible for recklessness and of facing sanction under the new legislation, were—not surprisingly—cautious about admitting whatever role they might have played in creating the situation. Faced with such understandable circumspection, I in turn found circumspection to be the best remedy. Tales offered up, in the abstract, about well-known moneylenders, and stories recounted, in general terms, about the "scams" practiced by furniture store repossession agents, proved easier to gather and discuss than did firsthand accounts from those subjected to the dealings of such lenders and agents, or from the agents themselves. People were more willing to give insights into their own and their families' histories of banking or saving money, and of buying items "on tick," than to recount the details of their current financial situation. They were also often more ready to comment on others' habits of profligacy or frugality than on their own. Topics eliciting positive attitudes, like savings clubs and funeral societies, were readily discussed, although their darker underside of unpayable subscriptions and unmet contributions was less available for commentary. Cross-checked against other sources, this information proved useful despite the awkwardness of the subject matter.

The nature of the topic also made it necessary to record examples from different settings rather than being deeply acquainted with particular locales, and to analyze practices in a variety of socioeconomic settings rather than sticking to one or two. Researching this topic thus meant exploring diverse contexts, places, and types of actors. Given that the ranks of those who aspire to join the new middle class, in both rural and urban contexts, far outnumber those who have succeeded in doing so, I undertook interview-based research and participant observation across a range of settings. My existing research base in South Africa, however, allowed me to locate specific ethnographic case studies and examples in a wider context, as with the extended case method (see Evens and Handelman 2006, 27). My informants included medium- to well-paid employees of the government based in Pretoria (Gauteng Province); low- to middle-income wage earners in Sunview, a neighborhood of Soweto, and Tembisa (Gauteng Province); and villagers in Impalahoek, a village formerly zoned in one of South Africa's homelands (now in Mpumalanga Province), where civil servants like teachers and nurses are neighbors of those who hold lower-wage jobs.[15] In all these settings, earners live cheek by jowl with large numbers of the unemployed, who often depend on them. While some informants sought anonymity, others were keen to be cited, and I have respected their wishes.

Issues in South African life are extensively commented upon, discussed, and engaged with by political actors and activists, and matters are widely reported in the press and narrated in fictional representations. This wider set of discussions formed an important backdrop to the case study material. Attending to this wider context, I moved beyond specific field locales to direct attention to policy discourses and the pronouncements of agents within the state, the corporate sector, and the world of charitable and nongovernmental organizations. I also spoke to employees in the banking sector and the owners of microlending businesses. Being attentive to those who seek to regulate or curb the activities of lenders, and those charged with advising borrowers, I talked to debt counselors and sat in on sessions they held with their clients, in Pretoria and Midrand (Gauteng Province) and in Cape Town and Knysna (Western Cape Province). To gain insight into the more subjective experiences of debt and aspiration, I read novels, written in South Africa's equivalent of nineteenth-century realism, like Mehlaleng Mosotho's *The Tikieline Yuppie* (1998) and Miriam Tlali's *Muriel at Metropolitan* (1988),[16] and I consulted works of investigative journalism like David Cohen's *People Who Have Stolen from Me* (2004) and Jonny Steinberg's *Thin Blue: The Unwritten Rules of Policing South Africa* (2008).

Underpinning the attention to policy questions and commentary was the requirement of my funder, the Economic and Social Research Council, that researchers be seen as having "impact" within the wider, nonacademic community. Aspects of the research were developed in preparation for presentation to the banking, journalist, insurance, and business community at a dissemination workshop in Johannesburg in September 2010, with the aim of challenging and providing nuance to state- or market-driven pronouncements about the problem of debt and its solutions. I hope and trust that my findings, presented in this book, will have some purchase among these constituents and in the world beyond the academy.

What Economists and Anthropologists Say

Economists and anthropologists have existed in an uneasy relationship: less a truce, more a state of studied mutual disregard based on ignorance. If some of the assumptions of the former have been called into question by events since the global financial crisis of 2008, many assertions made by the latter—about how economic arrangements are contextualized in social values and relationships— seem to be irrelevant because they have not been proved by hard facts and give no insight into broad trends. Studies of debt illustrate this pronounced divergence of approaches. Economists of South Africa, giving figures on the proportion of debt repayments to income for different kinds of earners across time (Ardington et al. 2004, 636), never question the underlying premise that "one has to pay one's debts" (Graeber 2011, 3–4). Graeber interrogates that premise, criticizing the deep-seated assumptions that lie at the heart of the global capitalist order. Something originally thought of as "reciprocity," in which gifts or favors, once given, are returned only after long delays or are transferred onward over the generations, has been transformed by the modern financial system, backed up by the power of the state, into a relationship of unequal power and of enduring hierarchy in the modern world: between first-world and third-world nations, rich and poor (Graeber 2011). To reject the power of that system is also, implicitly, to question the obligations that require borrowers to repay their loans. At a more local and modest level, Parker Shipton (2011, 217) critically interrogates the "self-evident truth" that "all loans and repayments should cancel each other out." Based on his studies in Kenya and other African settings, he explores the local ideas and values that underpin relations of debt, revealing irreconcilable differences between financiers' and bankers' views, on the one hand, and local "understandings about wealth, time, and the relation between them" (Shipton 2011, 215), on the other hand.

While admiring the broad sweep of Graeber's project, in what follows I do something closer in spirit to Shipton's. Rather than calling into question the very founding premises of capitalist arrangements and the repayments that these entail, I look at the specificities of the South African post-transitional context, with its mixture of liberalization and state regulation, and investigate how people—both those upwardly mobile and those who aspire to be so—have become engaged in debt and credit arrangements. I seek to establish whether and why they have, as the *Wall Street Journal* writer put it, been borrowing "to bridge their earnings and the lifestyles they aspire to have."[17] And if they give little attention to the longer-term consequences of being unable to repay their loans, I explore why this is so.

The book tracks a middle path between a more "economic" and a more "anthropological" approach. It uses summaries of survey-based material by economists while also exploring how far these are distinct from, can be used to explain, or require explanation in terms of householders' own views and practices. If giving credence to economists' accounts seems to be at odds with what anthropologists normally emphasize, it makes sense to do so in this context. In part, this is because analysts' and householders' attitudes and practices often *converge*. In a country where financialization is further advanced and deeper than in many other African settings, local people have to some extent internalized the views disseminated by financial institutions and the economists who work in and for them. South Africans' ideas about economic arrangements in general, and debt in particular, thus do not always contradict, or differ from, those held by the scholars and policy makers who analyze their behavior.

In 2012, the figures as reported by the *Wall Street Journal* presented a stark picture:

> Unsecured lending has nearly tripled in the past four years to $44 billion, or 10.5% of total credit, according to the central bank. Nearly half of consumers are at least three months behind on debt payments, says South Africa's National Credit Regulator, a consumer advocate that is charged with registering lenders. "The speed at which unsecured credit is being extended is ridiculous," says Nomsa Motshegare, the regulator's chief executive.[18]

If these figures were considered "ridiculous," they were not unpredicted. A series of accounts over the past decade or more had shown the extent of the problem—if that is what it was. Many were focused on the plight of the poor and jobless; others on those who, though employed, were at the bottom of the scale and were getting in over their heads. Regarding the former, one account points to a huge growth in borrowing during the early 1990s (Ardington et al. 2004). While this affected people at all levels, certain among their number seemed more vulnerable than others. The poorer were taking out loans from small lenders and retailers rather than the big banks, and (black) Africans were borrowing more from informal lenders than from formal institutions. Those from whom they borrowed included an estimated thirty thousand informal moneylenders, or *mashonisas* (Ardington et al. 2004, 619). Ardington and colleagues (2004) conclude that in cases where credit is used to "smooth consumption and cope with shocks," it helps to "manage risk." But such a use, they say, is unlikely for those who are already in poverty. These people get into debt to buy consumables at high interest rates rather than solid assets at affordable ones (Ardington et al. 2004, 607), so borrowing simply increases their vulnerability. Enabling greater financial "deepening" and thus facilitating more borrowing from banks, these authors argue, will help such people move away from their reliance on less formal and more exploitative loans and toward cheaper ones from financial institutions.

The debate about the benefits or otherwise of financial formality runs as a constant thread through discussions on the topic. Suggesting that "being banked" will not necessarily solve the problem is an account by economists Hurwitz and Luis (2007). They demonstrate that "the growth rate in credit consumption . . . exceeds growth in incomes" among the urban working class. These consumers, they show, often borrow at high interest rates to repay their other debts, are "overcommitted to numerous retailers," and "cannot afford the installments they are expected to pay" (Hurwitz and Luis 2007, 130). Although the authors strongly advocate consumer "education about basic money management, interest rates and credit costs"—an injunction that has certainly been taken seriously, as this book shows—they also recognize that "many of the causes of over-borrowing are socio-economic" (Hurwitz and Luis 2007, 131), and hence that something beyond education might be required. In contrast to Ardington and colleagues (2004), Hurwitz and Luis (2007, 108) conclude that overindebtedness has been facilitated rather than countered by the fact of "increasing market penetration into previously 'under-served' markets" (see also Porteous with Hazelhurst 2004, 89).[19]

Echoing the alarm about overindebtedness, a Consumer Debt Report of 2008 revealed that six million consumers, half of South Africa's labor force, were unable to pay their debts.[20] But the stark figures presented by surveys and represented in graphs are always subject to interpretation. Countering similar accounts which, in 2011, had shown how "household debt as a percentage of disposable income is at a worrying 76%," and that "consumer debt" stood at "R1.2-trillion, up from just R300-billion in 2002," a 2011 newspaper report by journalist Kevin Davie gives a rather different account. He cites Reserve Bank economist Johan van den Heever, who repudiates the use of the debt-to-disposable-income ratio and points to an important difference between short- and long-term loans. Items paid off over the longer term—mortgages, vehicles, furniture—complicate the picture. Using "interest paid" rather than "debt" as a percentage of disposable income yields a figure of just 7 percent rather than 76 percent. We must, he says, qualify the alarmist claims that "credit-fuelled lifestyles" are "a recipe for disaster."[21] This important argument reminds us of the claim mentioned earlier: that whereas buying consumables at high inter-est rates is unsustainable and ultimately detrimental, buying solid assets at af-fordable rates of interest can constitute the basis of a sustainable middle-class lifestyle (Ardington et al. 2004, 607).

These divergent perspectives on levels of indebtedness and their signifi-cance—drowning in debt versus rolling in riches, as Kevin Davie put it—echo the dichotomy of "debt is bad" versus "credit is good." Giving attention to both, it is Hurwitz and Luis's (2007, 131) "socioeconomic" causes that my approach, framed in anthropological terms, explores. But my concerns differ from those of the economists cited here, in that I switch attention away from examining the profile of specific income groups—especially the poor, vulnerable, and low-paid working class who have been the subject of these earlier analyses—to en-compass a much broader swath of consumers. For them—both the upwardly mobile and a larger grouping with similar desires and expectations—these causes necessitate other uses of borrowed money, besides the smoothing of consumption and coping with shocks. Anticipating parts of the argument that are yet to be laid out in detail, the situation is neatly summarized in this quote from a 2008 book by Jonny Steinberg, *Thin Blue: The Unwritten Rules of Po-licing South Africa*, in which—writing about a police officer in the post-1994 period—he captures precisely what these uses are:

> To ensure that your children attend a good school, you must buy a house in the
> suburbs. You have no reserves of cash, no investments, and so your entire house
> is bought with borrowed cash; the Reserve Bank governor's quarterly decisions

on interest rates, which once meant so little that you were barely aware of them, can now destroy your precarious monthly budget overnight.

And then there is the school itself; the decent ones cost money. There is private healthcare, increasingly obligatory to any suburban families. There is life insurance and a good retirement annuity. One cannot do without a car now that each family member must commute daily through suburban sprawl, and that, too, must be bought on credit. And when your children finish school, they must without question have the means to go to university. (Steinberg 2008, 105–6)

The people discussed in this book include many—like this police officer—who are unable to sustain their future dreams by their present earnings. They nonetheless aim to actualize expectations formerly reserved for those wealthier than they are, and buying now and paying later is one way to do so. There is a crucial time dimension in relations of debt, says Gustav Peebles (2010, 226), such that a consumer can "borrow speculative resources from his/her own future and transform them into concrete resources to be used in the present." But for South African borrowers, the use of these resources in the present is focused on achieving aspirations that may materialize only after yet further delay. Giving an account of these consumers, I explore the terrain between considering the kind of material debt that can be measured in percentage terms and understanding the things less easily quantifiable, felt to be necessary for the good life, which justify such debt. Local ideas of worth often challenge the tendency to measure all value by, and demand repayment in, its universal equivalent: money (Hann and Hart 2011, 49). Giving attention to these ideas will help me contest those analyses that represent all economic matters by listing contracts and transactions.

First it is necessary, however, to consider some of the contradictions of class and status in South Africa. If the state helped to forge the "new middle class" by employing its members in the public service and through affirmative action policies, it also encouraged its rise by liberalizing credit. But what kinds of people does this class—if it is a class—comprise?

Class: Marx and Weber in South Africa

This book deliberately erases the rigid distinctions that characterize some studies of social differentiation. Attempting to paint a broad picture, it looks across a wider range of income levels than classic accounts do, finding that certain habits, social practices, and expectations are characteristic across so-called class divisions. It follows the ways in which people themselves describe their position, as well as how analysts have categorized them. Combining the two presents a difficult task, but it is a necessary one, not only because anthropologists are pledged to capture local conceptualizations—how informants view their situation—but also because analysts' models and popular ones have converged, albeit often in complex and contradictory ways.

Concepts of class deriving from Marxism have held considerable sway. South Africa's political situation is such that the ruling ANC does not restrict itself to a nationalist project but is also embedded in an historic alliance with the South African Communist Party (SACP) and with the trade-union alliance COSATU. The ideology underpinning this alliance was, and remains, a strongly workerist one. It is devoted to overcoming the iniquities of a capitalist system that is identified as having benefited from the cheap labor of blacks over the past century and as continuing to do so. Marxism in South Africa thus goes beyond furnishing a model for use by sociologists, historians, and political scientists. It has also been embraced in the terrain of workers' political and economic struggle.

Matters are complicated, however, by the fact of recent social mobility, largely engineered by the post-1994 regime, such that it is now the *middle class*, broadly defined, whose members have greater influence in that alliance (Barchiesi 2011, 152; Southall 2004, 528). Political scientist Roger Southall shows that the ANC, burdened with the "massive expectations" of the electorate, needed to use its control of the state to fulfill those expectations, which it did in a variety of ways. One of these was its restructuring of the public services and public institutions, including parastatals, public commissions, and health and education professions. As a result, "the rapid increase of black representation within a public sector which . . . has expanded significantly has provided the basis for the substantial upward mobility of significant segments of the ANC's constituency" (Southall 2012, 10).[22]

But people may share the characteristics of several different classes at once, as Olin Wright (1997, 23) points out: "contradictory locations within class relations" arise in any analysis using a Marxist framework. Rapid change has recently brought these differences into sharper focus in South Africa, thus intensifying the contradictions. Pushing in one direction, there have been high levels of mobility over the past decade; pushing in another, there have been what a recent study describes as "lower class family and community members' attempts to . . . re-embed black professionals . . . back into communities of origin through the use of customary and obligatory mores of reciprocity" (Stauffer 2010, 210).[23]

Even though the dominance of Marxist-oriented ideas about capitalism and class, at least since the 1950s, remains an undisputed fact, it has been mediated by these "contradictory" pressures. But there is a further source of complexity and fragmentation. Since well before the workers' movement started to emphasize the importance of class identity and membership, social categories of a rather different kind were in evidence. Marks of status and respectability have been used in the creation of hierarchies based on small, internal differentiations, which sometimes have predated and have subsequently threatened to tear apart large-scale class solidarity. Ideologues in the struggle and analysts alike have, over the years, been much unsettled by this tendency. Of particular preoccupation to them has been the way the minutiae of social difference have marked off the black middle class from the broader black community.

The members of what Leo Kuper (1965) called the "black bourgeoisie" have been difficult to typify or categorize, even—or especially—to themselves. Starting with the period in which many of this elite group were founders of the South African Native National Congress (SANNC), the movement from which the ANC was born, they have tended to act in two contradictory ways. They have been leaders of the struggle against segregationist policy in its various guises, but they have also colluded with the rulers who—in cahoots with corporate interests—put such policy in place (Cobley 1990, 8–9). What inspired and intensified their resistance was the way they came to be lumped together with the broader ranks of the oppressed. But what made complicity attractive was being offered occasional concessions by the ruling interests. Illustrating this ambivalence, and giving eloquent voice to a blurring of class boundaries that still holds sway, though for different reasons, is an observation made about the 1910s by historian Philip Bonner. The members of the black petty bourgeoisie stood between and were pulled both ways by capital and labor. From a Marxist point of view, they seemed, as a class, to be "stunted and repressed by forces of colonialism and racism." For each person who possessed the necessary attributes to belong to this small elite grouping, "there was always a correspondingly greater substratum among the upper levels of the working class . . . who aspired to their position and struggled to get in." As a result, the black middle class experienced "a downward identification" toward those beneath them in the hierarchy (cited in Cobley 1990, 9).

In view of the marginal level of advantage that members of the "black petty bourgeoisie" actually held over their working-class counterparts, its differentiation from them was thus very slight. Yet sociologists and anthropologists like Leo Kuper (1965), Monica Wilson and Archie Mafeje (1963) and Mia Brandel-Syrier (1978), attentive to people's subjective consciousness of status hierarchies in a manner more Weberian than Marxist (Seekings 2009), became aware that people were intensely preoccupied with the outward and visible signs of lifestyle that demonstrate minute differentiations. (The Weberian mode of analysis, with its emphasis on subjective rather than objective criteria, thus fit the evidence neatly). These scholars were investigating how informants experienced their class position at a time—from the 1950s to the 1970s—when opportunities for difference had been even more stunted by the effects of apartheid policies, and when this "black bourgeoisie" was being forced into ever closer proximity with its working-class neighbors, by spatial segregation, inability to own property or pursue a decent education, and draconian restrictions on business. The more this happened, the more its members seemed set on emphasizing those features that would distinguish them from those neighbors.[24]

The Weberian approach certainly gave the most attention to these kinds of subjective measures of difference that underpin the existence of status groups. A Weberian analysis also, however, considers matters of economic class, exploring how "life chances" are shaped by "market exchanges" (Breen 2005). In the South African case, the market and commerce did not play a major role in shaping the black petty bourgeoisie during the period in question. It is certainly true that in the 1930s and 1940s a small black middle class did emerge, own property, become educated, and—in Johannesburg at least—engage in trade in the inner city. But the existence of that middle class was severely cramped and restricted. As time went by, the class did not, on the whole, come to comprise traders or businesspeople with any access to market exchanges: such access was purposefully denied and negated by the segregationist and, after 1948, apartheid authorities.[25] Instead, and increasingly as the century wore on, the black bourgeoisie consisted of state employees servicing the bureaucracies through which other blacks were administered, in a manner that further entrenched the ambivalence of these people's class position and fear of being accused of collusion.[26] All in all, one might apply a variant of the maxim famously attributed to Henry Kissinger: status differences in the black community were so marked and noteworthy because the "stakes were so low" and the range of options so narrow (Kuper 1965, 70).

If we skip forward to the postdemocracy period, we can see that these patterns and restrictions were to have long-lasting effects. Business and trade liberalized, enabling opportunities for black entrepreneurs and the rapid, "dramatic" growth of a new elite (Southall 2004, 529; see also Adam, van Zyl Slabbert, and Moodley 1998). But the dependence of that elite on state patronage through black economic empowerment, and the way this involved only a privileged few, has restricted its relevance for those outside the charmed circle: black enterprise remains, in effect, stunted in character. Whatever the salience of this "sudden appearance of black business magnates," Roger Southall maintains that they "constitute only a tiny, albeit highly visible, elite." To "gain a deeper understanding of contemporary South Africa," he suggests that we look "at the wider middle class" (Southall 2004, 529), a suggestion I take up in this book. The public service remained an important site where this wider middle class consolidated itself, later to expand after the mid-1970s and even more after 1994: upward mobility, then, was especially pronounced in the public sector.[27]

Setting aside the salience of Marxist or Weberian forms of class self-identification for the moment, how possible is it to measure the growth of that class in terms of objective measures such as income, property, and the like? And how does its size position it in relation to the vast numbers of the poor and unemployed, who have become much more numerous over the past few decades, resulting in South Africa's eventually outstripping Brazil, with the highest Gini coefficient in the world?[28] Several authors have used official data to answer these questions while cautioning against using such data to determine class categories and warning of the difficulties of arriving at an accurate assessment. Southall offers a cautious guesstimate that "by 2004, around 1.8 million African employees, or around twenty-seven percent of formally employed Africans, can be broadly defined as 'middle class'" (2004, 53).[29] The rise of that class, beginning in the mid-1970s, accelerated after 1994. Seen in spatial terms, this resulted in a situation in which "a racially desegregated middle class," with some of its members moving into the formerly white suburbs in urban areas (albeit not in large numbers, and differentially in the biggest cities), "has become separate from a black working class" and from the broader ranks of the unemployed (Crankshaw 2008, 1695, 1703; Crankshaw 2012; Steinberg 2008, 105–6). Confirming this, and moving beyond an urban setting, Seekings and Nattrass show how the upward mobility of a few was accompanied by rapidly falling formal employment, especially in rural areas and particularly in the former homelands (2005, 314–19). They also show how intergenerational mobility was largely determined, and chances further restricted, by which side of this division people were initially positioned (Seekings and Nattrass 2005, 331). In sum, they liken the system of differentiation in South African society, post-1994, to a game of snakes and ladders, with more snakes at the bottom of the board and more ladders at the top (Seekings and Nattrass 2005, 337).

On the question of blurred class boundaries and contradictory class locations, however, there is an important difference between the current period and the earlier one. Whereas the black middle class of the 1910s experienced a downward identification toward its working-class counterpart because of being spatially and economically compressed together with it (Bonner, cited in Cobley 1990; Crankshaw 2005, 362), a century later there is a tendency in the opposite direction. Wage-earning workers, and even those without salaries, are undergoing what one might call an upward identification toward those better off than they are. Many Sowetans, for example, now self-identify as "middle," stressing their in-between status, a position in flux but envisaged as upwardly mobile (Phadi and Ceruti 2011). Worldwide, a similar upward identification is in evidence (Berry 1985; S. Cohen 2004; Edwards, Evans, and Smith 2012; Zhang 2008). In India—to cite just one example—some segments of the working class have become socially and culturally middle class, and many people by the end of the 1990s were calling themselves "middle class" or "middle people" (Dickey 2012, cited in Fuller and Narasimhan 2014, 21). As in South Africa, this development was partly enabled by liberalization, but it also encompassed a strong reliance on salaries rather than self-employment in business (Fuller and Narasimhan 2014).

This new self-identification has salience for a discussion of debt in the South African case, and probably elsewhere. When Leo Kuper wrote his classic study *An African Bourgeoisie* in 1965, what rankled for a member of this tenuous grouping, given that his lifestyle, standards of respectability, educational expectations, and housing requirements were higher than those of people lower down the scale (even though they were all from the same neighborhood) was the "discrepancy between his earning capacity and his cost of living . . . his inability to meet the demands of modern times." These demands went beyond furnishing "the barest necessities of life" required to feed, clothe, and house himself and his family, to include—among other things—education (Kuper 1965, 16). Three decades earlier, Ray Phillips, a US-trained scholar of divinity who had worked as a social worker among black inhabitants of Johannesburg from 1918, had similarly observed a situation in which restricted means were available to bridge the discrepancy between earning capacity and cost of living (1938, 40). What marks off the present day, in contrast, is that a proliferation of credit sources, accompanied by a set of perhaps even more elevated aspirations, has created the conditions for much more extensive borrowing.

There has, then, been a blurring of boundaries between what were formerly considered strongly demarcated classes in "economic" terms at the same time as sharply increasing inequality between those at the bottom and those at the top of the pile. There has also been, across the board, an expanding emphasis on matters of consumerism and lifestyle and the status that accompanies these. These have important implications for how class is viewed in South Africa. While a strong Marxist-derived rhetoric remains in place about the need to overcome capitalism, and although worker organization remains robust and vociferous in promoting such a need, matters are complicated by the fact that COSATU now comprises a majority of public servants (Southall 2004, 534). The professions involved in COSATU already constituted an enclave for the black "middle class"—teachers, nurses, and the like—but the black proportion of those employed in them has expanded in size. Matters are also complicated by the fact that those involved in worker strikes—often those not organized by COSATU, since it is increasingly seen as representing that middle class rather than "real workers"—have needs and wishes above and beyond the requirements that Leo Kuper (1965) glossed as the "barest necessities of life" (see Saiag and Servet 2013). Two anecdotal examples suffice to give some idea of this. A 2012 report on a farmworkers' strike showed how the youths among them, all educated to secondary level, wished to attain, acquire, or defend the markers of a consumerist lifestyle, alongside pursuing further or higher education, despite being employed in one of the country's lowest-paid sectors: seasonal agricultural work.[30] In a 2013 radio discussion, participants cited surveys that showed that dwellers in the abject-looking shacks of Khayelitsha, near Cape Town, have pay television and consider it essential to wear branded trainers and drink branded whisky at Christmas.[31] Author and journalist Jonny Steinberg neatly captures the paradoxical and fluid character of the situation when he speaks of the "shifting sands of South African class formation" (2008, 100).

Whether experienced by people on the ground or analyzed by social scientists and policy analysts, class has not dissolved: a complex array of factors keeps it present in everyday practice and the public mind. But it has diverse and contradictory aspects, encompasses both Marxist and Weberian measures, and stresses both objective economic circumstances and subjective measures of worth and value.

Close Connections: The Household and the Economy

One concern of this book is to explore how small-scale, local-level practices pursued by ordinary people factor into processes taking place at a broader level. In doing so, it shares the approach of a range of recent writings in economic anthropology. Exploring "house"-based models of the economy is important, says Stephen Gudeman, since these relate to, rather than being distinct from, more corporate or contract-based conceptions (2008, 139). Keith Hart and his collaborators call for a "human economy" perspective: one that recognizes the household as the domain in which economy is situated and that focuses on the mutuality that grows out of living together (Hart, Laville, and Cattani 2010). Jane Guyer questions the way capitalism has been represented as counterposed to local forms of exchange that resist it; she calls for us instead to explore how economic concepts, which blur such sharp distinctions, emerge from "experience in the world" (2004, 158).

Such a focus may seem out of kilter with the times, especially in a setting like South Africa, where financialization has "deepened" and increasing numbers of people are in the grip of the formal money-based system, or when they are not, they seem to feel excluded from that system rather than actively embracing a local or community-based alternative. But the point made by these writers is to keep both sides in the same frame rather than neglecting one in favor of the other, analytically bracketing off an "informal" from a "formal" sector of economic activity or separating the domestic domain from the arena of growth and production. Where their insights are of particular value is in helping us take a fresh look at how contract-centered, market-oriented economic activity has penetrated the household or community, and conversely, how the mutuality of local arrangements has affected the world of contracts and business. In doing so, and particularly in pursuing the implications of these matters for borrowing and lending, we can gain some purchase on the importance of that house-based or domestic domain and start probing why it is that credit in South Africa has been used primarily for the purposes of consumption within that domain rather than for production outside of it, as policy makers originally intended.[32]

What one might call the "nonproductive" aspects of economic activities have been a matter of abiding concern in the anthropological literature on

South African societies. In the 1970s, scholars with a Marxist orientation challenged claims that the country's economy was "dual" (Houghton 1976) by emphasizing that capitalist profit was premised upon, articulated with, and only profitable because of domestic and/or rural cultivation and pastoralism. This was the "cheap labor thesis" (Wolpe 1972; Feinstein 2005, 245–51). (Despite insisting on this holistic, or "articulated" view, anthropologists' analyses, echoing other dualisms that have prevailed in South African studies, continued to focus mainly on the rural subsistence economy. Implicitly accepting a division of academic labor, they explored subsistence and the reproduction of the domestic domain, and they left matters of the market and the creation and exchange of value to economists.)

This Marxist-inspired account of articulated interdependence between production and reproduction might sound too neat and functionalist to be accurate—and it is. Various analyses challenged the insistence that capitalist profit depended on the subsistence economy—the domain of "reproduction" in the rural areas—and hence was reliant on "cheap labor." In an analysis with lasting influence, sociologist Belinda Bozzoli (1983) contested the assumption that rural households or villages would automatically yield up whatever labor was required. She noted that struggles within the domestic domain, the results of which were far from predictable, determined who would join the labor force and why. Challenging the ongoing accuracy of the Marxists' cheap labor thesis from a different point of view, economic historian Charles Feinstein showed that the key problem during the 1980s was that apartheid's unskilled and still largely migrant work force cost *too much* in relation to its productivity, rather than too little, achieving less for higher wages than their equivalents in other countries (2005, 245–51; see also Beinart 2012, 13).[33] Although the role of households and the sphere of reproduction—whether rural or urban—does not feature in his analysis, one is left to ponder whether one reason for the lack of productivity of members of that labor force was their commitments to those very same households. After cultivation and subsistence had largely been abandoned, whatever dependence there had been on rural cultivation was reversed, with workers' households and communities coming to rely increasingly on the money that migrants sent home. As the century wore on and unemployment rates soared remorselessly after the late 1970s and into the 1980s (Feinstein 2005, 245), remittances, dubbed "redistribution via private transfers" by Seekings and Nattrass (2005), were increasingly supplanted by their "public" equivalent: disability grants, child support grants, and the state pension on which large segments of the population came to rely (Ferguson 2010a, 175–78; Neves et al. 2010).

Whatever the outcome of struggles in the domestic domain or the direction of dependency between it and the sphere of productive work, it must be noted that the process of incorporation into a dominant capitalist system has been far more extensive in South Africa than in other parts of the continent. As Frederick Cooper writes, "Wage-labor capitalism, in most of Africa, takes place on islands in a sea of other sorts of socio-economic relations; in South Africa, wage-labor capitalism pervades the economy" (2002, 194). The (former) ubiquity of, and reliance on, paid work, has left in place an assumption that the main route to both a livelihood and citizenship is through employment (Barchiesi 2011). This remains the case, despite high levels of unemployment, which stood at around 25 percent in 2012, and despite a strong policy emphasis in recent years on small-scale enterprise as a means to solve problems of unemployment. This historical legacy has underpinned dominant assumptions about the nature of accumulation that render certain types of work invisible and make them undervalued, such as those performed in the household, in rural villages, or through "informal" employment. At the same time, the household, domestic, and community domain, once considered the domain of "reproduction" on which the economy rested, has shifted gradually to become one in which "redistribution" occurs.

The hegemony and formerly wide spread of wage work, then, left its mark in much the same way as did the Marxist model of worker struggle and working-class identity that arose out of it. If the shift to a more middle-class position and set of aspirations has introduced new complexities to what happens in the domestic arena, that arena still bears the mark of a century of proletarianization. It also bears the mark of earlier social arrangements, practices, and ideologies with a strongly gender-differentiated character. A model of the household or homestead as a center of both husbandry and thrift, and consumption and expenditure, has become consolidated, but it is characterized by stark conflicts and domestic struggles.

Historically, the broader homestead was an arena under the patriarchal control of a male head, and a wife held sway over her own individual house in a polygynous household, within which property was owned and devolved to members of the next generation.[34] At the height of South Africa's economic growth, when migrant labor still predominated and before the slowdown began in the early 1970s (Feinstein 2005, 143, 165), men's commitment to the homestead often took the form of consolidating wealth by investing in cattle (Ferguson 1992) and organizing costly rituals aimed at recognizing ancestors, thus building the communal solidarities in which the homestead was embedded (McAllister 1980). Women were more often concerned with the daily and yearly cyclical costs of running a house. As these costs increased and as dependence on men's migrant wages grew, the interests of husbands and wives diverged. From men's point of view, monies needed to be safeguarded through long-term investments in the homestead, including the propitiation of the ancestors. From women's point of view, monies needed to be diverted from these purposes and used for husbandry and everyday expenditure in the house. The long-term effects of these struggles are evident today, as Chapter 4 documents. To state matters starkly, wives (women) often conceptualize themselves as the bastions of the domestic domain, responsible for saving, thrift, and measured expenditure, where men (husbands) are seen as wasteful and as "eating" (wasting) household resources on nonessential spending. From men's (husbands') point of view, ceremonial expenditures and investments in the long-term future remain of key importance, but the fact that they are often unaffordable has made for a deep-seated sense of failure and of psychic, social, and cognitive dissonance.[35]

This brief and oversimplified sketch might be thought more relevant for the rural unemployed and marginalized than for the upwardly mobile suburbanites and their aspirant imitators mentioned earlier. It might be criticized for misrepresenting the situation, given that many women have brought up their children in single-parent households and without partners. Yet in broad outline its model of domestic and house-based arrangements, and the more recent overlay of gendered struggle, remain relevant, even if these have been interwoven with the concerns and preoccupations of sophisticated urbanity. The expectation of salary-earning men, whether in suburban or village settings, is that they will invest for the longer term—primarily in higher education for their children—while also procuring the material assets necessary for a decent life over that longer term. They must at the same time be mindful of the need to secure the futures of their unsalaried and unwaged relatives, thus securing the modern-day equivalent of the communal solidarities implied in the existence of the homestead. Wives, whether dependent or salary earning in their own right, may have similar priorities. But they are also attentive to the need to save for, and buy, consumables on a more humble—and practical—daily and yearly basis.

These divergent sets of expectations can have divisive and disruptive out-comes. This is especially the case when they are overlaid with the tendency of men, particularly when younger, to engage in multiple partnerships—legiti-mated as the modern-day version of polygyny.[36] In Impalahoek, for example, state salaries earned by public servants such as teachers play a key role in local economic arrangements. When salary-earning men become involved in rela-tionships with women other than their wives—and especially if they father children—this can constitute a major drain on such men's resources. This is said to be one major reason men get into debt. While at one level these re-distributive arrangements fund the entire political economy, they also lay the ground for further domestic disputes (James 2009; Niehaus 2012, 334).[37] A second complexity relates to changing ideologies over time, as is revealed by Grace Khunou's (2006, 2012) Johannesburg study of maintenance payments following divorce. As young men, initially bent on sexual conquest as "playas" (players), mature into adults, they leave aside their promiscuous ways and ac-quire sentiments about their responsibilities to play a "traditional" provider role. But these ideas are often out of kilter with the fact that their girlfriends and wives earn more than they do and are often reluctant to allow these men access to their children. This in turn results in disputes over maintenance pay-ments (Khunou 2006, 157–60). Again, images of saving, investment, provision, and thrift within the household are at play here, albeit in disrupted, gender-divided, and often conflictual ways.

Even in settings characterized by less domestic disharmony, becoming mid-dle class and moving into "the suburbs" can present particular challenges for the male, upwardly mobile recipient of a state salary, as is neatly captured in Steinberg's (2008) book about the "new" policeman. In contrast to what was the case for a member of the "compressed" middle class one generation back, with little in the way of mandatory expenditure after the rent was paid and the groceries bought, a young middle-class aspirant today is burdened with mul-tiple expectations. The "investments" needed not only to join the bourgeoisie but also to "keep your children there" are extremely costly, as Steinberg dem-onstrates in discussing the steep price of suburban housing, education, medical aid, and transport. These expectations often place an undue burden on domes-tic relationships. Themes deriving from these mismatched expectations, and their associated domestic conflicts, are an important theme throughout this book, surfacing especially in Chapters 1, 4, and 7.

In sum, when considering how economic arrangements originate in the "house" (Gudeman 2001, 2008), at the "human" level (Hart, Laville, and Cattani 2010), or through "experience in the world" (Guyer 2004, 158), we must also be attentive to the local specificities that make the South African situation unique on the African continent as well as different from mainstream settings of capitalism. The situation was one of widespread proletarianization, in which value was created only in the workplace and in which the household or house was spatially separate from that workplace. As that distinct arena switched from its role of "reproduction" to one of "redistribution," its activities of saving, spending, consuming, investing, and transacting in that domain have acquired a particular character. Overall, the earning of wages or salaries has been, and remains, validated. What occurs beyond the workplace, and is to some extent seen as parasitic upon it but is starting to surpass it in importance, is the processing and redistribution of those wages and salaries. This is a clue as to the importance, in South Africa, of "consumer" credit and to its predominance over forms of credit aimed at production.

Alongside these issues of the house and the domestic domain, it is necessary to return, once again, to the role of the state. From one point of view, the state helped create the circumstances that allowed for large-scale borrowing by facilitating the growth of the new black middle class. Conversely, one might equally say that the state created the circumstances that made for the growth of that class by pursuing liberalization and making borrowing easier. The state also attempted, somewhat belatedly, to protect the members of that class—broadly defined—by regulating the unintended consequences of their growth and borrowing. Considering these complex matters requires a brief discussion of the ethos behind and practices entailed in the politico-legal aspects of South Africa's transition.

Regulation, the Law, and Negotiated Transition

If South Africa's democratic moment was soon to be followed by class mobility for some of those previously held back, this was not—at least at first—the most immediately obvious way of striving to overturn the apartheid racial order. Nor did the elimination of the dual economy of credit, or the regulation of borrowing and lending, initially seem as urgent as other pressing problems. A number of more celebrated initiatives, legal or broadly quasi-legal in character, were put in place to ensure the restoration of certain rights to those previously denied them and simultaneously to facilitate a peaceful and harmonious coexistence in the new order. Perhaps best known among these was the new constitution itself, well known for enshrining a variety of rights (including many not yet recognized in other countries). Guided by the spirit of that constitution, other measures included the establishment of the Truth and Reconciliation Commission (TRC) and a program of land reform.

Apartheid was a system of state power. Its incidences of overt brutality were underpinned at a less visible level by an array of bureaucratic arrangements characterized by a more everyday, or "structural," violence. It is not surprising, then, that attempts to restore the dignity of its victims centered on reforming state systems so as to reverse the effects of that violence. The TRC, for example, held hearings around the country aimed at airing the terrible outrages committed by police, the security branch, and the army. To coax such perpetrators into the public eye, it offered them amnesty in return for their testimony. It also heard submissions from the business community, in the interests of uncovering various kinds of less obvious complicity with apartheid's system of racial capitalism. But this received less publicity than the hearings that recounted apartheid's ghastliest atrocities. As a result, many felt that these less visible injustices remained unaddressed. Activist groupings such as Khulumani have undertaken a David and Goliath struggle against Daimler AG, IBM, Ford Motor Company, and Rheinmetall for "aiding and abetting the perpetration of gross human rights violations by providing military and other equipment that was used by the apartheid security agencies to violently suppress widespread resistance to apartheid by the people."[38] These and similar initiatives resulted in a general acknowledgment of corporate South Africa's complicity in apartheid's repressive economy. Such a recognition, in turn, intensified the onus on big business to play a role in creating more "inclusive" markets, whether through an affirmative action hiring policy or by extending access to their products and services to poorer consumers, as by "banking the unbanked." Even here, although there have been attempts to act against business interests and corporations that operated in the shadow of the state, and although large corporations have attended to the need to frame "corporate social responsibility" programs and the like (Rajak 2011), the focus has mainly been on the overtly violent acts such corporations enabled rather than on the ordinary operations of capitalism and the market.

Similarly focused on redressing the abuse of state power was the land reform program. Apartheid's overtly brutal forced removals, conducted by the army and police and implemented in the name of state ideology, were those for which redress was immediately planned. But the program also made careful provision for people displaced by market forces. Besides compensating those resettled by the authorities in the name of the state's racial laws, land reform also redistributed land, or gave a place to live, to those rendered homeless by changes in the economy of farming. State and market forces were similarly intertwined when the program was implemented: government funds and advice were made available, but established property rights were respected through the market-driven "willing buyer–willing seller" model.[39] The retributive and restorative outcomes turned out, however, to be muted. Like the TRC, land reform had perhaps been too focused on the overt disruptions caused by state brutality to take account of those less obvious displacements attributable to the power of capitalism and ultimately far less easy to put right.

Perhaps because of the confusing interplay of forces and the resulting lack of clarity about "who to blame," reconciliation and reform were thus difficult to achieve. In the case of the neither the TRC nor the land reform program did matters turn out to be as clear cut as they might initially have seemed. As is shown in Richard Wilson's account of the TRC, a simple binary between domination and resistance had reduced "the complexities of a historically produced politico-legal context" and obscured the existence of "shifting patterns of dominance, resistance and acquiescence, which occur simultaneously" (2001, 222). In the case of land reform, that part of it which was implemented often laid bare and even exacerbated preexisting inequalities (James 2007; Falk Moore 2011, 13). In both cases, the difficulties of "reversionary legislation"—however well intentioned—were exposed (Falk Moore 2011, 14). The starkly oppositional image of a brutal state violating its people dissolved in the face of a more complex reality, with diverse groups, entrepreneurs, and business interests colluding or resisting by turns and always defying easy classification into a schema of perpetrators and victims.

What is the relevance of this for questions of indebtedness? The higher-visibility legal processes referred to here were instigated early on in the post-apartheid period and were aimed at overturning or remedying very obvious forms of "human rights" abuse of various kinds. However misconceived, patchy, or ineffective they might have turned out to be, they were celebrated for their lofty intentions. A concern with consumer rights, in contrast, is less "sexy" and less likely to be exported internationally. It has also taken longer to surface. Where other reversionary legislation had been passed in the 1990s and early 2000s, with special oversight ministries or commissions, those forms of regulation protecting the consumer or borrower, though likewise debated in the 1990s, were put in place (to tackle a problem that had taken longer to surface) only toward the end of the 2000s and left to the Department of Trade and Industry (DTI 2002, 2004) to instigate and monitor, as is discussed in Chapter 2. When the legislation was eventually passed (the National Credit Act of 2005), it did establish a new public institution of sorts—the National Credit Regulator. But that regulator has so far proved relatively ineffectual. The *Wall Street Journal* described the office as a "consumer advocate that is charged with registering lenders," portraying it in a manner that might be seen as failing to accord it much gravitas—and accurately so. It has not had the political or economic clout to do much more than register lenders and produce reports on debt levels.

Credit regulation also differed from the more visibly noble forms of legal regulation by virtue of its relationship to apartheid. Given that the new consumerism and its fallout affected those from all "population groups," or races, it was far from obvious that the new excesses of lending (which the act belatedly sought to curb) and the resulting "over-borrowing" had anything to do with the previous racist order. Indeed, this problem—if it was a problem—did not seem to be particularly South African in character. The everyday processes through which loans are granted, risks assessed, interest rates set, and property repossessed or wages docked when such loans are not repaid or when installments are in arrears for items bought on credit—all appear to vary little from one setting to another and seem mundane and unremarkable.

There was, however, something particular about South Africa's "credit revolution." It came on top of, rather than superseding, credit apartheid, and its effects were racially skewed. It is in examining the complex and compounded results of those initial restrictions on credit, the effects of their sudden withdrawal, and the outcomes of the later reimposition of regulation that I expand on the discussion of what Falk Moore calls South Africa's "reversionary legislation" (2011, 14). The legislation I explore, directed at lenders and borrowers, and aimed more at the world of business than aiming to address official injustice, affected an area relatively hidden until now.

Let me restate matters in simple terms. Reform and restitution were informed by ideas of rights restored that had previously been denied or confiscated. Reconciliation was informed by a somewhat different idea: of giving up the right to retribution and justice in the interests of peaceful coexistence in a new, nonracial order. Although both were aimed at bringing some closure, the ideals of restorative justice that underpinned these processes turned out to portray things too starkly, in binaries that oversimplified the situation. And whatever radically restorative intentions they may have had, these were ultimately subordinated to the politics of the "negotiated settlement," of "elite transition" (Bond 2000). In part as a result of that settlement, in which the interests of the market began to seem inextricable from those of the ruling ANC and its allies, the new prosperity grew apace, bringing new aspirations but also making them more difficult to achieve for many. Only after the transition, then, did a new set of problems and a new set of "rights"—those of the consumer—come into their sharpest focus. Regulating this terrain would prove as difficult as, if not more difficult than, the processes of reform, restitution, and reconciliation that had come earlier. As with those processes, but perhaps more so, any apparent division between perpetrators and victims would be blurred by the existence of actors with a wider range of entrenched interests—deeper roots as colluders and participants in "the system," with connections to the state and the market in equal measure—than was initially envisaged.

Set against the backdrop of the notorious racial segregation and denial of rights, and against the longer history of exploitation of South African black people by the forces of capitalism, this book explores the complex ways in which those forces currently manifest themselves. The present-day moral panic about consumer indebtedness, as this book shows, is not new; it has a long history. The immersion of South African society into capitalist relationships was swift, albeit uneven. Market arrangements arrived long ago, and people have become accustomed to them over a lengthy period. Wage labor has dominated the economy, and the formal or state sector has been extremely strong. This is not to deny that the recent advent of more recognizably neoliberal features has had severe effects. But there is a history, both of consumption and of people's engagement with formal banking arrangements.

The National Credit Act was motivated, no less than other legislation, by the state's aim to overcome the worst effects of apartheid. If the particular iniquities at which it set its sights were of less immediate interest than other more obvious ones, they were also, perhaps, more entrenched. The credit apartheid that the legislation aimed to overcome might have been implanted in capitalist arrangements of a widespread and thoroughgoing character, but it also had its roots in a peculiarly South African system of race-based exclusionary injustice. This book asks how far attempts to incorporate the marginal and previously politically disenfranchised, and to create a single economic framework from a dual one, have succeeded in changing the character of savings, consumption, investment, and property ownership. Or does the fact that so many intermediaries have a stake in the system as it is—in which money can be made "from nothing"—simply mean more of the same?

Chapter Outlines

The complexities of middle-class aspiration in the postdemocracy era, with its heightened competition and intensifying obligations, are explored in Chapter 1. The few who have well-paid and/or salaried positions are expected to help educate their siblings' children; they simultaneously strategize to remain beyond the obligations of marriage and the reach of their prospective in-laws. The many single mothers in this upwardly mobile group experience particular pressures and contradictions. Many who have achieved rapid mobility (and many who have not) have a sober and prudent attitude toward matters of investment and are all too aware of the need to save money where possible. They recognize the kinds of things that bring returns in the longer term, with education primary among these. The categories invented and surveys conducted by market researchers and advertisers thus belie the realities of consumer experience.

Chapter 2 shows how, after an initial period in which both borrowers and lenders seemed to benefit from liberalization, the state made belated efforts at regulation when things became unsustainable. The doors were opened, in a spirit of democratic engagement, to comment from widely divergent constituencies. But these seemed only to represent a starker form of the irreconcilability of the interests of borrowers and lenders, of regulation and the market. Based on a reading of the representations made to Parliament before the passing of the National Credit Act by corporations, trade unions, and civil society bodies, and on observations of debt counseling in action, the chapter analyzes the character of a society in which strong state intervention is required to maintain a market orientation. Mediating the stark opposition between borrowers and lenders, it also shows how many people who are not so well-off have been making an opportunistic living in that in-between zone.

Chapter 3 goes back in time to explore the longer trajectory of credit apartheid. Borrowing from both formal institutions and smaller (legal and illegal) moneylenders positions householders uneasily: to fulfill social requirements in one register, they acquire intensified obligations in another. Moneylending and money borrowing have involved an uneven mix. Under older systems, such as that of buying furniture on hire purchase, informal arrangements and community connection gave borrowers some flexibility and even allowed them temporary escape from their obligations. Under newer ones, technologies enable creditors to pursue debtors with inexorable swiftness and efficiency. Credit postapartheid thus has an increasingly uniform, financialized character. In the face of debt, borrowers experience deeply ambivalent feelings about entrapment and enslavement.

While there has been an anthropological cottage industry in studying rotating credit and funeral associations, Chapter 4 moves beyond a preoccupation with the institutional structure and adaptive functions of such groups. The chapter explores whether and how these clubs help people save and how they express and enable social mobility in a rapidly formalizing economic setting. It also shows how clubs occupy a point of intersection of the two modalities. One comprises all those things associated with upward mobility in postdemocratic South Africa: modern roles in the family, high levels of education, property ownership, and the ability to invest money in a rational manner. The other thrives in pockets of apparent informality, customary mutuality, and lack of logic, where sociability predominates; housewifely thrift is kept separate from the rapid money flow of the market; valued items or commodities tied to the domestic domain are ring-fenced and protected; and egalitarian mutuality is valued.

Going beyond the individual topics and tendencies laid out in previous chapters, Chapter 5 illustrates how these things dovetailed at a particular moment: during South Africa's "credit crunch" of 2007 and 2008. Examining how far people have gone into debt to achieve their aspirations, it investigates the effects of the economic slowdown and shows that these differed widely between sectors of the population, even between neighbors. Household planning in the domestic domain was still possible, especially for savings club members with an annual or cyclical arrangement structuring their savings contributions, but many clubs were experiencing defaults. People were nonetheless continuing to trust in the clubs and in funeral societies to hedge against shocks, often using complex arrangements and pairing these up with formal insurance. Relying on more formal channels, some people were borrowing from banks. Consumers were alternately using their bank accounts and letting them become dormant, paying off or avoiding paying the money they owed to retailers, sometimes taking out more expensive loans to pay off cheaper ones, and borrowing from moneylenders or becoming lenders in turn—sometimes all at once.

A key area in which ideas of the free market and mutuality are at odds—the property market—is the topic of Chapter 6. Policy makers insist that secure title to property coupled with mortgage financing will provide essential collateral to underpin functioning credit arrangements. But the inalienable rights assured by custom and the South African Constitution are at odds with this: rights to housing are protected from the market, especially where repossession is threatened. Factors that mitigate against individual ownership have also inhibited the abilities of single women to improve their lot through property purchase or ownership. The ring-fencing in of some property has knock-on effects for small-scale entrepreneurs: it has affected the growth of small businesses and impeded the social mobility of their owners. Since their moneymaking activities are hampered by factors that perpetuate South Africa's dual economy, they are left to make a living through other means: mainly by "recruiting people." Credit apartheid thus has complex determinants and effects, ranging from domestic struggles at the intimate level of the household all the way to state policy and the law.

Chapter 7 explores the financial education which many advocate as an escape from the debt trap. Self-improvement and self-transformation discourses emanate from the secular world of advice and the religious one of the churches. In different ways, both seek to bring about transformation while also giving people the psychic means for self-reflection about what those changes might mean. A new language emerges in which participants articulate the experience of success while also coping with difficulties in achieving it. In the case of neo-charismatic churches, aspired-for self-betterment coexists with consolation for those who cannot seem to progress. Self-help books and advisers, in contrast, insist on the benefits of honest self-disclosure. By forcing responsibility on the individual, they deny the socioeconomic context that has led people to become indebted in the first place or that might prevent them from taking such advice.

The conclusion to this book draws various threads together and wraps up the analysis. It reflects on the apparent absurdity of a situation in which consumers' borrowing is registered with the credit bureaus, yet lenders lend indiscriminately and with impunity, and it reiterates a key theme of the book: that the paternalism of consumers' bank accounts being under "external control" must of necessity intensify the principle of advantage to the creditor that continues to underpin South African consumer law.

1 Indebtedness, Consumption, and Marriage

The New Middle Class

THERE IS A UNIVERSALLY held position, says Gustav Peebles, that "debt is bad, but credit is good" (Peebles 2010, 226; see also Gregory 2012). The present chapter aims to unsettle that assumption, and in the process it simultaneously explores—and challenges—other kinds of oppositions. Aligned with the alarmist perspective that views debt as a measure of social stress and unsustainability are claims about the dissolution of the social fabric and the "crisis of social reproduction" in South Africa (Comaroff and Comaroff 2001; Fakier and Cock 2007; McNeill 2011). This view highlights how normative relations, including and especially those between genders within the household, have been breached: neoliberal policy agendas have undermined men's masculinity by making jobs scarcer; household economies that were once supported by men and managed by "stay-at-home" wives have collapsed. For the unlucky majority, unemployment is prevalent, with its effects only minimally compensated for through extensive state welfare. The lucky few, in contrast, are seen as engaging in excessively opulent lifestyles. The former envy the latter because of their public displays of capitalist success.

Opposing this dyspeptic view, and aligned with the view that credit has its positive side, are perspectives that emphasize the positive transformation of society (Nuttall 2004; Mbembe 2004). Borrowing can provide the means to reframe one's lifestyle and social identity while also enabling the reconstitution of society at large. In the new postapartheid era, people explore new forms of consumption while also retaining or intensifying a desire for continuity in social, political, and economic process. Strategies labeled "traditional" often entail new social relations or older ones reconfigured: between elders and youths, Christians and traditionalists, mothers and daughters. These arrangements often take as their model, or are embedded within, the quintessentially moral and long-term reciprocal relationship of "good debt": affinity between families as expressed through the ongoing payment of bridewealth in marriage (Scorgie 2004).

Finding a midpoint between these opposing positions, we will see how, on the one hand, ties between families are severed in divorce, or alternatively never initiated because of the extreme expense of bridewealth and the onerous nature of obligations toward in-laws. Yet on the other hand, the entanglements in forms of commitment and webs of long-term obligation that Parker Shipton (2007) calls "entrustment" are acknowledged and pursued, and social investments made, at particular moments in the life course.[1] At the same time, while many decry an orientation toward careless consumption, householders often provide evidence of careful husbandry or take out loans to ensure the future well-being of their families. Neither of these pictures on its own—a dismembered society versus a reconstructed one; the spendthrift consumer versus the frugal householder; the overindebted person versus the borrower aiming to reposition him- or herself—presents a complete and accurate account of the rapidly shifting terrain of relationship, ambition, dependence and ostentatious display in South Africa. But in combination they can tell us something about the social terrain and those who are placed within it.

The New Professionals: Frugal or Fragile?

In the course of my search for those who might be considered representatives of the new middle class, I find myself sitting in the smartly apportioned and air-conditioned office of Abigail Mlate, on the fifth floor of an office block in central Pretoria. Our conversation ranges across a variety of topics: her upbringing and education, her family, her plans for her daughter's future. We also talk about the differences between her mother's generation and her own. The daughter of a policeman and a schoolteacher, Abigail was raised in a single-parent family by her mother, who paid for her education in its entirety. The private school she attended, in one of South Africa's former homelands, Bophutatswana, a little way to the north, gave her a good educational grounding and paved the way for her to attend university. For a while she worked in a middle-range job in social welfare, but soon afterward she did a postgraduate degree, and shortly after that she was appointed to a senior position in a government department in Pretoria.

There are several features that distinguish Abigail's story from that of someone who might hold a similar government job in another country. One is the speed of her upward mobility. Compared to the career trajectory of her mother, Abigail's own rise was positively meteoric. As with many young black South Africans in similar circumstances, her elevated position and her swift promotion were in large part due to opportunities forthcoming after the country's apartheid racial order was overturned in 1994. Another thing that distinguishes her position, closely but inversely related to the rapidity of this rise in status, is the fact that several close family members—aunts, nephews, and nieces—share neither her educational qualifications nor her upward trajectory. Her aunts are domestic servants, who are experiencing some difficulty in putting their children through school. She is often asked to provide help (in material and other terms) to these relatives.

But there are also complex threads that tie Abigail's story to longer-standing social arrangements. If there is a shift in class positions evident in this story, it is the one that occurred not in her own life course but in that of the previous generation. The difference between Abigail and her cousins owes itself to her mother's having "pulled herself up" to become a teacher, in contrast to her aunts (and their children), who remained in menial work.

A further striking continuity between the generations can be discerned if one looks at the careers of the spouses of Abigail's mother and Abigail herself. Both marriages linked people of similar social status, but both dissolved quite swiftly. In Abigail's own case, her partner was a university graduate, as she was. One of the key moments of disagreement between them came when he objected to her "wasting money" on her own further education rather than saving it for the education of their daughter. Rather than accepting this line of argument, Abigail saw it as a sign of his unwillingness to accept that his partner might become better educated than he. He could not accept that ultimately she might, as a result of her superior achievements, be unwilling to kowtow. "It's that patriarchal thinking that 'If she gets this master's [degree] then she will be better off than me. And I'm the man here so she will have to listen to what I say,'" as Abigail put it.

The wealth and investment habits of the new black middle class—which Abigail in many ways seems to personify—have been a matter of growing interest to those in the commercial world, and it is worth briefly outlining the reasons for this. The various tags used to typify the group—"black diamonds" (Mda 2009), "coconuts" (Matlwa 2007) and "cheeses" (Skhosana 2012)—

emphasize material consumption and lifestyle but also refer to race (Posel 2010). The "black diamond" tag, in particular, was more or less invented by advertising agencies and commercial market research organizations such as the Unilever Institute, inspired by the need to profile—so as better to target—new categories of consumer; and later it was taken up in the media and portrayed in stereotypes on television soap operas.[2] This profiling, originally crude, but increasingly sophisticated, involves the use of ten living standards measures (LSMs), each "defined by a number of criteria, ranging from income and housing type to car and phone ownership" (Chevalier 2010, 79).[3] Where under apartheid the state was the agent responsible for categorizing people so as better to divide and govern them, it is now corporations that pigeonhole people so as better to market goods and services to them. By means of this class and lifestyle profiling, attempts were made to bring more people within the ambit of visibility and to enable them to be reached by advertisers.

While advertisers have tried to separate such people from their money, critics show how the use of such labels is misleading. Discussing the "black diamonds" in Durban, Sophie Chevalier says the emphasis on lifestyle diverts attention from "what is really at stake in society and politics, in this case the persistence of racial stigma and of a behavioral standard based on the white minority" (Chevalier 2010, 84). The argument that members of the newly liberated nation would have done better not to squander money on luxury consumables is addressed by sociologist Deborah Posel (2010). Such critiques, she says, echo those of an earlier, apartheid-era discourse, when being black was closely associated with specific types of food, furniture, crockery, vehicular transport, and the like. Those who aspired to own or consume items normally thought of as "for whites" were greeted with ambivalence: praised for being more civilized but also regarded with suspicion since their behavior amounted to the imitating of their "betters." The unexpected association of political freedom post-1994 with the "freedom to consume" can be understood, she argues, since its opposite, political repression, had meant being excluded from the consumption of anything but bare necessities (Posel 2010, 173).[4]

Within the ranks of those reckoned as "belonging" to the black diamonds (albeit now known by other names), some view the categorization, and similar ones, as having some validity, whereas others view it as invalid because of its lack of attention to social nuance (Krige 2009, 2011). The new reflexivity of those labeled in this manner—and the fact that many have a "voice" as journalists, radio presenters, writers, and commentators—has given them confidence to respond critically, calling attention to the precariousness and lack of economic sustainability that underpins their lifestyle. Members of this putative category are "no-carat diamonds," wrote Jabu Mabuza in the *Financial Mail*, "nothing more than a glorified consumer group," especially given their lack of material assets and real prospects of advancement through business.[5] Their wealth—such as it is—arises through the state's affirmative action and black empowerment schemes and is soon squandered by the consumption of "luxury goods acquired through debt." Disliking the emphasis on this new class, since it is not their work that in reality underpins the economy, Mabuza states that market surveys of this group are used by industry "to instil a false sense of aggrandizement and achievement in the black diamond market segment" (cited in Krige 2009, 23).

This emphasis on the flimsy material underpinnings of aspiration was reiterated in a more recent altercation in the pages of the *Mail and Guardian* newspaper. Young hip-hop star Jub Jub, a member of the consumption-oriented middle class whose family had moved out of Soweto to Johannesburg's southern suburbs and later went to the United States, acquired a drug habit that, on the family's return to South Africa, led to his being jailed for killing several youngsters during a misguided drag-racing stunt. Essayist and journalist Bongani Madondo wrote critically about the empty "bling" and excess embraced by those in this upwardly mobile group.[6] Countering Madondo's criticism, a letter to the paper echoed the points made by Mabuza, noted previously: what was really of note in the story was not the "bling" but the "precariousness of African success after apartheid" and the "fragility of new black wealth."[7] That this fragility consists in part of overreliance on credit, in the absence of other alternatives, is suggested by Sophie Chevalier in her study of Durban's "black diamonds." Despite benefiting from bigger (mostly state) salaries, members of this class have few options available to enable them to actualize their access to the wider range of goods that has become accessible to them. They have little in the way of "capital, savings or inheritance to draw on, and must go into debt if they wish to consume on any scale" (Chevalier 2010, 78).

However much the state might have acted to bolster and establish the new middle class, then, and however important the new social meanings of the new forms of consumption engaged in—and the indebtedness entered in to help engage in those meanings—some view its fragility as overweening. From Abigail's story, however, it is clear that her position is neither as precarious nor as oriented toward the flashy and unsustainable expenditure of money, as some media accounts on the topic have suggested. Displaying a self-reflexivity that is characteristic of people in this new position, Abigail has considered opinions on the "new black middle class," of which she acknowledges that she herself could be reckoned a member. Acknowledging the role of state employment, she draws attention to the circumstances that have enabled the rise in her own fortunes, to "the political climate currently, and . . . issues around broad-based black economic empowerment programs that government has introduced." But alongside "the political change—the opportunities that are open to us— what we call disadvantaged groups," she also emphasizes the fact that she went to a good school and to university. In short, she recognizes both the dependence of her success on the postapartheid state, which gave her the chance of holding a high-level job, and the much earlier investments in education by the farsighted individual efforts of her mother. As Abigail put it, her mother "had certain expectations . . . 'if I put my last money on my two daughters, I know hopefully one day they will become better people.'" In many of my subsequent discussions with people in relatively senior jobs in government or the state-owned enterprises, I find that many of them fit a similar description. It was their parents, pre-1994, who made the educational investment necessary for them to later take up positions as part of the post-1994 dispensation. Inter-generational mobility over the past few decades has been largely determined, and opportunities restricted, by which side of the class division people were originally positioned on (Seekings and Nattrass 2005, 331).

Making clear the robustness and enduring character of intergenerational strategies, Abigail's future plans for her own daughter echo those that her mother had for her; she puts a similar emphasis on judicious expenditure and investment. Repudiating her ex-partner's idea that spending money on her own education would preclude funding that of her daughter, Abigail's strategy encompasses both. She intends to send her daughter "to a good school" and to provide her with higher education. But she also states matters in a more tradi-tionally middle-class vein that balances privilege with due consideration, grati-fication with necessary delay, and liberal agency with context and structure. She stresses the importance of her daughter's individual "free choice" while also emphasizing the need to educate her daughter about the financial constraints that might narrow that choice:

> I explain, and I have noticed that when you talk to her and explain to her—my
> daughter is not the kind of child that will start crying in a store because she

wants all these toys. My cousins are amazed, because I always talk to her. She always knows that when she asks for something she needs to acknowledge the fact that mummy has money, or mummy doesn't have money. And if I do have money, I tell her, "This month I think I can be able to buy you that thing that you want." And through that engagement I have noticed now that she starts to understand that you don't just get things just like that, you plan things. And it really helps, because I'm never frustrated when I go shopping with her. She won't sulk. She must realize that you have to work hard, that you have to have delayed gratification.

Abigail thus points to the importance of taking a measured attitude toward consumption. Further stressing this, she points out that, as a single mother, she often faces pressures to match the expenditure of those who raise their children in couples: "You want to keep up with your friends who have husbands, to say 'I need to show them . . . I am adequate, I can take my daughter, I can have the same life they have even though I am a single parent.'"

It is necessary, then, to spend money in the here and now to meet social expectations and challenge negative views of single parenthood. But this is balanced by emphasis on the importance of future planning and investment—in part to counteract the possible disadvantages of being unmarried.

There is an emphasis in Abigail's story on the strength of mother-daughter bonds. The story also shows her connection to—yet partial independence from—a wider set of kin. This complex intertwining of causalities and themes extends beyond the boundaries of both the new black middle class, whatever it is called, and of its longer-standing or "old" equivalent. Whether the much-written-about "black diamond" category is merely putative and "media-invented" or has elements of objective fact, similar narratives can be traced in a much wider setting. Encompassing both aspiration for one's own family and concern for a more extended set of kin or neighbors, Abigail's story neither confirms prophecies about the imminent success nor bears out those about the drastic failure of the newly upwardly mobile in the new South Africa.

Those who have well-paid or salaried positions, like Abigail, are experiencing intensifying claims on their resources, but they are balancing those against new bids to acquire freedom and independence. They may be expected to help educate their siblings' children or to provide upkeep for other members of their natal families, but simultaneously they find themselves escaping, or striving to remain beyond, the potentially crippling obligations, expenses, and constraints of marriage. Individual narratives of status mobility, like Abigail's, show the importance of life-course events such as marriage: challenging it, however, some state their plan to remain permanently outside the bridewealth circuit and the reach of prospective in-laws. Such narratives also illustrate the particular pressures and contradictions experienced by the large numbers of women responsible for bringing up their children alone: both those in this upwardly mobile group and those beyond it.

Village Aspirations

My encounter with two friends, Thandi Thobela and Anna Mohlala, provides a village-based counterpoint to the story of Abigail. Having contacted Thandi on her mobile phone, I arrange to meet them for a glass of Coca-Cola in the noisy cafeteria adjoining the Impalahoek supermarket. Raising our voices to make ourselves heard above the chatter of voices, we talk animatedly, enjoying this reunion after our meeting on a previous field trip. We share information about our respective children. Thandi has three. Her oldest child, a fourteen-year-old son, lives with her in-laws in Pretoria, where he is being educated. She is separated from her husband, but his parents are caring for her son. Anna has one child, whose father died some years back. Showing something of the unstable character of couple relationships, a second male partner recently jilted her by text message.

Our conversation echoes many of the themes that Abigail emphasized. Both Thandi and Anna are single mothers who have lost—or achieved independence from—unreliable male partners. Both see education (for themselves and their children) as a route to upward mobility. Both also stress the need to communicate openly with their offspring—in classic middle-class fashion—to impart the importance to them of elevating one's status while remaining frugal in one's habits.

Our meeting also emphasizes the importance of employment by the state. Here, however, it does so because of the frustrating absence of such employment—despite some promises of its possibility. Working as a volunteer for a local state-funded nongovernmental organization (NGO) is thought of as a route to a job in local government (James 2002; McNeill 2011, 115). The fact that such jobs infrequently materialize does not lessen the importance given to them. Reliance on, or at least the eventual expectation of, state employment is ubiquitous for young women. It is a means, perhaps the only means, to realize the upward mobility to which they aspire.

On our previous meeting, both women had been employed as trainee journalists in a local newspaper run by an NGO. But the project turned out to be short lived. The friends bemoan the skittishness of local job prospects. Before being employed at the journalism project, Thandi had briefly worked in the shop of the microfinance lender Lohen, situated a few storefronts away from the supermarket where we are sitting. Anna had worked as a volunteer helping to organize home-based care for those with HIV/AIDS, for the state-funded Bushbuckridge Consortium. She trusted that the experience might give her an edge when applying for employment in the same or some related organization, or help her to get a job in a shop or local business. But she concludes gloomily that "jobs advertised are always given to relatives of the employer," or that the employer, "if he is a man, will ask you to sleep with him before he will offer you the job." Both had felt positive when the journalism project started and found their work there stimulating and inspiring. But the extreme dependence of such projects on the vagaries of funding and often on the personal circumstances of the project leader—in this case, a foreign-born woman who suddenly got divorced from her South African husband, precipitously ended her involvement, and left the country—means that they often turn out to be as insecure as other local forms of employment.

Thandi talks with optimistic cheerfulness, nevertheless, about her own family background and her plans for her children. Her parents are both state employees, and her family places great importance on education. Two of her siblings were educated to tertiary level at the family's expense; one works as a nurse, and the other is a public prosecutor. "Family politics" of an undisclosed nature prevented her from being similarly educated. Undaunted, however, she has enrolled as a part-time student with the University of South Africa, South Africa's distance learning university, to study information science. She hopes by doing this to better herself and enhance her job prospects. She also feels optimistic about her son's chances of educational success, and she stresses the importance of communicating openly with him to enhance that success. Like Abigail with her daughter, Thandi insists on giving her son clear messages about frugality and the importance of not living beyond his means: "If I don't have the money I don't buy. I say, 'Sorry my boy.'"

But in Thandi's case, unlike Abigail's, investment in children's education by the parental generation did not marry neatly with the frugality and self-discipline of a Weberian Protestant ethic (Weber [1905] 2002). Although both of their mothers were teachers, income and expenditure for Abigail's mother were commensurate, whereas for Thandi's mother they failed to match. Instead, sending a second child to university, on top of other expenses, proved the proverbial straw that broke the camel's back and drove Thandi's mother to borrow from a moneylender after exhausting all other more formal lines of credit. Judgmental about what she sees as her mother's profligacy, and holding up her own attitude in contrast, Thandi leans across the table and jabs it with her finger, emphasizing the need not to live beyond one's means. She plans, she says, to warn her own children about the dangers of doing so.

My discussion with Thandi and Anna has an upbeat feel. I get a strong sense of what it is that both aspire to. Being single causes them some anxiety, but it also signifies independence (Niehaus 2012, 334). Aiming for (in Anna's case) or maintaining (in Thandi's) a respectable and modern status, acquiring job security, and ensuring a good future for their children are paramount. If these women are not "black diamonds," they nonetheless share the values that are held by the members of that putative category. But the tale of Thandi's mother's indebtedness and of Thandi's employment by a microlender gives me a sense of the darker side that might accompany such aspirations. Drawing attention to what seems like the unsustainable aspect of these, their account echoes some of the critical points made by Mabuza in his coruscating critique of the "no carat diamonds."

On a more positive note, these women's values and aims are very similar to those described by journalist Tim Cohen, reporting in *Business Day* in 2005. He focuses in particular on women in the new middle class:

> [They] are the beneficiaries of economic growth and, to a certain extent, government assistance. They are fixated on the education of their children and will go through enormous personal hardships to ensure that their offspring land feet-first in the middle class. They are the backbone of social development and progress; hard-working, law-abiding and dedicated. (cited in Krige 2009)

This discussion centers especially on urban women, but my conversation with Thandi and Anna reveals that such values motivate women, as well, among those living in villages of the former homelands and whose class position is less certain.

"Things" or "Care"? Consumption Versus Investment

One line of argument has it that black people were newly subjected, at the moment of democracy, to pressures to consume useless and unimportant luxury goods, and that if only those could be curbed, frugality would prevail and people would start to live within their means. Debates over the social meaning of consumption outlined earlier indicate that there are some truths in this assumption. But it fails to recognize how the most important kinds of expenditure for the middle class—whether new or not so new—are not necessarily frivolous but often encompass investments now regarded as mandatory. These include life-cycle events: both the shorter-term expenses of weddings and the longer-term ones entailed in marriage payments. Burying relatives with due dignity is also important. Higher education, often outstripping the other events in expense, is likewise crucial. While some informants were increasingly ready to stay single to escape from the expenses associated with life-cycle rituals and obligations, few denied that going to university had been essential to their own success.

On the one hand, then, there are those who purchase luxury goods in an undeniably extravagant manner, the complex social meaning of which refers to the deprivations of the past (Posel 2010). On the other hand, there are those who—again as a result of earlier financial hardships—husband their resources so as to invest them and secure themselves in the long term. While these may sound contradictory, they are not disconnected. Decrying the competitiveness that has been seen to lead *some* into excessive displays of wealth is one means by which others assert their own frugality. In some cases, like Abigail's, people speak positively about their ability to deny themselves—and their children— the opportunity to indulge in such consumption, thus evoking the need for delayed gratification in order to save up for the more important things in life. At the same time, many reflect upon the way in which social mobility, particularly when linked to marriage and the expectations and costs that surround it, might actually bring more costs than benefits.

Competition, many people tell me, is a kind of fatal flaw in contemporary South African life. It is also the main reason people get into trouble with debt. The idea of status competition is invoked repeatedly by people I interview in a section of the Soweto neighborhood of Sunview. In the same spirit of self-reflexivity that informed critical comments on the formation of the black diamond category, discussed earlier, many middle-class and not-so-middle-class people have a keen and critical awareness of the existence of competition. Far from seeing it as modern, they view it as an almost intrinsic failing of "African culture." As one man puts it, "People are pressurized by competition in the township; if someone has something, someone else will want to have [it], without considering the cost"; another pointed out that "people want to be equal with other people." According to a third, "People are challenged by other people, the pressure comes from society." These pressures are said to be the reason people will relinquish their view of the longer term, abandon prudence, and spend money they have not earned and do not possess. "People cannot wait and budget, they are in a hurry for everything," says one. Another observes that the advantage of credit is that "you can immediately get what you need without any delays," but the disadvantage is that "you are working backwards instead of progressing. . . . People are just quick to get things without calculating the cost."[8] Other informants, including those holding well-paid positions in the government, echo these views. "Some of us are too inclined to worry about what others think, and want to be seen to have the same things as other people," Geoff Matlatsi tells me, again describing this sense of status anxiety as something specifically "African."

Further illustrating the critical and self-reflexive manner in which this competitive consumer complex is viewed, a postgraduate student and junior lecturer at Pretoria University, Bongile Cengimbo, tells me about the impression she gained when as a child she moved with her parents from a rural village in the Eastern Cape province to settle in the informal settlement of Orange Farm, Gauteng, some twenty miles south of Johannesburg. Unlike Abigail's story, Bongile's upward trajectory, taking place in one generation, has been more precipitous, as is evident from the fact that her family still lives in this low-income area. "Neighbors compete and feel under pressure to show that they are living in the correct way," she tells me. This generates both competition and—paradoxically—imitation. "If you take three neighboring houses in Orange Farm, going into one of them is just like going into another: you feel as though you are going into the same house. All the consumer items—DVD players, washing machines—are exactly the same as each other," she says. While competing for status might be thought to entail a striving for distinction, acquiring the same items as one's neighbors speaks of a rather different tendency. It is something more like "keeping up with the Joneses" than striving to surpass them. This paradoxical relationship between a wish to express income discrepancy and a wish to possess identical commodities is commented upon by Krige (2011, 280–84). In his account of a middle-class beer-drinking club, the very fact that young professionals have chosen to get together to imbibe a "yuppie brand," Castle Light, speaks of the fact that they are marking the growing disparities between their home-based lives in Soweto and their work-based ones in the upmarket area of Sandton. Celebrating inequality in this way counts as positive competition, but Krige points out that this can easily degenerate into its negative variant. *Jealous* is the word commonly used to characterize both those who promote competition by showing off and those who feel slighted by—and desirous to imitate—such status display. Unlike its use in common parlance elsewhere, *jealous* thus applies both to those who fear being envied and to those do the envying. A variant of what is elsewhere called the "tall poppy" phenomenon, jealousy is associated locally with ambivalent attitudes toward those who are better off. It is known in Soweto, says Krige, as the "PhD syndrome," or the "pull-him-down syndrome" (2011, 292).[9]

Competition, consciousness of relative status, and fear of gossip—important in their own right as sources of indebtedness, or as elements of a "folk" critical commentary on the problems of debt—also have an important relationship to marriage in settings of rapid upward mobility. Showing that these are well-established themes in accounts of social change in South Africa,[10] and that they can place severe pressure on prospective husbands, a 1998 novel called *The Tikieline Yuppie* by Mehlaleng Mosotho illustrates, for a more recent period, how marrying "upward" can exacerbate such anxieties. Its protagonist, prefiguring typical post-1994 stories of status advance, is the Sowetan Tseke, the university-educated son of a lowly domestic worker mother who has a job as a salesman in a cleaning products corporation. His impending marriage to a woman he met while at university puts him under immense pressure. His future in-laws have niceties of behavior and rules about good manners that alert him to the fact that they claim to be of superior status to his own family. This sense of inadequacy makes him vulnerable when he takes his fiancée shopping, and she insists on buying shoes and a dress that are inordinately expensive. When he objects, she clinches the argument by saying, "I won't allow you to shame me on my wedding day. I don't want township gossips to cure their boredom with my name." Experiencing a sense of panic, and against his better judgment, he agrees to the purchases, using both the credit card he had just been granted and the year-end bonus he'd deposited in an account "and vowed not to touch it until he really needed it," to cover the expenses. Doing so conflicts with his sense of obligation toward his own mother, who possesses few of the attributes of affluence so cherished by his in-laws (for an account of the items of furniture he buys for his mother, see pages 55–56).

Incidentally, the story of Tseke gives insight into a key concern of those in the post-1994 middle class. As a person from a poor background with newfound (relative) affluence, he is expected to spend his earnings to honor two discrepant sets of social obligations: one toward his future wife and her parents (who in this case are richer and of higher status than his family) and the other toward his own blood kin (whose status and wealth is increasingly lower than his). Where such countervailing obligations might have been precariously balanced against each other to form a sort of equilibrium in traditional settings, they have become increasingly difficult to reconcile in situations where sharp inequalities prevail.

If we return to the question of critical accounts of consumption, we can see that what served to prompt these in South Africa—after the period when Tseke was facing these dilemmas—was a period in the mid- to late 1990s, well before the worldwide credit crunch. At this time there was a sense that too much credit had been offered, too freely, by South African financial institutions.[11] Frank Pule, a Sowetan, points out that South African firms were "throwing credit" at people. "When we bought our house, we then qualified for R500,000," he tells me. But he and his wife decided to buy a house that cost only R130,000. The bank insisted, "'Here is R500,000, it's up to you how you use it.' Ours is that we want it paid back. But you have a credit of R300,000—if you want to buy a car, a house, this and that, or if you want to go on holiday, or go to the World Cup—they will give it to you."

While acknowledging the very real sense of pressure—both from friends and acquaintances and from financial institutions—that these examples suggest, one should be careful about accepting stereotypes too readily. Informants in Sunview decry in abstract terms the problems of excessive consumerism. But—in a manner reminiscent of Abigail, Thandi, and Anna—they talk of the need to practice prudent financial acumen in particular cases. If they have taken out personal loans, these are often to pay for their own or their children's education rather than because they have yielded to the pressures of "competition" over possession of sofas or brand-name shoes. "The quest for things," observes Posel, "can be an expression of care and support for others, as much as a crass self-absorption" (2010, 162). One might add that the quest for *ready money* may be driven by care and obligation rather than simply by the wish for "things." This is where credit, in many cases, has played its part in enabling the upward trajectory of the new middle class.

The case of Soweto resident Mrs. Ngunyula is a good example. She, like her husband, is a waged employee of the transport corporation Transnet, a parastatal. They have two school-age children and one who is studying at university.

She speaks with frustration of the way she has been bombarded with offers of store cards, insurance deals, and "free" mobile phone credit by a variety of companies. But she has not proved easy prey. Although she often feels uncertain about her consumer rights, and especially ignorant of how to take action to uphold those in the face of bombardment by advertisers, she is aware—and critical—of the dangers of rampant consumerism and of getting into debt to participate in it:

> At my workplace, there are people who have wallets full of cards—Foschini, Truworths [two large clothing retail chains]—and it is a problem when the end of the month comes. People are mad. People must wait for credit, take it and get it again. They only earn R3,000 a month. Go to Truworths, they wear nice clothes, fashions . . . now, it is summer, there are winter sales. You will be buying things for R3,000. After, when you look at it, there will be summer sales. One person in Truworths has R5,000 credit, at Foschini another R3,000. When they count, they will owe R50,000. When it comes to groceries, it is the 15th, 16th, they will have no money.

She has observed people's readiness—here expressed as "I" but meant by way of an abstract example—to buy even small everyday items of foodstuff on credit: "I need peanut butter. I will go to Shoprite [a supermarket chain], and swipe the card, even for bread."[12] Such items, she insists, ought to be bought only with cash, even if that means abstemiousness:

> If we have no bread, I tell the children they'll have to eat soft porridge and *morogo* [wild spinach], I have no money for bread until I get paid. But if I have a credit card I will go and get the littlest thing, and swipe it. I see a lot of women, they are crazy. . . . [T]hey must pay this, pay that. The shops will phone you, "Ma'am, you know that you must come and pay us R850. You owe it, you did not pay last month."

In contrast to this all-too-ready commodity consumption that she condemns among her peers, Mrs. Ngunyula has chosen to pursue a prudent strategy of investing in the education of her children above all else, despite slights from her neighbors and acquaintances:

> My first priority is . . . "You must go to school. I want to be proud of you." They criticize me for what I wear. But when I have given you something I feel better. . . . Some at my workplace have shoes for R1,000, but their children don't

even have shoes. I want to be proud of my children. I try by all means to pay the little money I can.

But even such priorities, she notes, can carry the danger of landing one in debt. At one point, keen to help educate the children, she was persuaded by a salesman to buy a series of school mathematics guides on hire purchase. After almost completing their installments, the debit orders mysteriously ceased, only to recommence some years later:

> We paid until there was only R800 to pay. Then they no longer took installments. . . . After about 4 or 5 years, people came, saying, "You owe the company for the book." We said, "Yes, but we have not heard about you, what you were doing, what was going on?" In our pay slip at the bank . . . they dropped it, for 4 years, we don't know why. When he came back, it said we owe again R5,000.[13]

There is clear evidence here of levelheaded opposition to the whirlwind of attractive branded items and the pressures to buy these capitalist offerings. The desire to participate is juxtaposed uneasily to a resistance to "giving in," in a manner reminiscent of the ambivalent feelings experienced by subprime mortgage borrowers in the United States.[14] But even the more farsighted expenditures—on school or university fees or educational books—have the very real potential to get people into trouble (Niehaus 2012, 337–38), especially when combined with illicit ways of collecting payments (for an account of some of these, see Chapter 2). In their attempts to meet these obligations, people are often forced into further indebtedness at the hands of moneylenders, as happened in the case of Thandi Thobela's mother above.

Elsewhere on the social spectrum one sees the same paradoxical combination. Profligacy is acknowledged, but it is disavowed in particular cases. Statements like those of Mrs. Ngunyula are made not only by members of lower-middle-class waged families in the township, but also by more rapidly upwardly mobile people living in the suburbs, that is, by members of the new middle class as it is more commonly understood (Crankshaw 2008; Steinberg 2008). People recently employed in high-ranking positions in government departments, like Abigail Mlate, speak to me disparagingly of the bad borrowing habits of their peers and of how their peers put pressure on them. Abigail withstands the pressures, for the most part, but admits to having an inconsistent response. The time disconnect evident in the "buy now, pay later" ethos features in her remarks:

It depends on my mind-set whether I give in. . . . You find yourself really wanting to . . . keep up with the Joneses. So you find yourself going for expensive things, furniture, because, when they visit me, I want them to see these couches. . . . So you start using your credit card, and at the end of the day it is to your detriment. Because they come and see those couches, and it's only at that point in time they will say, "It's nice" and then forget about it—and you are the one that's left with the debt. . . . Giving in is just not on.

In a later conversation, Abigail's friend Geoff Matlatsi, also a government employee, tells me about the skewed value system that has led his cousins to spend huge amounts on prestige items like expensive cars while continuing to live crammed together in cramped township houses. They in turn mock him for continuing to drive an old Toyota rather than buying a Mercedes. Despite his relatively well-paid and important position, he prefers, he says, a more modest style of living. He chooses to invest in building a house back in the rural area that he hails from and to contribute to the education of his niece. His account counterposes a quest for "things" against "care," disparaging the former (Posel 2010, 162).

In a similar vein, lecturer Bongile Cengimbo points to the way her neighbors in the informal settlement Orange Farm, though living in shacks, buy expensive appliances and brand-name clothes on credit. They, too, mock her for failing to spend the money she earns on items of opulent display. Unable to accept that she prefers a simple lifestyle and is not keen on consumer goods, they ask, "Now you have a job, when are you going to buy a car? When are you going to buy your own house?" She is ridiculed by her friends at university, too, for the fact that she eats simple food, associated with her rural background, like *samp* (maize) and chicken giblets. They protest, "But you could eat whatever you like!" Why, they wonder, does she not spend time sitting around tables in cafés, eating expensive meals, as they do? For Bongile, as for Geoff, it is the obligation to help pay for relatives' education that takes first place. Her insistence on doing so is not, or not simply, a sign that she is choosing to act out of philanthropic motives; rather, it is indicative of her farsighted future orientation. There is little option but to help put her two younger sisters through college, she says, since they will likely ask her for money later in any case. Better to help them get educated now, so that they can eventually earn their own living (see Stauffer 2010).

One force that can exert pressure on people to spend most intensely, both Geoff and Bongile point out, is prospective marriage partners and/or future in-laws. The alliance itself, the wedding, or the kind of lifestyle to be lived thereafter can involve considerable costs. In a manner earlier commentators have noted, and echoing the conundrum of Tseke in *The Tikieline Yuppie*, such expenditures can also detract from one's obligations to one's own natal kin: something that has long been the case (see Brandel 1958). For precisely this reason, both Geoff and Bongile indicate that they have more or less resigned themselves, at least in the short term, to steering clear of marriage.[15]

Getting married or avoiding marriage, paying or failing to pay bridewealth, are matters of central importance. A consideration of them brings us to a broader discussion of how debt and indebtedness factor into other socially important meanings in the everyday life of the family and household: how different obligations and imperatives are balanced against, or converted into, one another, and how people either switch between cash-based and short-term imperatives and moral or longer-term ones, or erect barriers between the separate spheres, thus making them incommensurable.[16]

Marrying, Separating: Conflicts over Bridewealth and Household Responsibilities

Aspiring to become middle class, which encompasses a far wider set of people than those who have "made it," can entail considerable ambivalences. One source of such ambivalence concerns the obligations and dependencies that marrying sets up between in-laws. Equally central, but appearing farther down the line once the nuptial knot has been tied, is the complex negotiation of roles within the household. The latter sounds typically modern, but speaking of the former—bridewealth—might seem anachronistic and irrelevant in a discussion about a phenomenon as contemporary, monetized, and commodity-related as the rise of a new middle class, in whatever setting. In South Africa, however, there is still a real sense in which the quintessentially "moral," enduring relationship that indebtedness ought to entail (Parry and Bloch 1989) is considered, at least in ideal terms, to be that between in-laws. The protracted and delayed transfer of wealth that occurred in the event of marriage in rural society (Krige and Krige 1943; Kuper 1982) provides an archetype of, and model for, relations of debt in their longest-term form. This ideal still holds true, as Impalahoek village teacher and resident Solomon Mahlaba points out to me. (Although himself a speaker of seSotho, it is the widely used township term *lobola* that he uses):[17]

People have been in debt since time immemorial. . . . In marriage, when I pay *lobola*, I don't pay the whole amount. I am in debt—I owe the family of my wife. They have the right to follow me up, and send people, even to send the chief to collect the debt. . . . They might even allow you to have children, and when your first daughter gets married, you are paid *lobola* for your daughter, you will then use these cattle to pay your in-laws.

Bongile makes a similar point. In earlier times, she says, "the role of *ilobolo*[18] was to establish relations between two families. There could be a period of time over which it could be paid—and the bride's family would also make counter-prestations." According to this view, one ought never to borrow money to make marriage payments, since to do so would be inappropriately to incur further long-term social obligation in what is, in and of itself, precisely such a relation. This statement, while revealing the existence of a continuing ideal, conceals changes that have long since transformed the bridewealth relationship. Besides the facts that money has replaced cattle and that the level of payment required has gone up considerably, economic considerations—particularly among the vast majority of South Africa's unemployed in both rural and urban areas (Hunter 2006; White 2004, 2011) and even those who have jobs, but inadequately paid ones, in urban settings (Krige 2012b)—have led to the decline of bridewealth payments.

These changes do not, however, mean "new kinds of possibilities, even freedoms": rather, they imply "exclusion, inequality and private frustration" (White 2011, 7). A young man who is unable to pay bridewealth to marry, but also, himself, is living evidence of unpaid bridewealth in the previous generation, typically lives with his mother's people rather than with those of his father, and he has no opportunity to be reconciled with his paternal ancestors. Apart from the psychic disconnect this implies, it also causes distress in other areas: although "completed bridewealth payments are a distant dream for most young men[,] . . . they nonetheless are trapped in endless accountings of outstanding debts and fines to their partners' relatives" (White 2011, 7). While this sense of debts unpaid and unpayable might hang over many men who have no hope of a way to redeem the situation, there are also those who, despite their minimal earnings, are so committed to paying bridewealth that they take out commercial loans from microlenders, despite a general consensus that this ought never to be an option.[19]

These matters, of grave importance for those who are low-paid or have no employment, also remains a matter of concern for those higher up the scale.

In South Africa's intense hothouse of change and mobility, they often excite fierce debate and contestation. For one thing, exorbitant costs have prompted criticism. Once a man—who is nowadays usually independent of his family—has raised the money for the marriage payments, he is also obliged to pay for the "white wedding" soon afterward, rather than waiting another few years, Bongile Cengimbo told me. The cost of *ilobolo* in Bongile's case, given her education, would be estimated at about R50,000, and the wedding itself would cost about R250,000. In earlier years the cost of the former was sometimes reduced in consideration of the latter, which the bride's parents often covered (Brandel 1958; de Haas 1987). While she understands that her parents would want to demand this payment from any prospective son-in-law, Bongile also feels that the huge debt with which he would be saddled to carry forward into the future would make the arrangement unsustainable. Her sentiments echo those expressed in disputations as long ago as the 1950s, in which parents were often viewed as unduly acquisitive (Brandel 1958). It is these conflicting sentiments that underpin her resolve to stay unmarried, Bongile tells me.

Such costs have appeared particularly extreme since 2000 or so, and indeed they have increased sharply over the two decades prior to that. We can see this if we compare Bongile's stated estimates with the case of the unhappy "yuppie," Tseke, in Mosotho's novel. He and his girlfriend have a child out of wedlock, and his prospective in-laws put pressure on him to bring his family to visit, to negotiate the marriage payments. After a somewhat formulaic complaint by the woman's father about how her education has been interrupted, the "cattle" are negotiated at the lower price of R3,000, instead of the R4,000 that would have been appropriate for a university-educated woman who had not yet given birth. Confirming such amounts, research by de Haas (1987) in Natal recorded occasional payments of up to R3,000. (It must be borne in mind that any comparison is somewhat difficult to draw, however, since the South African rand was worth far more in the 1980s than in 2010.)

Whatever the finer details, it can be seen that marriage payments, added to the cost of a wedding, are considerable. Some see them as a crippling expense that it is unfair to expect men unaided, men and their immediate families and/or uncles, or even men and their wives to bear. Such matters are discussed with passionate intensity by callers to the radio phone-in program *Morning Talk*—held in English on SAFM, an English-language service with a predominantly middle-class audience—that I listen to one day. One woman complains about the way *ilobolo* can serve to sour relationships between in-laws. The bride's parents, she says, are typically acquisitive, demanding amounts that are excessive. Because of their immoderate demands, the future husband often gets into debt. This may impede his ability ever to buy a house for the couple, because it impairs his credit record.

Most contributors to the phone-in program are men. Maintaining that such payments are part of "culture," they echo the somewhat benign and functionalist account: *ilobolo* originally had good intentions and effects in setting up long-term relations between families. But they concur with the female caller's claims about the crippling effects of such payments in the present day. One indeed goes against the grain by claiming that the new phenomenon of parents demanding huge amounts because of having educated their daughter is *not* part of culture but rather "part of capitalism." His view is reiterated by another man who feels that sons-in-law are virtually held hostage by their wife's family. Bridewealth ought to be "abolished," he maintains, on the grounds that "it is a form of trade." The reason many people do not marry, he says, is because they cannot afford *ilobolo*. It would be better if couples simply exchanged gifts, since this would make it possible for them to give what they are able to afford.[20] Such suggestions are not new. There are records from the 1950s and later the 1980s suggesting that "tokens" would be preferable to large payments: but brides' parents—and sometimes brides—have argued that this might devalorize the bride and delegitimize the marriage (Brandel 1958; de Haas 1987).

The male callers to the program, then, it seems, share the feelings of extreme pressure experienced by Tseke in *The Tikieline Yuppie*, but in an intensified form. For Tseke, what imposed impossible constraints are not the marriage payments alone but also the expenses of the ceremony, the food, and the like, and worse still his future wife's demands for particular kinds of high-status clothing. For callers to the phone-in show, both pose an obstacle, with *ilobolo* looming particularly large.

The picture of modern *ilobolo* that emerges, then, is one of considerable financial constraint alongside whatever longer-term moral ties it is intended to confirm. Added to the other elements of mandatory expenditure for the upwardly mobile (or even the "old" middle class), it can in some cases be akin to the straw that breaks the camel's back. There is a paradoxical element here, in that such payments are intended to cement long-term bonds and consolidate family solidarity and relationships between affines. But anecdotal evidence suggests that they can have the opposite effect, because—as in Tseke's case—they pull people in two different directions. If Tseke had fulfilled the expectations of excessive consumption imposed by his in-laws, this would have lessened his ability to help sustain—through the purchase of consumer items—his own mother's need to keep up and confirm her expectations of respectable status, as he felt strongly obliged to do. Relationships of "entrustment" (Shipton 2007) may thus be more conflicted than they first appear, especially as income discrepancies are growing exponentially.[21]

The matter of marriage payments is one that largely concerns family members beyond the immediate household. But after marriage, making decisions about household expenditures might be thought to center more closely on the needs of the immediate family, and on their children—especially for a middle-class (or proto-middle-class) couple. And this is indeed the case, to a degree. But even here the requirements of other relatives often need to be attended to, and this redistributive pressure can draw resources away from the marital household (Stauffer 2010, 210). Couples need to agree on how to balance the imperative of earning an adequate living for the family's day-to-day needs with that of investing in the future. It is the frequent failure of such negotiations that in part accounts for the prevalence of single female parents in the cases discussed in this chapter. "Support for conventional notions of the importance of the two-parent family in the African middle class," whether or not because of experiences like these, "is only lukewarm," according to a recent survey (Schlemmer 2005, 7; see also Khunou 2006).

In exploring this topic, it is remarkable how far particular gender stereotypes come into play. Women, whether single or married, are often typified as those who are most concerned with the everyday care of their families, but also as attending to longer-term investments in their future well-being, most typically via education. Soweto resident Mrs. Matsimbi, for example, has been the parent who considers it of paramount importance to insist on getting her children a good education, a priority with which her husband does not agree. In the case of her two younger children, educating them entailed busing them out of Soweto at considerable cost to attend a "better" school in the neighboring Indian area, Lenasia. In the case of her daughter Rivoningo, it meant the far greater financial sacrifice of paying university fees. Mr. Matsimbi has different priorities, believing that Rivoningo ought to have gone out to work to help support the family after she finished school. In part because of the disagreement, but also because of the general pressure on the family's scarce resources, the family often struggles to meet this commitment. Rivoningo regularly finds herself debarred from the library or ineligible to receive her exam results on the grounds that her fees have not been paid. Only when her mother is paid her annual year-end bonus are the payments completed and her library access reinstated.

I get some insight into similar conundrums as I drive along one day, again listening to the phone-in program *Morning Talk*.[22] The matter up for discussion is how much it is justified for married couples to keep their finances separate. Judging from their accents and concerns, most callers are black and well educated. Expressing the most typically middle-class view is a caller who says that both he and his wife used to have separate bank accounts that they kept secret from each other. But both eventually came clean about it, and each now respects the other's right to keep discrete financial arrangements.

But some express their opposition to holding separate bank accounts on the grounds that it speaks of lack of trust. This trust relates to nonagreement on how household income ought best to be spent, with classic gender stereotypes being brought into play. But in other cases the trust has to do with disputes about how, and whether, to redistribute income to the wider family and to relatives.

Concerning trust in the former sense, one male caller claims that women are concerned with the upkeep of children and family members, whereas men spend money more selfishly, on high-end commodities. But he defends his right to do so, stating emphatically, "I would rather let a *tsotsi* [criminal or gangster] use my credit card than my wife." Countering this, a woman phones in to give her perspective: "my husband is reckless and stupid, so of course I need to keep a separate account."

Somewhat more revealing are those callers whose mistrust was caused by the spouse's use of household monies to support the broader family. One man states that he would not oppose his wife's having her own account if she did so purely to fulfill her role of caring for their children. Where he does object, though, is a case in which a wife would keep money hidden so that she can contribute to her natal family. This he thought was wrong. Calling this "abuse," he maintained that trust needs to exist between spouses to ensure that this will not occur. The next caller gave a rather different perspective on the same phenomenon, saying that he previously kept money secret for the same reason—so that he could pay his mother. (It later emerged, however, that his wife knew all about it and had no objection.)

Such comments indicate a wide range of contrasting practices and attitudes, and they cannot on their own be taken to indicate any specific trends. But where there is dissent over the existence of trust and what it ought to entail, it points to the kinds of conflicts that might eventually lead to marital dissolution or divorce, as in the cases of Abigail and Thandi. The considerable expenses of getting married, added to lack of harmony over how and whether to privilege in-laws' claims, children's requirements, or the needs of the wider family when disbursing household income, make for a potentially conflicted financial situation. Such matters have a particular relationship to the predominance—clearly visible in the cases of Abigail, Thandi, and Anna—of single (female) parents in the new professional class or those aspiring to be professionals. They relate, in turn, to matters of family property. As is discussed in Chapter 6, being married or not can influence whether a daughter is able to contribute to, and inherit, such property.

Conclusion

Members of the new middle class have been said to combine modern consumerist aspirations with a connection to "traditional roots," including a sense of obligation toward family and parents and a commitment to the payment of bridewealth (Bisseker, cited in Krige 2009, 21). A similar aspirational ethic exists within, and serves to inspire, a broader group than that which might be typified by the use of marketing surveyers' living standards measures (LSMs). For them, the effects of competition to consume, pressures to invest, the sharply increasing costs of marriage, disagreements over expenditures, and intensifying claims by the broader family on household resources are considerable. For those public-sector employees like Abigail, however dependent they are on a state income, such demands may be manageable. But managing them can lead to disconnecting from, and repudiating, the claims of a husband and of in-laws. Those who are lower down the ladder handle conflicting obligations in other ways. In sum, such pressures contribute in complex ways to the formation or maintenance of the new professional class, to the aspirations of those beyond it, and ultimately to its experience of indebtedness—the broader topic of this book.

My critical analysis of stereotypes used to characterize the "new black middle class" leads to the topics of later chapters and highlights how this class and its concerns are linked to the contradictory character of the South African state. Its "neoliberal" dimension allows and encourages free engagement with the market and advocates the freedom to spend, even to become excessively acquisitive of material wealth. But it simultaneously attempts to regulate this in the interests of those unable to participate in this dream of consumption while outsourcing the means by which such regulation is attempted. The responsibility to practice "self-discipline" (something Abigail, Thandi, and Anna already embrace) is placed on borrowers themselves, as Chapters 2 and 7 indicate, but without recognizing the complex sets of reciprocities in which they may be embroiled. When individuals do succeed in placing themselves beyond such obligations, the discourse on financial constraint and on such "self-discipline," albeit fitting, may entail new problems. How far the powers that be—whether market or state—play on precisely such obligations, and whether this mismatch between self-discipline and obligations is accidental or more systemic, will need to be judged from what follows.

2 Regulating Credit
Tackling the Redistributiveness of Neoliberalism

I AM IN THE SMALL Knysna office of the Black Sash, South Africa's premier human rights organization.[1] I am talking to Xolela May, a consumer rights activist and lawyer. He is one of a small network of people spread across South Africa whose strong sense of indignation about the credit conundrum and commitment to the cause of the indebted have driven him to play a key role in designing and implementing arrangements to help alleviate their plight and to regulate the activities of creditors.

He gives me some of the background, recalling the origins of his activism. Having grown up in the black township of Langa, he says it was a daily occurrence for neighbors, having become indebted, to be taken to court by their creditors. He'd observe the sheriff of the court arriving and doing an inventory of the family's possessions prior to confiscating them, while they stood by helplessly. Although Cape Town was host to several law clinics and human rights law organizations, Langa residents had no idea how to contact any of these: their plight was an "issue of powerlessness," according to Xolela.[2]

He later rose above his humble origins to study law, worked for a while at the advice organization Legalwise, and eventually joined the Black Sash. At the time, he tells me, a wide variety of providers were feverishly extending credit to people formerly denied it. Debtors were being taken to court in record numbers, and repossessions were being carried out to an even greater extent than Xolela had seen in his youth. What he noticed, in particular, was how legal practitioners acting on behalf of creditors were routinely ignoring particular sections of the relevant legislation—the Magistrates' Court Act of 1944—which might have afforded some protection to debtors: these lawyers were "likely to go to the last stage, so they can have profit."

On the basis of his experiences with indebted people in Knysna, in Western Cape Province, Xolela applied in 2001 to the Department of Justice to house a help desk in their offices, on behalf of the Black Sash. The matter with which he concerned himself most thoroughly was a particular section—section 65—of the Magistrates' Court Act of 1944: the legal framework governing garnishee or emoluments attachment orders, by means of which outstanding debts were being collected directly from a debtor's salary. This framework, he says, provided debtors with greater rights than were normally recognized:

> [It] makes a provision that before any court order can be made in respect of the financial attachment of the emoluments—which is the wages of the debtor—the court has to make it a point that that debtor has remained with sufficient means in order to maintain himself and the family.

Xolela's aim was to monitor and advise consumers who were ignorant of their existing rights. He found that debtors (in "their first time to go to court") were being intimidated into agreeing to unsustainable debt repayments. In a scenario where a debtor has a monthly income of R800, he ought to have "sufficient money left over" after repaying creditors to meet his needs. Instead, such a debtor would agree to give up half his income to repay his debts. As a result of the help-desk program, Xolela and other Black Sash officers built up cordial relationships with local attorneys and counseled creditors against the illogical pursuit of debtors unable to fulfill their obligations. Xolela explains:

> This person is unemployed therefore there is no way you can proceed with the matter. You can suspend any legal action on this matter, because, if you continue, what will be the point of you proceeding with the action while you know at the end of the day you are not going to recover anything? It's a waste of your resources.

While still operating the Black Sash help desk at the Department of Justice, Xolela was also playing an important role in the process under way to draft, conduct consultations on, and eventually pass the key piece of legislation that was intended to remedy many of these ills—the National Credit Act—along with its new debt counseling scheme.

Xolela gives a frank account of both the advantages of the act and its unexpected—and undesirable—outcomes. With great canniness, many lawyers, less able than previously to earn money from pursuing penniless debtors on behalf of creditors, "have changed their hats to own . . . debt counseling agencies," he says. Others similarly switching roles are those who previously acted as debt collectors or debt administrators. The earlier arrangements had been governed by the Magistrates' Court Act, introduced to South Africa on the basis of a precedent from the United Kingdom. The flaw of this act was that, for amounts of less than R50,000—the size of debt incurred by most of the debtors whose cases Xolela deals with—bankruptcy or sequestration (referred to as "insolvency" in South Africa) was not an option. The legislation excluded this possibility, and insolvency was in any case too expensive.[3] The intention of the new act was to provide a system more affordable to those in this category by stopping harassment by creditors, allowing debtors to reschedule debts, and giving them some breathing space in which to make payments while also preventing further indebtedness. Debt administrators, however, were often "unscrupulous individuals who wanted to benefit" by exploiting the desperation of poor people. Spotting the possible end of the old and the onset of the new, they too have entered the debt counseling profession, which they see as a new business opportunity, alongside or to replace that of debt administrator.

My encounter with Xolela illuminates several matters that have been puzzling me in the course of my research so far. It explains something of the dedicated reforming zeal which motivates a number of activists: those who might, in a previous era, have concerned themselves with what appear to be more fundamental human rights abuses but in the current one have homed in on consumer rights—and in particular the rights of those in debt—as a key issue of concern. It provides insight into the character of the legal arrangements governing indebtedness that prevailed during apartheid, and shows which aspects of those arrangements seemed to require reform or abolition, but it simultaneously illustrates the difficulties of replacing the old with the new. In light of these difficulties, my encounter with Xolela illuminates the personalized, entrepreneurial, episodic, and often piecemeal character of the steps taken to put these new arrangements in place. These steps have often generated unintended consequences, producing new problems that in turn have required fresh legislative arrangements to remedy. Reforms were always thus—but there is something about the character of the state and the law in South Africa, I realize in the course of my research, that marks them off as particular, even "exceptional"

(Bernstein 1996). There is great readiness to produce innovative policies in the name of social justice and equality, often on the basis of lessons learned from elsewhere. But entrenched interests often find new ways to assert themselves or to dress up in new clothes, dodging the potential restrictions that reforming initiatives threaten and taking advantage of them to create new opportunities. What eventually results is a mismatch between creditors (who operate with the backing of states and global finance) and powerless debtors (Shipton 2011, 232–33).

I am vividly reminded of my conversation with Xolela when, four years later, I read with horror about the massacre of miners at the Marikana platinum mine. South Africa found itself on the front pages of the world's press in 2012 when police shot and killed thirty-four miners during a strike by rock drillers at the mine. There was horror at the authorities' use of lethal force and at how their force echoed earlier killings in the apartheid era—most notably those at Sharpeville some fifty years earlier. But underpinning the episode was an opposition rather different from the earlier one, in which the politically disenfranchised were faced down by officers of an authoritarian state. Attempting to identify the character of this opposition, a spate of analyses followed the initial condemnation. Among these was the revelation by several newspaper reports that the miners, not necessarily in the lowest pay bracket, had unsustainable levels of debt. An additional feature making this doubly burdensome, indeed intolerable, was the manner in which their numerous creditors were ensuring repayments. Miners' pay, automatically transferred into their bank accounts at month's end, was being transferred out again with equal ease by those to whom they owed money. Shortly after payday, exactly as Xolela had described, many of them simply had nothing left to live on (Barchiesi 2011, 217). The Marikana killings, then, involved a disenfranchisement that was apparently more "economic" than "political" in character.[4]

Until then, the problem of indebtedness had tended to be framed in terms that isolate people and call them to account as "consumers," rather than uniting and leading them to group action or solidarity as "citizens." This suggests that there is something characteristically individual about the phenomenon of indebtedness in the current era. But in the Marikana worker protest it ended up translating into terms that involved confrontational solidarity. There had in fact been strongly political aspects about the way the "debt problem" was framed from the start. Trenchant criticisms of creditors and financialized lending have not been lacking among those who hold office in South Africa's ANC government (Department of Trade and Industry 2002, 2004). The minister of trade and industry, Rob Davies, spoke at a press briefing soon after the shooting about credit providers' "outright preying on the vulnerabilities of low income and working people," and he undertook to implement more controls to check such activities.[5]

One illustration of the deeply "political" character of the credit problem and its proposed solution was the fact that numerous groups of actors from across the board had been consulted in successive drafts of the bill that eventually passed into law. Broadly speaking, those consulted divided into lenders and borrowers, respectively, corresponding more or less with the classic Marxist division between the sphere of capital and that of labor. Perhaps not quite as clearly aligned but tending overall to represent borrowers (and labor) more than the reverse, there was input from the Black Sash, the organization where Xolela worked.

There is a further important dimension. The story of a struggle between capital and labor, while certainly true, needs some qualifying. South Africa's economy came to be dominated, during the twentieth century, by well-established sectors of Afrikaner capitalism ("maize") and English capitalism ("gold") (Trapido 1978, 53). Having participated differentially in the processes of proletarianization that created a cheap black labor force, the two had a decades-long struggle over which would have preferential access to that force. (Both are being in part replaced by a more ethnically hybrid, if still mostly white and English-speaking capitalist sector of "finance.") At the same time, a succession of governments with nationalist agendas, first Afrikaner (post-1948) and later black African (post-1994) have needed to keep themselves close to and ensure the uplifting of other less-easily-definable parts of the electorate. Alongside the clientelistic distribution of jobs and distribution of social grants (Ferguson 2010b; Neves et al. 2010), intermittent attempts have also been made, particularly since 1994, to encourage and accommodate the needs of the increasingly large section of the electorate bent on making a living in the interstices of the system. Marking the advent of liberalization, these operators are framed and encouraged as "small to medium-sized entrepreneurs" (Barchiesi 2011, 128, 135). Their activities, not always strictly legal, have long been tacitly tolerated in a "dual economy" in which brokers and commission-based agents mediate between mostly white-dominated capitalist enterprise and the largely black world of workers, the unemployed, and the poor (and—more recently— the swelling ranks of salaried public servants).

Runaway Liberalization and Belated Regulation

Although for half a century lenders have been entitled to recoup their money from borrowers' bank accounts, the process through which they suddenly started doing so in earnest is a key part of this story. It is the South African version of a broader global trend in which "as lenders re-toughen their terms in an effort to cover their costs while reaching smaller-scale, poorer borrowers, older and more familiar issues about where usury begins also resurface" (Shipton 2011, 231).

The gradual evolution of the state's approach to credit and consumer rights has involved a number of halting steps. It tries to help its citizens better themselves and even become rich; it endeavors to keep open opportunities for small-scale sellers, agents, and intermediaries; and it attempts to curb excessive enrichment by those who prey on the more vulnerable. In the process, the state not only confronts agents set free by those tenets of liberalization but also, in some cases, is haunted by genies let out of the bottle by its own attempts to regulate these forces.

Ostensibly to open up the market for small borrowers, who were previously excluded from opportunities to start small enterprises because of their inability to borrow money from the big banks, existing legislation restricting the interest rate was removed in 1992.[6] Removing the restriction was to enable lenders—in theory, equally small—to run viable businesses catering to the needs of such borrowers, thus creating opportunities for both. Putting a ceiling on the interest rate, as the Usury Act had previously done, would allegedly make it impossible for legitimate microlenders to impose a full-cost-recovery interest rate and cover their expenses. Such small lenders, some of whom had already started emerging in the 1980s, would allegedly be unable to stay in business, and would close up shop or go underground and turn into "loan sharks," offering more expensive credit. It would be to the unsavory practices of these illegal lenders that the poor would then be exposed and vulnerable (Daniels 2004, 846–47).

Out of this action arose an unforeseen consequence—one of the "most dramatic developments in the landscape of access" (Porteous with Hazelhurst 2004, 77). Instead of borrowing to set up businesses, the previously deprived population started taking out loans aimed at helping them engage in consumption. Mark Seymour, a spokesman for the microfinance industry, who I meet in his offices, tells me that "a host of lower-income individuals in South Africa who couldn't access formal credit from the banks" are able to borrow from a sector that can, at last, "price for the perceived risk of granting credit to these people." A new tranche of businesses, quick to respond to promising opportunities, came into being overnight. "From 1992, we started off with zero, up to 2006 we ended up with about R34 billion worth of industry," says Seymour, showing me a graph that illustrates its growth from 1992 to 2008, with the final figure "around R35 billion in terms of gross loans outstanding and around R40 billion in terms of annual disbursements" (see Figure 2.1).[7]

While the opportunities were not limitless, since this initial period of "breakout" was followed by one of "consolidation" during which several lenders went out of business, there was concerted marketing and take-up of loans. Not all participants in this new sector of enterprise were new to lending, and not all of those who were new remained small in scale. Several of the retail banks opened up microlending arms, and some small operators consolidated to become bigger ones. An anecdotal account from someone who observed this process at the time describes the situation in terms that are vivid, if not entirely complimentary:

> A large number of unscrupulous lenders piled into the market. Later, an outfit called ABIL [African Bank Investments Limited] bought out these and other small microlenders. There was a case of someone who borrowed R20,000 from his father and started extending loans at a bus depot. He lost the first R20,000, then told his father he had figured out how to do it properly and borrowed a further advance. Within a short time he had made enough money to buy a house in Johannesburg's upmarket suburb of Sandton, for cash. (Fieldnotes, 27 July 2008)[8]

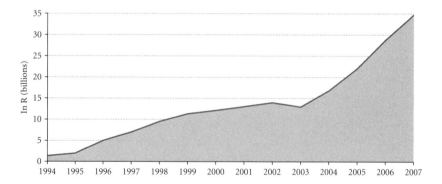

Figure 2.1 Growth of microlending sector

Source: Mark Seymour. Reprinted with permission.

David Porteous, who at the time was in charge of Finmark Trust, an organization partly funded by the United Kingdom's Department for International Development (DFID), with the philanthropic aim of "democratizing finance," identifies a key feature of this new credit landscape.[9] Although it might on the face sound unstable, even "bubblelike," lenders were not in fact unduly exposed to the risk of non-repayment (Porteous with Hazelhurst 2004, 77). This is because they were able, with state sanction, to collect debts through the payroll (especially, in the case of civil servants, via the electronic Persal system through which salaries were paid) or from borrowers' banks by taking their ATM cards and using their PINs, a practice widespread at the time and only later outlawed. As outlined by economist Jimmy Roth, wages paid directly into employees' bank accounts enable employees to "borrow without collateral" or "use their expected wages as a collateral substitute" (Roth 2004, 78; see Anders 2009, 76; for Malawi, see Maurer 2012; for elsewhere in Africa, see Chapter 3).

Whatever the description appropriate to characterize these events of the 1990s, the newly burgeoning credit industry was criticized for its recklessness. The results were certainly negative for the many consumers who had started responding to offers of cheap credit, in the manner that Xolela May described. The offers were coming, newly, from microlenders, clothing retailers, and upmarket grocery stores and car dealers, along with the more customary offers of hire purchase from furniture retailers (see Chapter 3). If we match this narrative with Xolela May's account, it becomes clear that many of those debtors unable to fulfill their obligations for which he set up his help desk came from exactly this group of newly enabled borrowers. It is generally agreed that the overall result has been—in what has become a standard phrase used to describe the situation—detrimental to the financial "wellness" of many (Cash 1996, cited in Bahri 2008; Crous 2008). It has also been productive of a deep sense of "helplessness,"[10] and related to social ills such as suicide (Niehaus 2012, 337–38), divorce, and homelessness.[11]

On the supply side, there is an ethnic-racial dimension to the tale, as outlined in the Introduction. If anxiety about problem borrowing was focused on the newly enfranchised members of South Africa's public service, the attempted regulation of supply focused in particular on a group whose establishment of small-scale lending enterprises had been a response to its own recent disenfranchisement—that is, members of the white, Afrikaans-speaking minority, mostly supporters of the apartheid government, many of whom had been rewarded with civil service jobs in an earlier period. Being offered retrenchment packages, under the black economic empowerment (BEE) scheme, to leave the civil service and make way for black employees, many invested in establishing microlending businesses (James 2012, 24; Krige 2012, 85). It was to curb the excesses of these newly established entrepreneurs—to which the removal of the exemption clause in the Usury Act had initially given rise—that the National Credit Act was formulated. To state matters simply, the public service had been newly restaffed by black Africans, leaving many of its former white Afrikaner employees to seek alternative ways of making a living. Many of them did so by moving into the microfinance industry, and many eventually became registered microlenders. State monies were flowing into the bank accounts of black civil servants, out of which the new entrepreneurs were making efforts to divert them.

The runaway developments and their unintended consequences led, in turn, to the state's clamping down in 1999. A notice revising the initial exemption to the Usury Act was promulgated. It outlawed the deduction of employees' wages directly from the payroll (thus leading to the collapse of the building society Saambou, whose extensive microlending arm had relied on precisely this process, and the near collapse of another large bank), and it outlawed the use of ATM cards to recoup loans from borrowers. It also established the Micro-Finance Regulatory Council (MFRC) (later the National Credit Regulator) and initiated the process that eventually led to the passing of the National Credit Act, with its aim of curbing reckless lending (a phrase used to characterize all creditors but initially aimed in particular at the behavior of the new microlending industry).

Debating the Bill

During debates and hearings on draft versions of the National Credit Act, during which organizations, businesses, consumer rights groups, trades unions, and the like, were invited to comment, there were fierce battles over topics like the interest rate and credit scoring. Underlying the tone of moral rectitude in the submissions made by financiers and business representatives—common in debates on matters of credit and debt, as Parker Shipton (2011, 226, 232) has indicated in his book *Credit Between Cultures*—was "the self-evident" truth, that "all loans and repayments should cancel each other out" (Shipton 2011, 217). Stridently challenging this assumption were the submissions by consumer rights groups, trade unions, and those claiming to represent workers' interests (as well as those of the poor and unemployed). They demanded protection from usurious practices and requested debt information amnesties. They were also, perhaps, requesting protection from the spendthrift behavior of their members.

Blurring the boundaries between these two opposing sides, those speaking on behalf of business often expressed more empathy for workers and consumers than for themselves. Nowhere was this more in evidence than in ongoing disputes about whether the capping of the interest rate would benefit borrowers (by reducing recklessness) or, conversely, disadvantage them (by distorting the "free market"). This came to the fore, for example, in discussions about whether a person "who already has a high debt level" but is faced with an unanticipated life event would be allowed, under the new legislation, to take out a further loan.[12] Business representatives argued strenuously that allowing such extra loans ought not to be counted as "reckless." To allow such loans, however, the interest rate—in their view a neutral, quasi-scientific instrument that enables the competition of the market to provide for self-regulation—ought to be "uncapped" once again and remain unregulated. Failure to do so, said Johann de Ridder, of African Bank Investments Limited, far from protecting borrowers, would "distort supply" and re-create the very same "dual credit economy" that it was imperative to eradicate.[13] In a similar vein, the clothing retailers' submission maintained that capping the rate—to which their sector was currently subject—restricted their "ability to take on more risk by offsetting the additional losses with the improved interest income." They asked to be allowed to charge rates similar to those of UK stores like Harrods, with its annual interest rate of 28.9 percent. Invoking the interests of openness and free market competition, they argued:

> A customer who was not happy with the interest rate from one provider could obtain funding from another provider to settle the debt with the original provider and in so doing reduce the cost of credit to the consumer. This approach will stimulate competition in the market place and will reduce the cost of credit to the consumer.[14]

Such familiar arguments about the character of the free market are criticized by Graeber: "we have all been asked to accept . . . that 'the market' is a self-regulating system" (2011, 363) and to ignore that markets rise and fall in response to state decisions about the interest rate.

Opposing this position, and supporting stringent regulations and the capping of the interest rate, the trade union federation COSATU aimed to protect its wage-earning members from what they saw as the rapaciousness of unscrupulous lenders. Where industry submissions used the shadowy figure of the loan shark (*mashonisa*) as their ultimate weapon and threatened that capping the interest rate would again drive borrowers underground and put them at the mercy of such lenders, the COSATU submission countered that it was precisely the lack of regulation that was likely to cause registered (mostly white) microlenders to engage in exploitative lending practices. They warned of the danger that these microlenders might start to "increase their interest rate on loans, and further exploit the vulnerable and poor, but legally so!"[15] These lenders are the villains in their account; the (black) moneylender or *mashonisa*, informal and technically illegal, is described in contrast as a more community-minded figure (see Chapter 3).

Fierce debate also took place over creditworthiness. Members of South Africa's governing tripartite alliance (ANC, SACP, and COSATU) had long clamored for an amnesty on credit information, which would allow debtors a fresh start concurrent with the act's coming into law. Building on this legacy, COSATU was demanding "access for all, to financial services, including an amnesty for those listed by credit bureaux." Citing the undesirability and destabilizing effect on the financial sector of having "millions of citizens excluded from access to credit, many for trivial amounts and because of exploitative interest rates, lack of affordable credit, discrimination or joblessness," the COSATU submission maintained that "apartheid credit practices and massive exploitation of the poor did not end with the fall of the apartheid regime—they flourished after 1994 and so did credit blacklistings." Since rich people formerly transferring assets offshore had recently been offered an amnesty allowing them to repatriate these, COSATU maintained that it would be fair to offer an equivalent amnesty to the "two million blacklisted adults"—many of them COSATU members—whose status was creating a "serious national problem." Protesting that credit bureaus were "selling information to agencies to screen potential employees," a claim borne out by independent investigation,[16] the union federation claimed that this was unacceptable and unconstitutional, as it threatened to increase unemployment and relegate "jobseekers to further economic hardship." At the very least, failing an amnesty, they demanded that credit information be used only for the purposes of assessing creditworthiness and that sale or use of credit information for other purposes should be an offense.

Submissions on this topic by the business community had a predictably different thrust. The Credit Bureau Association maintained that the bill was already biased in favor of debtors and against the interests of creditors. Arguing that credit is not a "right" but a "market instrument, access to which must be earned," they pointed to how impairing the "free flow" of credit information would be injurious, ultimately restricting credit itself. The section of the bill to which they objected was the one requiring that, once a clearance certificate had been issued recognizing a consumer's having satisfied all obligations, the "credit bureau must expunge from its records . . . the fact that consumer was subject to debt re-arrangement." This, they claimed, would have the unintended consequence of removing "risk predictive behavior data":

> Credit providers will not have the consumer's full credit history when assessing the consumer's debt repayment behaviour and there will be no way for a credit provider to establish if a consumer has a pattern of non-payment and of having his/her debts restructured. Lender confidence in the information held by credit bureaux will be low, resulting in lenders devising other means of protecting themselves against the risk of bad debt.

This was disingenuous, however. During the credit boom of the 1990s, lenders had already "devised other means" of protecting themselves against such risks. This involved gaining direct access to borrowers' bank accounts in one way or another.

A further area of disagreement concerned the ambiguous aims of the act: it was intended not only to protect vulnerable and financially uninformed borrowers from reckless lenders but also, in the new spirit of affirmative action or BEE, to open up new possibilities for black business in fields that had previously been dominated by whites or members of ethnic minorities from South Asia or elsewhere (see Chapter 3). Such opportunities included those of debt counseling itself. But these—especially salespeople's insistent efforts to sell on credit while visiting employees' places of work—would themselves require regulation and necessitate consumer protection. Defending such direct selling, one submission by a microlender, Balboa, points to the central role of selling on credit in providing a livelihood for black people: either those formally unemployed or those combining this means of livelihood with other income-generating activities. The submission points out that the reason "commission driven agents" visit the "work places of potential consumers to enter into loan agreements" is largely because such "consumers are not able during office hours to attend at the credit provider's physical premises," and that worldwide trends in direct selling indicate that "it is certainly convenient, speedy and efficient both for the credit provider and the consumer for the loan agreement at times, to be concluded at the consumer's work premises." Prohibiting such a practice, the submission anticipates, will result in the closure or complete (and costly) restructuring of "many small credit operator businesses relying solely on agents to sell their goods and/or products to employees at their work." It evokes the following scenario should this prohibition of direct selling take place:

> The thousands of agents currently operating within the South African framework would immediately lose their jobs resulting in catastrophic implications for their families and extended families. It is clear that the purpose of the clause is to prevent harassment and consumers' making sudden and rash decisions to enter into credit agreements but by preventing business being done at work or at home a large section of the economy will effectively be destroyed overnight.[17]

While there was no countersubmission on this particular point, Balboa's claims point to the contradictory character of the legislation. For every piece of protection offered to borrowers, one of the semiformal income-generating opportunities so characteristic of those "formerly marginalized" would be forfeit.

Overall, then, members of the business community were reiterating the familiar claim that only by securing market freedom can consumers be best served. The countervailing position among reformers, who recognized the need to counteract the "advantage to creditor principle" that had formerly dominated laws concerning indebtedness (Boraine and Roestoff 2002, 4), was that debtor consumers require protection (Wiggins 1997, 511), even perhaps from their own profligacy. Fitting with this view, the demand for a "credit amnesty," more accurately a "credit information amnesty," was in fact met by the Department of Trade and Industry for a period in 2006. The department focused on deleting records of default judgments. Provided that there was only one judgment and that the total amount owed was less than the threshold of R50,000, it removed "adverse information" for amounts less than R500. A second amnesty was proposed in 2013, but journalists and credit providers predicted that it would have a contradictory effect, making lenders more cautious when lending money to those in lower-income groups and allowing the indebted to end up further in debt to informal lenders.[18]

In most respects, the act as passed maintained the appearance of an uneasy truce. Unresolved issues, already partly addressed by "other means," would need to be attended to in alternative ways.

New Legislation, Old Scams

In what appears as a classic opposition of market forces and state regulation, and of capital and labor, some complicating factors belie the stridency of the claims made by the two sides that were debating the National Credit Bill. The specter of the loan shark, perhaps predictably, is condemned by business as the figure of illegality against whom all ought to be united, but it is defended by unions as a communally embedded creature, striving to make a living and even offering protection against the worst ravages of retail credit. More ambiguously, the community-based direct seller of items on credit who earns a commission seems to epitomize the figure of the small-scale entrepreneur whose efforts the government has been keen to promote. Her lending is a by-product of the way she makes a living, which is barely sufficient to distinguish her clearly from those to whom she sells (and lends) when selling "on tick" (on credit) to those with low wages.[19]

What complicates matters further is the behavior of another set of actors who make their living by enterprise, in a manner whose borderline legality—or full-blown abuse—seems easier to condemn, yet might be regarded as inextricably a part of the system, given that they operated with some impunity under the rubric of the previous laws. The existing legislative framework of the Magistrates' Court Act was much more detailed and restrictive (albeit poorly understood and executed, as Xolela told me), whereas the new legislation, in the modern legal spirit of mediation, was less precise. It was the fine-grained specifications of the earlier legal arrangements that opportunistic and canny operators had used to their own advantage. Legislating against these practices—and not only against the reckless provision of credit—had been one reason the act was drafted and implemented. But if the existing laws were barely enforced, what were the chances that the new act would be any better implemented?

The protagonists of these practices ranged from lawyers who had been discredited but who were nonetheless operating as debt administrators, through unregistered "credit repair companies," which fraudulently offered to expunge the names and records of consumers from the credit bureaus, but failing to do so, to retailers such as those selling furniture or clothes on hire purchase (installment plan), apparently legitimately but engaging in unsanctioned and illegal practices to collect outstanding repayments. Adding to their ranks, the establishment of debt counseling as one of the remedies the act proposed led inevitably (according to the law of unintended consequences) to the establishment of rogue companies and individual operators that offered such services. As indicated by Xolela, it is in many cases the dodgy administrators, operating under the previous set of laws, who have adjusted to the new regime by retooling themselves as debt counselors.

These practices all rely on the ease with which creditors, or their agents, are able to reach into debtors' bank accounts. That is, they rely on the "other means," identified earlier, which protect creditors from the risk of non-repayment. But these "means" have been extended, taking them beyond the parameters of the law. Chief among them, as I am told by legal aid expert Frans Haupt and his team at the University of Pretoria, is the garnishee or emoluments attachment order.[20] Such an order requires that an employer enable a creditor to take a monthly repayment directly from the salary of a defaulting debtor employee, with the creditor bearing a 5 percent charge. The order is granted by a magistrate and served on the employer of the debtor by a sheriff.

The problems with this system go beyond the familiar and much-decried inability of consumers to live within their means. Many practices used by debt collectors to attach workers' salaries are frankly illegal. Awareness of these prompted major employer BMW, with funds from the German Development Funding Agency (GTZ), to commission Haupt and his team to investigate these in detail (Haupt and Coetzee 2008; Haupt et al. 2008). One of these "terrible irregularities" concerned the use of signatures. Although the debtor must sign the consent to judgment as proof that he or she has agreed to the arrangements, according to Haupt, "if you have a legally and financially illiterate consumer he will sign anything, especially if you harass him at work." According to Haupt, debt collectors paid on commission were also forging debtors' signatures or leaving them off altogether:

> Imagine I am a debt collector. I employ . . . ten or twelve field agents who must approach the debtor to get this consent to judgment . . . to an emolument attachment order. I, as a collector, pay these guys . . . a commission on the amount of money that they collect. . . . We came across cases where . . . I must collect from Mr. Jones, and I bring back the consent signed by him, and nobody checks if that is Mr. Jones's signature. . . . A person would say, "That's not my signature," then he'd show us other documents he'd signed, and it was obviously not the same signature. You do not need to be a handwriting expert to see this. Or people who say, "I never signed this document." You'd trace the witnesses. It would turn out that the document had been signed by a witness, but not by the person in question.

There were further irregularities. Debt collectors and creditors, making applications for such orders, were deliberately approaching magistrates' courts that were inconveniently situated—often hundreds of kilometers from where either the employer or the employee was based—thus making it impossible for a debtor to challenge the order to have it rescinded without incurring huge travel costs and/or legal fees. The area of jurisdiction is clearly spelled out in the act: "it is where the employer conducts his business or resides, the idea being that the employer can assist his employee going to that court to have this emoluments attachment order amended or set aside." But debt collectors had been exploiting the "lack of knowledge among the clerks of court" of this fact.[21]

Even without such forays into illegality, the impact of garnishee orders on employee well-being has been acknowledged as extremely worrying. One of the unsustainable repercussions of a garnishee order comes about once a debtor starts borrowing from new sources to pay her original creditors. Each of the new creditors then queues up to apply for a further garnishee order on her salary. This results in a situation where "a large part or even all of the consumer's salary goes to the creditors, leaving the consumer with no or insufficient means to pay for his living expenses and support his family" (Smit 2008, 2). As orders proliferate, so do the negative effects on the "wellness" of employees, including "absenteeism, stress-related illness, pilfering, theft, violence, family problems, reckless gambling, alcohol abuse, unfounded demands for pay increases" (Haupt and Coetzee 2008, 82). Many debtors resign from employment and cash in their pensions to settle their debts rather than retaining them for use in retirement (Smit 2008, 2). Even when granted legitimately, then, the use by of such orders by queues of creditors, together with other kinds of debit orders placed on wage earners' incomes, has been much decried as a source of general social malaise. Many people have been driven simply to abandon their bank accounts and open new ones, I am told by Rebecca Matladi, a community education officer with a nongovernmental organization. This practice had become endemic and was often repeated as creditors continued to pursue them from one account to the next.

Also enabling ready access to debtors' bank accounts was the system of "debt administration," in theory supplanted by but often in fact coexisting with that proposed by the National Credit Act once it was passed. The problems which debt administration was designed to remedy arose, in the first place, from the readiness with which creditors could request consents to judgment and procure emoluments attachment orders allowing access to the debtor's

salary or wage stream; this arrangement was based on the "advantage to creditor principle," which had long been recognized as needing reform (Boraine
and Roestoff 2002, 4). Yet the remedy simply consisted of more of the same,
resulting in debtors' going further into debt. Administrators, once appointed,
would be paid by means of yet another such order, diverting funds into a trust
account so that they could distribute those to creditors. But administration orders themselves had grown "into an industry" (Smit 2008, 1–2) whose rewards
arose largely from malpractice and inadequate policing of the law. Administrators, unqualified and unregistered, often overcharged their clients, or failed to
pay creditors as they had undertaken to do, with outstanding interest from the
unpaid debts then accumulating to the detriment of the debtor. In one case,
administrators extended a loan to one of their clients, added themselves as a
creditor, and "distributed the better part of the client's installment to themselves and the remainder to the client's other creditors." In other cases, "administrators were attorneys who were struck off the roll or were themselves under
administration" (Smit 2008, 14).[22]

Perhaps more shocking were the commissions awarded to the administrators for each payment made. The charging of fees was not in itself illegal, but
in practice there was "fundamental distortion" of the legal framework as originally intended. The court had ruled in 2005 that an administrator was entitled
to only one "collection fee" of a restricted size, but debt administrators added to
this the fees they were able to glean each time they were granted (yet another)
emoluments attachment order on the salary of the debtor: this time for the
purposes of transferring money into the trust account (which would then, in
turn, be paid to the creditors in question). In theory, an employer might take
5 percent; an administrator, 12.5 percent; and the attorneys acting on behalf of
the creditor, 10 percent. According to Smit (2008, 11), "At this rate it is not surprising that administration orders cause debtors to go further into debt." It was
these circumstances that had led to Xolela May's concern, echoed in the Black
Sash's submission, that consumers ought not have to make repayments that
leave them with an income less than the minimum subsistence level.[23]

The reforms were intended to fulfill similar aims to those of debt administration, but this time without the crookery and sharp practice. The idea
was to provide for debt reorganization in cases of overindebtedness. Under
the leadership of Gabriel Davel, appointed microlending regulator and later
chief executive officer of the National Credit Regulator, a new set of procedures was pioneered. "Debt review," of which debt counseling was a key aspect,

was envisaged as bringing to book those credit providers—especially the microlenders identified earlier—who had been engaging in reckless lending and (as an inevitable accompaniment) in queuing up to place garnishee orders on debtors' accounts.[24]

Prescient warnings were made by several of the 2005 submissions, however, against expecting miracles to result from "wonderful legislation." Cost would be one impediment, the "administrative burden" another.[25] Rather than passing new legislation, why not amend the Magistrates' Court Act by making it mandatory to have judgments "dealt with in an open court of law" rather than being given, often fraudulently, by uneducated clerks of the court?[26] Perhaps insufficiently noted was a more fundamental question: would it be possible to reform what was, in effect, a system of "external judicial control" (Haupt et al. 2008, 51) over debtors' finances and salaries or wages, one biased in favor of creditors (Wiggins 1997), to yield one in which individuals, with the help of appropriate advice and guidance, eventually took control themselves, in the way normally expected of a modern, responsible citizen? The perhaps idealistic philosophy of regulator Davel was that "regulation works best when it persuades players in the industry to accept responsibility for their own decisions" (Porteous with Hazelhurst 2004, 94). Much effort was expended by state and nonstate actors to implement systems of financial education and "wellness" to persuade *borrowers* to do this. Making *lenders* accept such responsibility might require more stringent means. It was hoped that credit agreements found to have been "reckless" from the outset might be suspended and made unenforceable by the courts, thus freeing debtors from eternal bondage, but this proved extremely difficult (of which, more later).

Debt Counseling—A Brave New World

Expectations that this "wonderful legislation" might curb creditors' worst excesses were certainly idealistic. But the cards were not automatically stacked in their favor, as my observations of and discussions with debt counselors have revealed. Some debtors had an earnest desire to fulfill the terms and stick by the letter and principle of the law, but the process of getting numerous creditors to agree on an acceptable payment schedule by which a debtor might also abide proved difficult and time consuming. In others cases both creditors and debtors showed extreme levels of recalcitrance: many of the latter simply used debt counseling as a delaying tactic. In sum, the submissions cited earlier, with their opposing claims—either that the legislation would end up serving the interests of the market or (contrarily, and more predominantly) that it favored credit users over credit providers—must be read with circumspection. The complex processes were not skewed in either direction: what they achieved, instead, was a stalemate. The "credit users" they ended up serving, however, were not predominantly those low earners, workers, and the self-employed or unemployed who were originally intended as the primary beneficiaries of the act.

The processes involved in the new schema are as follows: the counselor is required to go through clients' basic needs to identify the amount the client needs to live, setting aside that amount before deciding on a realistic set of repayments to be offered to credit providers. The providers are required to respond within five days, usually sending a challenge or counterproposal. The debtor, once officially under debt review, must be allowed sixty days' grace from those providers before the final schedule of payments must be agreed and put into practice.

National coverage of debt counseling, however, is patchy, and often worst in rural areas, and the training of practitioners is inadequate. The service was initially thought of as most appropriately provided by the nongovernmental, charity, or donor-aided paralegal sectors: by offices such as Knysna's the Black Sash, where Xolela May works. This idea was later jettisoned, partly on the grounds of inadequate capacity—"Law Clinics and NGOs simply would not be able to manage," Frans Haupt tells me—but also on the grounds that it ought to be framed as an income-generating activity that would benefit the unemployed rather than a charitable or overly professional one. The initial requirement that its practitioners have at least two years' experience—in legal or paralegal services, consumer protection, and the like—would exclude too many.[27] The restrictions were lifted, eventually leaving only the almost laughably paltry requirement that candidates undergo four days' training and sit for an examination on the fifth. This resulted in a bifurcated provision. Those targeting the higher-end market possibilities offered by this activity—the "richer indebted"—were unaffected: they have operated offices as "an add-on to an attorney practice, a financial advisor practice, a book-keeping practice: those people have a lot of background and experience. So for them a week-long course is fine . . . they have the capacity, they understand the system," as Frans Haupt tells me. Those, however, who target the people with fewer resources, and/or who operate in more remote or marginal areas, are often poorly trained:

We have had people taking consumers' money as a deposit . . . and debiting it away as a fee, and without the job being done. Then we have complaints about people who had to wait a very long time, and in the meantime they are still being harassed by the credit provider, and they didn't hear anything from the debt counselor. The normal problem that you have when you start a practice is you take on too much because you want to make money, especially in the beginning when your overheads are high—investing in hardware and software, computers and stuff. So they tend to take on a lot of clients, and they can't really service them properly. Some proposals, and even court applications, were simply not up to scratch.[28]

If debt counseling was as much a means of livelihood as one of relieving financial stress, and if in rural areas the setting was already one of poor regulation and borderline illegality, then it is perhaps unsurprising that those formerly benefiting opportunistically from the indebted in one guise were reconfiguring themselves to do so in another. But even this shift of occupation has been slow. Demonstrating that provision has been patchy, there is a commonly shared perception that this "law has not reached" the rural areas. No one has heard of any debt counselors in my rural field site in Mpumalanga. Instead, people refer me, with an ironic smile, to the makeshift posters advertising the consolidation of debt or the expunging of credit records.

What becomes clear is that those most likely to seek counseling are not the previously disenfranchised or poor and marginalized who were the intended beneficiaries of the act. Instead, they are those—both white and black—in receipt of regular monthly payments. But perhaps this was no bad thing. The salaried were, as Daniels argues, the ones most in debt (2004, 842).

The Audit Trail

A key area of expertise distinguished trained from inexpert or "rogue" debt counselors: the need to keep detailed records and track an audit trail. What makes it particularly necessary to keep such records is the emphasis on flexibility in the new legislation. The old system of debt administration had a rigid, rule-bound character, with its judgment orders readily given by clerks of the court. Under this system, frequently abused and misused as I have indicated, a debtor had little protection against the process whereby a rapid succession of automatic deductions were made from his or her salary. Once the clerk of the court had agreed to these, further negotiation was neither required nor possible until all payments had been completed. Under the new regime, in contrast, a debt counselor must negotiate in person between a debtor and what might be multiple creditors. Part of the rationale, as explained by Frans Haupt, is to preempt forms of negotiation between a debtor and any single credit provider, especially a bank, which might ignore "the interests of the non-banking creditor—the medical practitioner, or the microlender."[29]

Figure 2.2 shows a case example concerning two of the "big four" banks and illustrates such an attempt to negotiate. The attempt foundered because, in the course of negotiation between a client and one of these banks, it failed to take another of them into account. In the process, each in a series of telephone calls, faxes, or e-mails sent to each of a series of creditors to negotiate acceptable terms of repayment with them had to be noted. Communications with the client, made to convey the negotiated terms to her, likewise needed to be recorded. Once the proposal was outlined, each creditor was notified and asked for comment, and then further negotiation was required. Much of the counselor's time was spent trying to get in touch with unreachable departments or low-level employees who work in creditors' offices (themselves having typically received minimal training about the processes brought into being by the new legislation) or being referred back and forth between credit providers (CPs) and their lawyers.

Although the net income of this borrower was R15,000 odd, taking her above the law clinic's normal ceiling of debtors owing R10,000, they had nonetheless agreed to take her on as a client. The two banks were Standard (STD) and First National (FNB). Having first requested that their client be put under debt review in 2007, the clinic's counselor made a debt restructure proposal in January 2008, which was accepted by STD, but the clinic was "still awaiting response" from FNB several months later, necessary to get a "consent order" agreed to and an application to court made. After a flurry of (mostly unanswered) phone calls to an employee at FNB, a court application was drafted. The requisite form (Form 17.1) was sent to STD, and the debt counselors made a note to themselves to ensure that the debtor continue to make the restructured payments, as promised. By March 2009 she had started a new job and had paid off some money on all her accounts. In April 2009, STD requested that the Form 17.1 be sent again, starting the debt review process over. The item-by-item list of actions, taken from the "audit trail," documents the frustrating delays (Figure 2.2).

Even for a client with a relatively simple set of creditors—here, only two, and among the "big four"—it is difficult, then, to procure a mutually agreeable

Figure 2.2 Actions undertaken by debt counselor, June–October 2009

June 2009

- Phoned the attorneys for STD. They told me that the account was handed back to STD and that I must phone them about it.
- Phoned STD Legal Dept. to ask if any payment arrangements have been made by this client—No answer.
- Phoned STD—the client has been making payments, but not the actual amounts that were previously accepted in the proposal of 2008. He said the client should re-apply for Debt Review by sending form 17.1 and 17.2 to them again, indicating that the client had previously applied for Debt Review and that the Proposal had been accepted.
- Phoned STD and asked for COBs [certificates of balance, detailing account balance, payment due, interest rate and term of loan], because the client has been noted as under Debt Review again. Received COBs from STD. Sent e-mail to client that I have received the COBs and a proposal will be sent to her CPs.
- Phoned client and asked her to send her salary advice for use in the proposal. Received salary advice from client.
- Phoned client—told her that the amounts for the living expenses that she gave in form 16 are not the same as the amounts in her expense list.
- Sent both lists to client to check correct amounts. Received proof of payments from client. Phoned client to ask which expense amounts are correct. She will look at it and get back to me.

August 2009

- Still no reply from client about correct expense list, so I used the highest amounts in the proposal and sent a copy to her to check the information before we send it to her CPs.
- Received fax from attorneys acting on behalf of STD—60 days have expired from the date of application for Debt Review.
- They say they are waiting for a court order placing the client under Debt Review—the final termination date is only on 21 August. They will only be taking legal steps then.
- Phoned FNB to ask for COB—He said they cannot provide a COB to me because the client's first application for Debt Review in 2007 has to be formally terminated first.
- Phoned client and told her I cannot send the proposal only to STD. I have to include FNB too (even though she has an arrangement with them). Asked her to provide me with the FNB statement that she received from them, because they will not send me a COB. I told her it was urgent.
- Sent e-mail to client—need that statement from FNB in order to draw up the proposal to send to STD.
- Received e-mail from client—sent reply to her that I still need that statement of her FNB account
- Phoned client. She asked if it would be better for her if the account was handed to the bank's attorneys so that the interest will be stopped. I told her that will not stop the interest. When I receive the FNB statement, I will draw up a new proposal, and then we'll have to apply to make the debt restructuring proposal an order.
- Received e-mail from client—the bank phoned her and wants to repossess her car.
- Phoned client to ask about the e-mail that she sent. She is unavailable.
- Client phoned—she says the person who contacted her was from STD
- Phoned STD—no answer.
- Phoned STD's Legal Dept. Anne from STD's Legal Dept. phoned back. She has since seen that there is a dispute marked on this client's file as she has re-applied for Debt Review and

(*continued*)

Figure 2.2 *(continued)*

STD has stopped all legal action taken against the client, so if she receives any notice of execution, she must just ignore it. Phoned client to tell her this.

September 2009

• Sent e-mail to client asking for FNB statement again. Client phoned. She said she just spoke to Jabu (FNB) and I must phone him for a statement.
• Cannot reach Jabu, so I phoned FNB—She said I must fax proof from the Law Clinic that I need a statement.
• Sent fax to FNB. Phoned Jabu—I haven't received any reply from him. No answer. Phoned FNB—cannot find Jabu—asked them to send a COB to me. Received COB from FNB.

October 2009

• Client sent e-mail to ask how her case is going.
• Sent proposal to CPs and to client.
• Received e-mail from STD—they need the vehicle finance details to consider the request.
• Phoned STD—no answer, so I sent an e-mail to him asking what asking what details on vehicle finance he still needed.
• Received reply from STD to forward the details on the insurance on the vehicle finance from the client. She sent this to me.
• I forwarded this document received from the client to STD.
• Proposal rejected by STD—they sent a counter-proposal with lower installments and interest proposed.
• Phoned FNB to ask if the proposal had been accepted—she says they have no record of the proposal, so I sent it again.
• Phoned client to tell her about the proposal being accepted by STD.
• Sent e-mail to STD that the client accepts their counter proposal.
• Forwarded all these documents to the client.

Source: University of Pretoria Law Clinic. Reprinted with permission.

Note: COBs = certificates of balance (detailing account balance, payment due, interest rate and term of loan); CP = credit provider; FNB = First National Bank; STD = Standard Bank.

arrangement. It took this client two years (which encompassed the starting and restarting of debt review, since the deadline of sixty days had elapsed on more than one occasion) before the creditors finally agreed to her repayment proposals and the court approved them.

Reforming Persons: Deserving and Undeserving Debtors

When hearing about the difficulties that cause clients to get into debt, counselors often find themselves going far beyond the technical skills of debt rescheduling to embrace the role normally associated with advice of a more therapeutic kind. When I visit debt counselors Rethabile Tlou and Richard Mutshekwane at their modest offices in Midrand, their accounts vividly illustrate this point. "Just when you think you've discussed everything—'here are all the creditors, this is my pay slip'—you find that the real stories start to pour out: there's a divorce pending, or the children are giving me a hard time, or this and that," Rethabile tells me. While counselors are supportive in such cases, they can also become impatient with recalcitrance. The act is written "nicely," so much so that it can encourage backsliders, she says.

Richard confirms that "the system has been so crafted that it gives everybody a chance." This evenhandedness is built on the assumption that undertakings for repayments made by debtors and the responses by creditors are made "in good faith," and there are indeed occasions when the requisite spirit of collaboration is in evidence. "There has been a lot of give and take" between debtors and creditors, he says. Equally, however, there can be evidence—from both parties—of lack of "faith." In the case of creditors, Rethabile complains, their counterproposals are often nitpicking and unreasonable:

> You've got ten creditors to satisfy, this one tells you, "No, I'd rather not have R50, I'll have R53." But why must I change the whole agreement? Or they will say, "Go ahead and do a proposal based on this." . . . So I go ahead and I do it. Then they say, "You had no right to go and reduce my interest rate," and I say, "Tough luck. This is according to the rules that *you* wrote."

Considerable efforts were likewise necessary to exact compliance from client debtors. "We forget," says Richard, "that these people are the worst insofar as committing to anything." Counselors find themselves alternately threatening creditors and morally blackmailing them in their efforts to get them to cooperate. Rethabile continues:

> You have to tell them, "The moment I reject you and the creditors know, you lose the house, you lose the car, they can do anything they want. They can sell everything, they can even sell your clothes. They've got the right to do that." You need to constantly remind them that these are the powers you have. . . . And you can just say to the client, "Why do I have to phone you, beg from you? You are not acting in good faith. You don't deserve to be on the program."

Even those client debtors who do not prove to be unreachable often make their rescheduled payments for only a short while, stopping after two or three weeks. Clients' files are often closed on the basis of their non-cooperation.

Although the act was designed to balance the needs of creditors with those of debtors, it is recalcitrance by the latter that debt counselors find themselves addressing. The far greater muscle of creditors makes it difficult to "reform" such creditors without recourse to robust legal proceedings. But here these creditors—mostly large banks or retailers—have the edge because they are able to hire top lawyers. Reform of legislation had been turned into the attempted reform of persons. In their attempts to rectify debtor behavior, debt counselors used a rhetoric emphasizing "merit" and the quality of being "deserving," pointing to the way a reformed debtor "ought" to behave. They celebrated cases in which debtors comported themselves appropriately in compliance with their injunctions.

Conversely, borrowers seen as having excessive appetites invited opprobrium. One such client was from an upmarket Johannesburg suburb, and Rethabile and Richard give her advice about living within her means:

> Accounts with Investec [an asset management firm], accounts with Standard Bank. You could tell that this was a typical case of keeping up with the Joneses. "Oh, my kids will not like this . . . if I tell them that they've got to drop their standards." How was she going to tell Investec Bank that she was under debt review? A pharmacist . . . she moonlights to make ends meet.

This client, like many others, was hesitant about committing herself to the process: "She is still thinking about it. She thinks she can handle it. It's like any addiction: you think you can handle it, but it overwhelms you. We've got many people, we send them forms, but they never come back."[30] Such a borrower is deemed to be "not taking responsibility."

I am told about a similar client by Mareesa Erasmus, a debt counselor working in the Pretoria University Law Clinic. The client had "retail accounts, personal loans, bank accounts. And with every possible institution she has a credit card . . . sometimes more than one at the same place." In negotiations with the relevant credit providers, Mareesa had challenged them for their original profligacy in having extended credit to this woman:

> "Don't tell me you guys are not guilty." But they say, "Oh, it was before the act." . . . I asked one, "What happened in 2006? She has a number of new credit agreements starting just then." . . . What happened in 2006 was, they would send invitations, send credit cards to clients. . . . She was too weak to reject them. She said that if *they* thought she could afford it, maybe she could.

"Credit," in this case, "has been just dropped at her door," says Mareesa. The client owed a total of R485,000, was earning a salary of R19,000, and had been paying her monthly living expenses—which she had estimated at R53,000—by living "on tick." She was "85 percent overindebted." According to Mareesa, initially, at least:

> She said she was doing fine—paying accounts with accounts. . . . Take the Absa Credit Card to pay Nedbank, take Nedbank Credit Card to pay the Standard Bank, and so on. She'd turn them around until she got to a point where she realized this was not going to work any more.

But even after this client's application for debt review, Mareesa was struggling to get anywhere with the case. The client fit the profile of someone who was "not doing anything to reduce their expenditure," who was "still living a luxurious lifestyle—not abiding by the suggestions . . . made when we drew up the proposal." Frustrated by the client's noncompliance, Mareesa's only option was to go to court to request a reduction in the interest rate on the client's behalf, yet she knew that without a visible sign of her commitment "to reduce expenses," this would likely not be granted.

Keen to get some rulings made and some precedents established in this all-important piece of legislation, Mareesa knew that whatever case she did take to court would need to be selected with care. Rather than featuring a resolutely extravagant borrower, it would have to involve one who was making strenuous efforts to reduce her owings and expenses. The client who seemed to fit the bill was a member of the black professional class but had fallen on hard times. Having earned R25,000 as a dentist but having lost her job, she had remained unemployed for six months and had found a new job earning only half the salary. But she still owed R130,000 on her car. In marked contrast to the client mentioned earlier with multiple credit cards, this client had made efforts drastically to reduce her living expenses to R5,800—"for everything, rent, petrol, etc. insurance"—but, having no other way of getting to work, she was reluctant to give up her car. She had been paying a third of her monthly income in repayments to the vehicle-finance wing of Nedbank, leaving approximately another third to distribute to her other creditors. After she had approached Mareesa to help with debt rescheduling, the two of them had worked out a proposal to submit to the vehicle financers:

> We offered R2,900, [and] they came back and said, "No, we want R4,030" . . . I have a lot of problems with vehicle finance, in terms of making a suitable offer . . . but at the same time not being unfair towards the credit providers. Other credit providers are more reasonable. I discussed this with my client and

she said, "Is that their final offer?" I told her, "I think we should take it to court, but there is a risk." . . . She instructed me to continue, she wanted to take their offer, pay the R4,030, keep the car, and see what she could do with the other credit providers.

"Now," Mareesa tells me, "she is trying to get extra income" by doing extra lecturing work. "Because she now realizes that the only way she is going to get out of this is to improve herself. . . . And that is something in which we try to motivate the clients, as well. Sometimes, we say, 'You can do better.'"

Being subject to the vagaries of fate, combined with a demonstrated willingness to tighten the belt, made this client appear more deserving and enhanced the chances that she would have her argument accepted in court, should matters fail to be resolved without such recourse. This case, Mareesa reckoned, had a greater chance of success than that of the suburbanite with multiple credit cards. This client was not "living in luxury" but "on the minimum." Mareesa was hopeful that the court, in such a case, would "recognize what is going on and make an order that is fair."[31]

Small Successes and Ways Forward

The reforms, debt counseling in particular, were thus having little effect. Small but significant successes ought not to be denied, but some of the reduction in borrower and lender excesses that followed my fieldwork owed themselves more to the unemployment accompanying the global economic crisis than to the new regulatory framework.

Given that many problems had arisen from inadequately policed legislative arrangements already in place, some minor victories were won through judicious strategizing or addressing the shortcomings of the old by applying the new, and—crucially—ensuring its enforcement. While many practitioners bemoaned the fact that most magistrates were ignorant of the act (often asking counselors' advice on how to apply it, for example), the canniest among them, I hear from NGO officer Dawn Jackson, made efforts to select only those magistrates who *had* made it their business to learn the new procedures.[32]

Protagonists of the new legislation recognized the need to curb the worst excesses of the old. Noting that existing frameworks were proving to have considerable staying power, they took action against those who abused them. In one case, the team at Pretoria University Law Clinic was determined to stymie a single creditor—a mortgage lender—who had shown signs of trying to jump "to the head of the queue" by applying to the clerk of the court to get a garnishee order on a debtor's salary. Had the creditor been able to push all its competitors aside in this way, this would have disadvantaged the client himself. By taking his home loan out of the total reckoning of monies to be distributed, it would have made his debt review implausible and rendered him unable to benefit from debt counseling.

Incidentally, this attempt by individual creditors to outmaneuver one another was in evidence long before the introduction of garnishee orders. A similar situation obtained some seventy years previously. Social worker Ray Phillips quoted a black pastor, Rev. Henry M. Nawa, who was experiencing difficulty collecting overdue "church fees" from his congregants:

> When you come to get the fees you find the furniture man who wants to collect and other Native men to whom money is owing and to whom promises have been made. The ones who come first get the money, the rest are put off with various promises until a later time. (1938, 40)

In that earlier period, however, the creditor who wanted to jump to the head of the queue was obliged to stake a claim by arriving in person. What has since made debt collection a much more streamlined and impersonal affair was the ready issuing of garnishee and administration orders on debtors' bank accounts.

Fraudulent debt administrators, still operating under the old scheme, also became a focus of concern. In one case, the University of Pretoria team was approached by a client who, previously seeking relief through debt administration, was switching to do so through debt review and debt counseling. The client, along with two others, had been put under an administrator who, despite having the money paid directly into his trust account from the salaries of these clients via the garnishee system, had made no payments to the clients' credit providers. The law clinic acted, attempting to repossess the property of the administrator. But the clinic found that another creditor had beaten them to it (in the case of his office furniture) and that his household effects did not belong to him and thus were not eligible to be confiscated. The administrator was reported to the police for fraud. He was being dealt with, in this case, using the means normally deployed against recalcitrant debtors. In a reversal of the old proverb, gamekeepers had become poachers, and sanctions imposed under the new regime were being used.

What of the clash between the interests of creditors and debtors that had caused early difficulties to debt counselors? I hear from Rethabile Tlou a year after our first meeting that "the various parties have got together and agreed on some rules," that both a mediating agency—the National Debt Mediation Agency (NDMA)—and a special tribunal have been set up to keep cases away from costly litigation and out of the clutches of undertrained magistrates, and that new forms of software have been developed to enable paperless operations. She complains, however, about losing work to the flood of new debt counselors, some of whom had turned out to be rogues. Two had been prosecuted for taking people's money. "Different people do this job for different reasons, but the good ones, . . . and the NCR [National Credit Regulator] in general, will get a bad name because of these bad ones," she notes.[33]

Where the aims of the reforms had been achieved, this was more because of the broader economic slowdown than because of these reforms themselves. The amounts of credit on offer has been drastically reduced, independent consultant Marlene Heymans tells me when I meet her in 2009. Mortgages and unsecured credit have both halved. Banks are reining in, either refusing credit where they previously offered it or giving it at much higher rates of interest—around 15–20 percent per month for a short-term loan. Borrowing, at least from formal lenders, has thus decreased. We discuss the extent and effects of debt counseling. Whereas previously only three thousand people per month were applying for counseling, figures gathered by the National Credit Regulator (NCR) indicate that three times as many are now doing so—although not all were accepted. The amount of indebtedness accounted for by debt review and debt counseling has increased sharply. In contrast to June 2008, when there had been a "structured redistribution" of indebtedness of R11 million per month, the figure, she tells me, has climbed to R160 million per month. (At the same time, the number of credit-impaired consumers has grown considerably.)

Given that the global recession hit at around the same time that the act became effective, however, "the whole picture is distorted by the loss of jobs," Heymans told me. "This is what is leading people to fall behind on their payments, and this leads to the increase of people going to debt counseling."[34] Having least demonstrable impact is that aspect of the act relating to reckless lending: "around half of credit providers . . . have taken it to heart. But for the others, it's a case of 'what chance is there of being found out?'" Such attitudes are fostered by the fact that the courts have failed to rule definitively on the matter or to provide any case law. In one case where debt counselors took creditors to court, they used a local and inexperienced lawyer, whereas the banks brought in "four senior counsel." The court found against the debt counselor, awarding considerable costs to the banks.[35]

Cases in which the court found against creditors for reckless lending are few and far between. In one, Absa was found in 2010 to have extended a home loan to a person who was soon to retire and would clearly have no means to repay it.[36] In another, a debt counselor took African Bank and other credit providers (including Absa, FNB, and Nedbank) to court on behalf of several debtors— some of whom had repayment commitments amounting to between 79 percent and 160 percent of their monthly income—and secured a guilty verdict.[37] A third case showed that illegality was present in the heart of the financial sector and demonstrated the determination of borrowers to become indebted "at any cost." An officer in African Bank's branch in Dundee, KwaZulu Natal, was alleged in 2012 to have been accepting bribes from customers in return for approving their loan applications. In addition to the R15 million lost to the bank through this fraudulent activity by its employee, the NCR asked the National Consumer Tribunal to fine the bank R305 million for reckless lending.[38]

Overall, then, the act's lack of bite in regulating lenders seems to have become generally accepted. Rather than trying to police them, Rethabile's approach has now become one of reforming borrowers:

> The person *must* pay back, and must make an effort to do so. Don't look at it as "They had no right to extend the loan"—this is beside the point. Instead, I try to encourage people to pay back. Make an effort—it *has* to be a painful process. Otherwise they won't learn the lesson. You need to make sacrifices. Forget about movies, eating out three times a week. The only way is to pay in as much as I can. This way I get a lot of acceptance from creditors. I try to practice a system that makes sense.[39]

Conclusion

This story of credit reform has been quintessentially South African. Attempts to liberalize the economy and provide opportunity, coupled with the promise of freedom (including the right to consume), unleashed a wave of credit provision. Both borrowers and lenders initially seemed to benefit from liberalization, but things soon became unsustainable. Subsequent, belated efforts were made by the state to curb the worst excesses. Reformers were optimistic that, with perfectly designed intervention, the thin but steady trickle of credit essential to a liberal vision of well-being might be sustained without trans-forming into something that might impair financial wellness. In a setting where "neoliberal means interweave with and facilitate redistributive ends" (Hull and James 2012, 16), the thing most likely to sustain that trickle, however, proved to be the processes of redistribution, enabled by the receipt of salaries paid regularly into bank accounts and by the readiness with which garnishee orders against these could be procured.

The reforms embodied a spirit of democratic engagement by opening the doors to comment from widely divergent constituencies. But these seemed only to represent in starker form the irreconcilability of the interests of bor-rowers and lenders, of labor and capital. Ultimately, the interests of the latter seem to have been predominant (Boraine and Roestoff 2002, 4; Wiggins 1997, 511), in denial of the idea that "lenders, like borrowers, should earn their trust" (Shipton 2011, 232). Mediating that stark opposition, however, there were the continual reminders that many not-so-well-off people were making an oppor-tunistic living in the zone in between them.

The earlier arguments about setting the interest rate (it was eventually capped at 44 percent), turned out to be misguided in the longer term.[40] The people originally targeted for recklessness—informal borrowers and the new, small-scale microlenders whose entrepreneurial energies had been unleashed by the initial liberalization—were not those whose borrowing or lending ended up being curbed (if anyone's was) by the act. But perhaps they had been the wrong target in the first place. Those intended ought, instead, to have been wage and salary earners, those gradually climbing up the ladder of class mobil-ity. If they were the ones in greatest need of rescue, they were also sustaining the most intense demands on their salaries—their greater earning power often meant that they were supporting poorer relatives—and thus the most likely to need to borrow.

The questions that remained unresolved, despite thoughtful submissions by stakeholders to the bill, were those being left to debt counselors to resolve. Some were hopeful that they might be able to have magistrates settle creditor-debtor disputes—and ultimately the interest rate—by law. But magistrates, schooled in the old legislation and too little acquainted with the new, proved unwilling or unable to take such action. Even in higher courts, where action might have been possible against the reckless excesses of credit capitalism that had failed to take heed of the information provided by the credit bureaus, the greater legal muscle of that capitalism was holding sway. Small successes by legal activists exploited areas of uncertainty between the old and the new, but none of these had yet proved sufficiently robust to qualify as reform. A few refashioned citizens, a few punished small-time commission agents and debt collectors, and the very occasional punishment of large financial organizations, seemed to be the most the efforts might yield.

The orderly attempts to control and rationalize clients' finances and lives by well-meaning counselors seems to be a long way from the harrowing account of the Marikana protestors who were killed over their debts. But the violence of Marikana is the sign that matters were left unresolved, and perhaps that their only resolution might be by further, and more overtly political, tussles between creditors and debtors, rich and poor. The earlier efforts to solve the problem by negotiations between these seemingly irreconcilable groupings had foundered. To understand more about why, we need to explore the underpinnings of credit apartheid.

3 "Ride the Camel"

Borrowing and Lending in Context

UNAMÊLA KAMÊLA (ride the camel) is a seSotho proverb. Debt is like a camel, explains Impalahoek resident Ace Ubisi. Be careful when you ride on its back, because it is easy to fall off and be kicked. His explanation draws attention to the sense of runaway danger coupled with violence experienced by those who have borrowed money. But in elaborating, he uses a different range of metaphors. The word for debt is *sekôlôtô*. It has its origins in the Afrikaans, *skuld*; its related verb is *go kôlóta*, "to owe." The use of this word from the lexicon of the settler farmers, like others from the register of commodified relations—such as *go bêrêka*, "to work," from the Afrikaans *werk* (Comaroff and Comaroff 1987), or *tšhêlêtê*, "money," from the Afrikaans *geld*—suggests that the phenomenon and experience of debt is profoundly connected to the domain of wage labor, in which blacks worked for whites.[1] People often use it, however, to suggest something more like a precapitalist relation: a labor contract with no end, a form of enslavement. *Skuld* also suggests guilt, even shame: emotions whose association with owing money were alluded to in Chapter 1.

Lerato Mohale, a female teacher who lives and works in Impalahoek tells me about her brother. Like her, he is a teacher, receiving a regular state salary. Having borrowed money from local moneylenders, or *mashonisas*, he has been risking the dangers of riding the camel. But more insidiously, he is effectively "working for" the lenders:

> He comes to me after one week, his salary is all gone—to the *mashonisas*. . . . Once or twice I tried to sit down with him, I say, "Let's pay all the debts so you can get out [get away] from the *mashonisas*." I told him to sell that car,

and to go to school on foot, because it is not far. . . . But he did not sell it. Next week the car will be at home, he will go to school on foot, because he will have no petrol.[2]

Borrowers like Lerato's brother have ambivalent feelings about lenders—many of whom hail from among their own ranks. On the one hand, as *skuld* (in its sense of "guilt") suggests, they often blame themselves or lay the responsibility squarely on their own shoulders for having been unable to curb their own consumption, or for spending money on frivolities and unnecessary things, rather than holding the moneylenders responsible for their misery. "You are a beggar," says one, pointing to the flexible terms and reasonable interest rates when compared, for example, with that charged by furniture stores for hire purchase and to the speed with which a loan can be procured. "You have asked for help so you can't argue," says another. On the other hand, people come either to resent their own enslavement or to denounce the weakness of relatives (husbands, brothers) for allowing themselves to enter into such long-term dependencies. The initial self-blame soon turns to anger, as I learn from another Impalahoek teacher, Solomon Mahlaba:

> They are helping and in a way they are exploiting. Because you are desperate when you go to them. They give you the money. They feed you in that moment. But in the long run they exploit you because the interest they are charging is so high. You won't ever finish paying. You pay and pay, and then you realize, "Now I'm being exploited." But at first it helps you.[3]

This sense of inescapable enslavement is associated with intimidation and violence in some cases, as with the classic loan sharks of film and fiction. Impalahoek resident Ace Ubisi, for example, has borrowed widely. He has been beaten up on several occasions, he avoids going near the shops in case he happens upon the agent of one of someone to whom he still owes money, and he once resorted to moving out of his house to avoid further brutal encounters with his many creditors. On occasion, *mashonisas* have been said to attempt to kill defaulting clients. Conversely, clients have also killed *mashonisas*. When an Impalahoek woman teacher who was a renowned lender died in suspicious circumstances, rumor had it that borrowers were responsible for her death. Confirming that this option is considered a possible means of escape, a participant in a Johannesburg meeting held by the Standard Bank's "community banking" forum tells me wryly, "That's one way of canceling the debt."

Such tales of violence and intimidation (in both directions) are giving way to something new: neither the brutality of the classic loan shark nor the retaliation of his client is now as inevitable as it previously was. A loan shark in any case is not as easy to define as much of the literature suggests; rather, the categorization is fluid and highly contingent. The term can refer to an actual person or to a business; it can describe someone who lends money only once or someone who builds up a reputation over time; it can denote both a large-scale and more permanent moneylender and a smaller or more sporadic one.

More in line with the insidiousness of enslavement, however, circumstances have recently conspired to place borrowers more inexorably in the grip of all kinds of lenders—both legal and illegal—than they have in some other settings (Guérin 2014; Villarreal 2014). These circumstances derive from a combination of sudden liberalization, deepening financialization, the banking of the unbanked, and companies' capture of personal data. What has resulted from these combined factors is a particularly inescapable debt bondage. The new regulatory framework has attempted to mitigate that bondage, but although formal (registered) lenders are legal and informal (unregistered) ones are not, there is often not much difference between the two. And since borrowers are often ignorant of the regulations, they use the term *mashonisa* to refer to both kinds of lenders.

This chapter explores the relationship between modern techniques and technologies of lending, borrowing, and extending credit, as well as the more social and less apparently formal arrangements on which they rely and that they also facilitate. Following Jane Guyer (2004, 158), I question the usefulness of a binary model in which capitalism is counterposed to local forms of exchange that resist it. The material presented here lends itself instead to seeing formalization as a dynamic and fluid process, which is extended piecemeal rather than uniformly and in a homogenizing manner (Guyer 2004, 157). Formalization and informalization thus occur in interaction with each other, producing a plurality. The South African context is admittedly one in which financialized arrangements long predated and still exceed those in other African countries. Black people, however, were earlier excluded through certain habituated patterns, credit apartheid, which were laid down during an earlier period. How far have those patterns laid the basis for later repayment arrangements, and to what extent, in more recent times, has the increasingly effortless flow of money altered matters? If credit apartheid remains in place, are its effects brutal like the kick of *kamêla*, or do they entrap borrowers in unending peonage, like the life sentence of *sekôlôtô*?

Habituations of Credit in South Africa

It is widely accepted that the discrimination for which South Africa is infamous, producing what some have called a "dual economy," extends into the terrain of borrowing and lending. The story of credit apartheid is closely linked to and begins with South Africa's patterns of racialized land ownership and exclusion. In this respect, South Africa's credit landscape differs markedly from the situation in, for example, many Southeast Asian and South Asian countries. Here, borrowers faced with agricultural shortfalls were often dispossessed by moneylending landlords, and in extreme cases indebtedness became a mode for lenders to dispossess their borrowers. Debt turned "nominally independent landowners" into the effective tenants of such moneylenders, "disciplined by the need for loans and the threat of foreclosure" (Murray Li 2010, 387). Other cases from South Asia, however, illustrate how lenders, rather than dispossessing borrowers entirely, cultivated their ongoing dependence, often beyond the lifetime of both the borrower and the lender (Martin 2010; Mosse 2004; Shah 2010). Long-standing relationships that combined paternalistic dependence and exploitation developed between low-caste or tribal people and their landlords, who in many cases were also those who lent to them.

South Africa's land dispossession, in contrast, being more definitive, failed to give rise to such long-lasting and personalized relations of debt, although these did develop in the interstices of the system as time went by. Following colonial conquest, there was a considerable period in the late nineteenth and early twentieth century during which black people—especially those who were or would later become members of the emerging middle class—made efforts to procure their own land. Some were granted title in recognition of their former occupancy; others formed syndicates and bought land via missionary and other intermediaries given that laws forbade black ownership (Cobley 1990, 157; James 2007, 53; Murray 1992, 37–44; Trapido 1978, 28). Given the extent and influence of nineteenth-century mercantilist capitalism in the region, the existence of numerous mining and land companies, the wide spread of settlers and traders across often remote areas of the country, and the prevalence of imperial banks, the opportunities for land speculation were considerable, and some black owners either lost their land after having borrowed against it or willingly sold it to pursue education and other modern investments (Beinart

1986, 265; Beinart and Delius 1986, 24; Murray 1992; Trapido 1978; Verhoef 2009). To cut a long story very short, the passage of several draconian laws (in 1913 and 1936—although they took decades to fully enact) secured most farmland for white owners. The eventual commercial success of some of those farmers (though by no means all) depended not only on the consolidation of the prejudicial laws preventing black ownership but also on a series of other measures. One was the pressure brought to bear on black occupants to be-come rent or labor tenants who, while continuing to cultivate, also worked for the farm owners (Beinart and Delius 1986, 33–34; James 2007, 6, 39, 131–39; Trapido 1978, 30–31). Another was the provision of state subsidies and the es-tablishment of state marketing boards (Beinart and Delius 1986, 29–42; Morrell 1986). But central among the mechanisms that eventually secured the success of white capitalist farmers and the demise of their black counterparts was the provision of credit on favorable terms to the former and the withdrawal of similar facilities from the latter (Beinart and Delius 1986, 29–30; Morrell 1986, 379–80).[4] For the blacks who remained on the farms, increasing restrictions on their time and decreasing access to the market, and to credit, eventually caused many to leave for the reserves, where others had resided all along, far from urban centers of commerce. The townward migration of black cultivators then began in earnest.

In the interstices of this racialized system, the stark exclusions of credit apartheid were accompanied by—and even laid the basis for—more person-alized arrangements through which it was partly mediated. When colonial authorities increased hut taxes, some black cultivators and pastoralists found themselves compelled to borrow from moneylenders (Carton 2000, 57). When faced with shortfalls, they borrowed from nearby traders or store owners (Krige 2011, 137; van Onselen 1996, 253; Whelan 2011, 88–89, 93–94). Blacks who settled in town, in contrast, had a wider range of credit sources. Rural-urban migrants with strong home connections borrowed from their compatriots, where migrants who were more settled (but unwaged) took out loans from neighbors who were earners: a practice that continues today (Krige 2011, 137). Alongside these informal practices, borrowing from shopkeepers or buying on credit became a widespread practice for both town and country dwellers. While the retailers belonged to the white settler constituency in certain areas, both rural and urban, in others they were ethnically marginal merchants who sold (and lent) to blacks in areas where their counterparts from more majority settler backgrounds did not venture (Beinart 1986, 266–67).[5] Predominantly, these were Gujarati-speaking Muslims from the Punjab and Jewish refugees from Russia and its borderlands (Hart and Padayachee 2000; Kaplan 1986; van Onselen 1996, 80, 93, 113, 186). Lest their dealings be thought to have been solely exploitative, van Onselen reminds us that these traders were "often sympathetic" to their black customers, themselves being "emigrants from societies dominated by peasant economies" (1996, 186). Some traders' enterprises remained as small "native" trading stores, probably combining such sympathy with profit in a fine balance; others expanded their businesses into large retailers, and from the 1920s, but increasingly so more recently, retailers began selling their goods on hire purchase (installment plan) (Kaplan 1986, 327, 167; Phillips 1938, 40–41).

While there may not have been a purposefully exploitative motive on the part of traders or credit providers, some members of settler society made considerable amounts of money by linking lending with labor recruitment. Traders' selling "on tick" (on credit) to black cultivators has long had the potential to drive these clients into migrant wage labor (Hourwhich Reyher 1948, cited in Whelan 2011, 94). In some cases this indebtedness was deliberately exploited. In Pondoland before about 1913, a system existed whereby rural cultivators were induced into work contracts or tempted to leave employment in one sector in favor of another, by local traders, doubling up as semiformal recruitment agents, who gave "cattle advances" against migrants' future earnings (Beinart 1979). In Bechuanaland (now Botswana), a British protectorate at the time, the relationship between wage advances and labor procurement was more direct. Agents recruiting for the South African mines "induced" locals to enter into contracts by paying them wages in advance, thus automatically indebting them (Schapera 1947, 108). These arrangements were open to abuse by those on both sides, with agents often extending such large advances that the borrower "remained in debt even after having worked for several months," and with borrowers often accepting advances from several agents at the same time, with no intention of honoring their debts to any of them (Schapera 1947, 109; Beinart 1979, 209). To counteract such practices, which might have led to unsustainable levels of debt for borrowers and to the collapse of agents' enterprises, regulatory measures were put in place by the colonial authorities. Officials viewed cattle advances, though enabling rural patriarchs to control the wages of young men, as exploitative and eventually abolished them (Beinart 1979). Such regulatory measures did not, however, result in migrants' getting free access to their earnings. Instead, a system developed of deferring part or the whole of a miner's pay rather than giving it to him at the work site (Schapera 1947, 106–7; First 1983). This was because authorities feared that cash received immediately would be too readily spent or diverted from "legitimate" uses (primarily the payment of various colonial government taxes and levies) or might encourage migrants to neglect or desert their families. The reliance on such measures, in which workers' earnings were subject to various forms of external or social control rather than being individually "owned" by workers themselves, proved to be long lived, as this book demonstrates.

In sum, then, the development of credit apartheid combined formal exclusion with some personal aspects arising from its reliance on various intermediaries and credit-offering agents. These arrangements have left an indelible stamp on their later versions. Doing fieldwork in the village of Impalahoek, I find that buying items and services "on the book," or *ka kgwêdi* ("on account," or literally "by the month") is a well-established practice. Local teachers supplement their earnings by hawking dinner services and other tableware, requesting that buyers pay in monthly installments and returning to reclaim the goods in cases of default. Independent salesmen—immigrants or visitors from Pakistan—travel around selling blankets and other goods, marking up their prices to cover themselves in case of default and visiting each buyer regularly to request this month's installment but offering their clients the opportunity to "skip" several months in cases of hardship. Householders run up accounts with informal *spaza* (small informal retailer) owners. Sellers of clothes, or fruit and vegetables, who cluster around the pay point on the day when monthly pensions are distributed almost never deal directly in cash. Instead, they ask grant recipients to settle last month's account using money from the welfare check, then immediately sell new goods to them *ka kgwêdi*. The presumed regularity of these benefits—though in fact delivery is sometimes uneven—assures sellers that buyers will eventually settle, thus enabling a routine delay to elapse between the purchase and the payment.[6]

The far-flung distribution of owings, borrowings, and advances within a community can mean that no one knows, at any given moment, what his or her "income" is, or how much money he or she has (van Wyk 2012). But some keep careful track of these processes. Ace Ubisi tells me that his mother was accustomed some thirty years ago to offer monthly credit for all her forms of commerce: letting out rooms to accommodate building workers, selling vegetables, prophesying. Memorizing the amounts owed to her by her diverse customers, she had no need to keep written records. Selective remembering and forgetting of debt has a distributive effect: it serves both to disperse obligations and entitlements widely within a neighborhood and to spread out the ability to pay across the month rather than concentrating it at month's end. When payday arrives, the cycle begins again.

Such practices, echoing Hart's (1973, 200) classic account of an informal store owner in Ghana, sound benign in their social embeddedness.[7] But they can have a more forcible, less voluntaristic side. Young Impalahoek householder Thandi Thobela tells me that her mother sells clothes to make a living, with customers often insisting that she extend them credit but sometimes failing to pay it back. Social pressures, however, eventually persuade defaulting customers to pay. Customers' wish to continue buying in the longer term can act as an effective sanction; failure to settle will legitimate the merchant's refusal to sell them further goods "on tick." Expressed in formal terms by economist James Roth (2004, 99), the "threat against default," as he notes in his study of credit practices in the black township near Grahamstown in the Eastern Cape, is "the termination of future contracts" (see also Cobley 1990, 48).

Similar community pressures serve to moderate informal moneylending, that much more easily recognized, and frequently demonized, form of credit. Before exploring such lending in detail, I turn to a discussion of two related practices. One is the buying of furniture on hire purchase, the arena in which many of the starker forms of credit apartheid—and the associated techniques of repossession, reckoning, evasion, and eventually financialization—took root in black communities. The other is people's use of banking facilities.

Buying and Selling Furniture: The Locus of Credit Apartheid

An aspect of black South African life that many outsiders find puzzling is the extraordinary predominance of large furniture retailers, mostly branches of nationwide chains, in rural villages and in black townships. In Impalahoek there are five of them in the same shopping complex. They compete with one another to purvey indistinguishable items—bedroom and lounge suites, DVD players, fridges, stoves—and all sell, more or less exclusively, on hire purchase. Supply by no means outstrips demand. Virtually everyone I meet during fieldwork in the village is paying monthly installments on furniture.

The origins of this system predated the onset of apartheid proper. It was described in the late 1930s, in terms that resonate remarkably eighty years later. Social worker Ray Phillips observed of Johannesburg that "on all sides one is informed that the 'hire-purchase' system of acquiring pianos and furniture is responsible for much of the indebtedness of the Africans" (1938, 41). He quoted an informant, Chaka:

> Since this instalment or hire-purchase agreement system was introduced Africans went into debt very fast. Indebtedness is increasing very rapidly among Africans. In my opinion the fault lies with the sellers or dealers in furniture. They do not care who comes into the shop, whether he or she earns £2 10s. 0d. per month, they give him or her goods worth £40 or £50, payable monthly at 30s. or 40s. per month. Then the buyer, after paying some accounts at the end of the month, is unable to make ends meet. He goes to another shop where he contracts another debt and so on continually. (Phillips 1938, 41)

Although Phillips blamed retailers for their immoderate readiness to lend and recognized that new forms of consumerism were also to blame, the major problem in his view were the low wages that black urban dwellers received.

As the century wore on, increasing numbers of people began to buy on hire purchase. The ubiquity of the system owed itself both to buyers' own restricted opportunities and to sellers' seizure of a new marketing opportunity. On both sides, but in very different ways, the story is one of inclusion in one register brought into being by exclusion in another. Urbanizing black people, seeking modernity and respectability but disallowed from owning property or from taking out mortgages, at least after the 1950s advent of apartheid in its most brutal and exclusionary form, invested instead in items of furniture—the "next biggest thing"—as a means of decorating and embellishing their council-owned township houses in Soweto and other black townships (Barchiesi 2011, 180–81; Krige 2011, 138, 172).[8] Their entry into entrepreneurial business having been similarly blocked, the retail sector was secured for white-owned trading business overall, but business opportunities were taken up in particular by the members of immigrant ethnic minorities mentioned earlier. It was thus in the trading store or retail outlet and its more specialized equivalent, the furniture store, that particular kinds of credit relations across the races evolved, with householders purchasing movable property "on the never-never" rather than immovable property with mortgages. Black clients and would-be consumers were driven into the waiting arms of store owners and businessmen who were themselves occupying a marginal position in South African society. Credit apartheid was also cross-racial credit—but of a rather particular kind.

There were parallels between furniture and house purchase: especially the way both were associated with marriage and starting a family. Buying furniture became part of the system of ceremonial gifts and countergifts associated with a wedding. Typically, when a man and his parents paid bridewealth to his in-laws, they would reciprocate by providing an item of furniture—most often a bedstead—as a "return gift" and as part of her trousseau. After that had been paid off, the new wife would then invest in a further item, paying that off in turn before buying yet further pieces of furniture, with the eventual aim of furnishing all the rooms in the house.

Life histories in Impalahoek and Sunview, Soweto, reveal that families' acquisition of furniture started with bedsteads bought by parents for marrying daughters, moved through bedroom suites, transistor radios, and wardrobes bought by those daughters themselves or their husbands, to lounge suites, and later—around the time that electricity began to be supplied in township areas in the late 1980s, but in some cases predating its supply (Meintjes 2001)—stoves, fridges, washing machines, and television sets. Buying such items involved considerable expense, and the practice described by Phillips (1938, 40)—whereby retailers offered "terms," and clients came to expect these—became the norm.

This business, associated in equal measure with forms of casual racism, paternalism, exploitative sharp practice and cozy familiarity, has been well documented by writers of fiction and journalism. Miriam Tlali's novel *Muriel at Metropolitan* (1988) and David Cohen's investigative journalistic account *People Who Have Stolen from Me* (2004) offer valuable insights here, augmenting accounts of current practices in my fieldwork sites. In contrast, Mendel Kaplan's book *Jewish Roots in the South African Economy* (1986), although useful in other respects, offers little detail on how hire purchase worked. This is perhaps unsurprising, given that the associated practices have been sharply criticized as laying the basis for credit apartheid (Department of Trade and Industry [DTI] 2002, 2004).

Buying such things as household goods and clothing has been noted in many other settings as an expression of urbane and cosmopolitan modernity (Besnier 2011; Ferguson 1999) and is not in itself a uniquely South African practice. What has been less well documented in these other settings, however, are the credit systems and technologies involved. Interest rates were and remain high (Schreiner et al. 1997), and added charges for credit insurance and the like often inflate them still further (DTI 2002).[9] A hi-fi system that would have cost R2,000 in cash was bought in 2005 by Muzila Nkosi of Impalahoek: "With various charges, insurance, et cetera . . . the amount I paid was R5,000."[10] In sum, credit for black people was offered only on unfavorable terms, in what has been called a "dysfunctional market" (DTI 2004, 22). Nevertheless, over the years many householders have been keeping up with their repayments in a measured and prudent fashion. They made sure to pay off each item before purchasing the next. The buying of furniture, then, arose in part within in a customary ritualization of the life course, entailed aspirations to suave urbanism and modernity, and exposed householders to gradually increasing expenditure—and expanding credit access—over time.

The rate of interest, coupled with the length of time between delivery of the goods and the final repayment—that is, the duration of indebtedness, which is typically two years—gives this system of commerce its characteristically uneven mixture of different registers. On the one hand, there is meticulous bureaucracy, record keeping, and regular mailing out of invoices in brown envelopes "with a window" to remind purchasers of what they still owe and to insist that they keep up with their monthly payments. In this sense the business is formal in character. On the other hand, this system involves personalized relationships. Much emphasis is placed on "trust": between different employees and the owner, to keep matters running smoothly, and between client and retailer, so that the former will act honorably by keeping up monthly payments while the latter will deliver a good-quality product. A policeman, Molepo, in Cohen's book, lectures an errant employee of Jules Street Furnishers. Himself a client, Molepo says he has faith in the store "to provide him with genuine bona fide quality brands," and "they—when they asked him what his job was and for whom he was working—trusted him to tell the truth and to pay the money he owed" (Cohen 2004, 63). This reliance on "trust" finds expression in another key feature of the business. Because owners were socially and geographically remote from their customers, who lived in black townships and rural villages, they relied heavily on intermediaries and agents, usually hailing from the African neighborhoods in which sales were being made.

There was a logic to these arrangements, especially in the case of the minority of smaller operators. These were family firms that remained small in scale rather than growing into massive conglomerates like their better-known counterparts (Kaplan 1986, 150–70). Being situated on the margins of the low-paid sector in both white and—more numerically significant—black neighborhoods certainly yielded profit (Cohen 2004, 18). But it also exposed owners to financial risk, given the low earnings and financial insecurity of its targeted buyers and the resistance of some buyers to making regular payments. To compensate for frequent defaults, and/or to pay for repossessions, the high costs of hire purchase for which the sector became notorious were built into the price of goods. Success in making money in the sector (despite these problems) and the ready availability of similar ethnically marginal traders who were not easily able to find work in arenas other than that of low-cost retail attracted high levels of competition. Mr. Bloch, the fictional store owner in Tlali's book, reports that "at every corner there's a furniture shop" (1979, 26). He nonetheless resolves to buy a new store situated near the train station where "hundreds of blacks pass every day," to hire extra employees, and to countenance taking ever riskier kinds of deposit from even more unreliable clients as down payments (Tlali 1979, 30, 116). This competition made business owners increasingly determined to increase their profit margins over those of their rivals while simultaneously driving down what they paid their employees and agents.

Those unable to make the monthly repayment were expected to approach the store and ask for extended terms, typically being granted a further year to pay off the item—at a higher cost. Accused of defaulting, however, many customers protest volubly that the records must have been inaccurate. In the case of his hi-fi, Impalahoek teacher Muzila Nkosi continues:

> I was paying every month, but I got a letter from the lawyers, saying, "You are not paying your installments." They charged me R2,000 for putting the garnishee order on my account. I approached the credit manager in the store, he said he'd approach the lawyers, but . . . they have never reimbursed me.[11]

Whether genuinely so or not, those deemed to be in default received warning letters, to which the habitual response was shame, fear, and denial. Xolela May, the Black Sash lawyer and human rights activist mentioned in Chapter 2, recounted to me his childhood memories of how customers, handed the notorious reminders of payment due or final notices, threw them away or hid them under the bed: "They would say, 'If it's in a brown envelope with a window don't give it to me' because they would know it's a letter of demand trying to recover an amount, and they ignored it. And that attitude persists even today."[12] Indeed, it was observing this mixture of humiliation, fear, and denial that had largely inspired activists like Xolela May to participate in devising the new system of consumer debtor protection.

Such attitudes had their roots, for the most part, in customers' inability to meet the installments. Difficulties in earning a living and covering all monthly expenses have exposed some to the shame of having items repossessed— although the confiscation of items is often temporary, since in many cases they are returned to their purchasers when payments resume.[13] Sowetan Dinah Zulu tells me that the store reclaimed the radio her mother had bought on hire purchase when, in 1987, her mother died, and her father, who drank to excess, failed to keep up with the installments. The arrival of the retailer's van and the threat of having one's furniture hauled out of one's house by rough-and-ready repossession men are embarrassments to be avoided if possible. Some clients, when visited by agents at their homes, have thus been ready to enter into complicit arrangements enabling them both to forestall immediate payment demands and to delay or escape the threat of confiscation.

The low pay and commission-based character of agents' work, combined with the perceived unfairness and exploitative terms offered to clients, lent themselves, then, to the emergence of forms of illegal activity, "scams," in which both family-member employees and agents conspired or entered into complicity with such clients (Cohen 2004, 42–46) or were tempted to do so (Tlali 1979, 82–83). From the agents' point of view, these enabled them to augment their meager commission-based livelihoods and make up for employers' reluctance even to pay for fuel (Cohen 2004, 61; Tlali 1979, 151–52). Cohen tells the story of one fruitless and hazardous trip by repossession men in pursuit of an electric stove. When they arrive, they find it has been sold on, and after driving still further into a more remote township area to find it, still unsuccessfully, they run out of petrol and are unable to make the return trip (Cohen 2004, 58–61). A further reason for agents' engaging in scams was to compensate them for the opprobrium they faced from neighbors and fellow members of the black community for being complicit in "squeezing money out of [clients] to swell the coffers of their white bosses" (Tlali 1979, 82–83). From the customers' perspective, collusion in such scams made it possible for them to escape, at least for a short time, the terms laid down and interest rates charged by the furniture outlets. Relying on such agents was what made such businesses, despite their extensive use of documentation, written records, ledgers, and the like (Tlali 1979, 58), strongly informal in character.

In Impalahoek, after a failed attempt in the 1970s to burn down a warehouse and destroy customer records—a common response by indebted consumers, as Graeber (2011, 257) points out—financially stretched customers started to engage in similar forms of agent-customer collusion. Some were ingenious in their complexity. Ace Ubisi describes a typical situation, using the name of a well-known store, Ellerines, which has a branch in a nearby plaza (in the period applicable to his account, larger chain stores had largely superseded smaller traders). In his telling, repossession agents ("they") are visiting an errant client ("you"): "On arrival they will tell you that for the past three months you never paid, and then they explain that, should you not pay within three months, they will come and repossess your furniture. Then you say, 'Yes, I agree with you—but I had some problems.'" Attempting to avoid having furniture carted out of the house, "you" will pay the agent a bribe to return to his employers and say, "There is no one in the house." If "you," unwilling or unable to pay a bribe, sign the form confirming that the goods have been repossessed, the agent embarks on a further scam. He "will take that furniture and sell it to another man or woman and say, 'This furniture costs R3,000 or R4,000.' That new buyer will buy straight from the agent—not from the furniture shop." The agent will pocket the difference between the amount owed by the original customer and the amount the agent was given from the new sale "and pay it at Ellerines as if it was the original owner of the furniture who was paying." The agent "will have an extra R2,500 for himself."[14]

Store owners and managers, faced with such ingenious schemes, found themselves in a sort of arms race. "Keeping abreast of the latest scam . . . is becoming a full-time operation," observed the owner of Jules Street Furnishers (Cohen 2004, 149). Their efforts to stay ahead of the game with each new sharp practice devised by employees or agents, and dismissal of them once the practices were laid bare, did not necessarily solve the problem for customers. The crooked agent that Ace Ubisi mentions to me, for example, was exposed and fired, but he continued to travel around to prospective customers, benefiting from the fact that "he still had the forms and the catalogs," and from villagers' ignorance of his dismissal. "He would . . . say, 'They will come and deliver the wardrobe, the table, and chairs. So give me a deposit of R200 or R100.'" Unsurprisingly, in this case, the furniture never arrived. Villagers' discovery, on visiting Ellerines, that they had been tricked, provoked such outrage that the errant agent left the area to go into hiding.

Overall, then, the scenario in the furniture businesses was one in which formality and informality combined in an intricately intertwined web of habitual practice. As with forms of illegality elsewhere, such practice underpinned and perpetuated a structural cycle in which the interdependence of each actor overdetermined the character of the system as a whole. A further contributing factor, after the lifting of authoritarian government and the liberalization of the economy in the 1990s, was the fact that various forms of illicit practice had "woven" themselves "into the daily fabric of social and business life" (Cohen

2004, xiv, 169–70; Steinberg 2001). But the character of the business itself incorporated some practices of borderline legality, as pointed out in Chapter 2.

Partly for these reasons, by the early 2000s, despite banks' efforts to abolish credit apartheid by extending financial formalization to all sectors of society, Cohen maintained that the "traditional business model" of selling furniture on credit still remained in place to some degree, in contrast with the more familiar worldwide scenario in which "all risk of nonpayment is transferred to the credit card companies" (2004, 18). Being obliged to shoulder these risks is what has given the enterprise its oddly contradictory character, combining bureaucracy with violence; sentimental community mindedness and trust with toughness and lack of sympathy.

But how did this "business model," centered on hire purchase, lay the basis for later ones—and what important differences can be discerned? As Chapter 5 will show, in the 2000s the "model" was starting to be supplanted. The range of credit options—and the range of actors who offered them—was proliferating. Consumers were beginning to get into debt to clothing retailers via store cards,[15] and to microlenders rather than to furniture retailers, often using microloans to buy appliances rather than procuring credit from the furniture stores themselves. Indeed, many of the latter—such as members of the JD Group, which started out as furniture retailer Joshua Doore—later expanded and branched out into financial services and microlending as an equally or more profitable aspect of the business. Lending was becoming increasingly formalized and financialized, and customers' being banked meant lenders bore less risk.

Banking Practices: Work Cycles, Life Cycles, and Marital Arrangements

The attempted undoing of credit apartheid involved a concerted effort by various agencies, including financial institutions themselves, to "bank the unbanked." Expanding business so as to include both "those at the bottom of the pyramid" (Prahalad 2006) and those who if not poor were politically disenfranchised, these agencies claimed that access to financial products would benefit such people (Krige 2011, 142; Porteous with Hazelhurst 2004, 4–6). Attempting more effectively to reach prospective clients, South Africa's banking sector intensified its efforts during the late 1980s and early 1990s to reach those parts of the market previously reluctant to use its services. While this initially involved various banks competing with one another in search of greater profit, the state later intervened, requiring all banks, in the early 2000s, to sign the Financial

Sector Charter and to provide a basic savings and transmission account, known as Mzansi, intended for the poorest, including those without a regular income. After market research concluded that "banks seemed to be intimidating, frightening, behind glass barriers, and nobody could speak indigenous languages," new branches were set up in urban townships and later in rural areas. This was done at relatively low cost, in part by switching all money transfers to ATMs, hiring staff to show new customers how to use ATMs, abolishing the uniquely high South African bank charges normally made on every transaction, and offering "prize draws" as inducements.[16]

My fieldwork showed, however, that many of those in need of banking facilities had long been aware of and made use of them, commonly combining the use of formal banks for savings and transmission purposes with hire-purchase arrangements and informal money borrowing to pay for things in advance. As shown by the "financial diaries" research project, households were using a complex range of strategies (Collins 2008; Collins et al. 2010; see also Zelizer 1995). Bank accounts were often used for saving, but in a manner that hindered rather than enabled an easy flow of money. The opening and closing of successive accounts often paralleled other time-specific patterns or reflected spatial disjuncture. Such jerky discontinuities went hand in hand with the stops and starts in an uneven history of employment; paralleled the geographical distances of South Africa's migrant system; accompanied the switch from one spouse to another; or reflected the domestic distrust that went along with more stable, albeit conflicted, relationships. Bank accounts were, in effect, single rather than multiple use, and it was often for the way they blocked, rather than enabled, the ready flow of money that they were specifically deployed.

Their use was combined with other arrangements, often intricate and requiring considerable skill and powers of recall to manipulate and manage. In a modern version of a much older practice (Ferguson 1992), people with multiple commitments to kin or spouses made their money inaccessible by putting it in fixed deposits. In the 1930s, Phillips's informants were already doing a version of this by holding certain money back from creditors: "the only time I save is when I force my way into debt and see that I place something in the bank" (1938, 41–42). Alternatively, many arranged with their employers to help them commit to enforced savings practices (Krige 2011, 137), put money aside with a retailer in the "lay-by" system (making a deposit on an item in the expectation of paying the rest of the price within a set time period or forfeiting the deposit [Roth 2004, 72]), or bought furniture on hire purchase.

Retailers have been criticized for such techniques, but buyers often use them in a canny manner, showing a strategic awareness of the advantages to be gained from economic formality (Krige 2011, 137). At the time of writing, however, the self-crafted "enforced saving" option was increasingly being replaced by an externally driven "enforced borrowing" one in which lenders would gain the upper hand.[17]

Illustrating the male and more rural-oriented perspective on banking and its relationship to both employment and marital history is the story of Ace Ubisi. Ace took the path—well worn at the time when he reached working age in the 1970s—from the Lowveld to find a job in the mines in the coal-rich area of Witbank, northeast of Johannesburg. At the mine each employee was given a monthly pay slip to submit to the "time office" in exchange for cash. Ace opened a building society account to put aside some money, about R30 monthly. Sending money home to the mother of his child required him, like others in his position, to engage in a separate part of the formal financial system. He drew cash out of his account, using it to buy telegraph orders that he sent home from the post office. His wife redeemed the orders at the local post office at Impalahoek. Other male wage earners, and later their female counterparts, while similarly using banks to save money, often opted to send cash rather than engaging in the bureaucratic procedures offered by the post office, using trusted drivers of locally owned and operated minibus taxis as couriers (see Maurer 2012, 597).

When Ace later separated from his wife and fathered children with a new partner, he opened up a different account with Standard Bank, which he kept active for some time. At this point in his marital trajectory, sending money back was more sporadic. Perhaps justifying his dwindling commitment to his rural household, as his life in Witbank necessitated new expenses, he remitted wages only to supplement the amounts earned and provided by his mother for the upkeep of his partner and children. When he later returned home and was no longer earning, his bank account—which still contained about R200—became dormant, and it remained so by the time of my fieldwork. He was notified that he would be required to return to Witbank, where the account had originally been opened, to reactivate it.

Although the story told by urban informants resident in Soweto is characterized by fewer extremes of geographical distance, similar discontinuities are nonetheless evident. People open bank accounts when jobs are secure, and those accounts later become dormant when jobs are lost. Differential levels of education and financial literacy between men and their wives, or members of the older and younger generation, affect people's use of financial institutions. Sowetan Mr. Leroke, for example, whose wife had no dealings with the bank, used the bank account of their better-educated, salary-earning daughter as a means to transfer earnings to the household and to secure the well-being of his dependents. In other cases, the conflicting demands on the income of men and women, and associated disagreements about household responsibilities, made it necessary to keep stores of wealth fenced off from each other. The mother of Soweto householder Dinah Zulu, for example, kept an account separate from that of her father. He, a truck driver, was the family's principal wage earner, with his wages being paid into his account at Saambou.[18] But he was irresponsible, drank excessively, and often failed to meet his obligations. Unable to gain ready access to his wages, his wife, like many women of her age and generation (Bozzoli with Nkotsoe 1991), earned a peripatetic living beyond the wage sector, making ready cash by selling cooked food to punters at the horse races. Her bank account with Standard served a dual purpose: it allowed her to deposit her earnings so as to save part of them, and it enabled her to pay the installments on the various items of furniture that she bought, successively, on hire purchase and paid off one by one over the course of her working life.

While the case of Dinah's parents reveals mistrust between marriage partners and shows how bank accounts were used to safeguard and ring-fence earnings in the 1970s, her own case illustrates that couples even under less discordant circumstances—as they do anywhere—keep their monetary arrangements and engagements with the formal financial system discrete. Dinah's husband, a policeman, earns a monthly salary that is paid into his bank account. She describes herself as "not working" but earns a separate income as an informal tailor. She, like many non-wage-earning women, makes use of arrangements beyond the formal sector such as savings clubs, not only to earn money but also to save, store, gain intermittent access to, and distribute it (see Chapter 4). Under the new dispensation, she acknowledges, "the banks do allow you to have an account—the Mzansi account is for people who are not working." But she tells me with a laugh, "I did once open an Mzansi account, but I don't have money to put in it." That others echoed her experience is evident from a news report stating that the numbers of such account holders gradually declined during the first decade of the twenty-first century. Banks had expected such clients to expand their usage of financial services to credit cards and personal loans, but they were disappointed.[19]

These examples show that those within the informal sector who might previously have had no reason to open bank accounts often responded with alacrity to the banking sector's new marketing initiatives by doing so. But they also warn against oversimplistic assumptions, often embedded in such marketing strategies, about the discreteness of the formal and informal realms or of the separation between higher, middle, and "mass" markets. Those with Mzansi accounts do not necessarily belong to the "masses," but they are in some cases— like that of Dinah Zulu—the wives of salaried employees. If they use these or allow them to lapse, their doing so correlates not simply with income bracket; it also reflects a variety of relational, marital, spatial, and educational discontinuities. As shown by Parry and Bloch (1989) and research elsewhere in Africa (Shipton 2007; Guyer 2004), the flow and transmission of money can be stopped, restarted, and interrupted depending on the circumstances.

But the patchy unevenness of these arrangements was beginning to change. Starting in the 1990s, increasing numbers of employers required that wages or salaries be paid into bank accounts, with civil servants in particular being paid via the state payroll system, Persal. In the course of that decade, the Department of Social Welfare, in an effort to enable similar regularity of payment, encouraged those receiving pensions and social welfare grants to open accounts (Breckenridge 2005; Porteous with Hazelhurst 2004, 50–53). The grants payment system was being further streamlined in the 2010s as I was writing this book (Vally 2013). Where banking had previously been used to keep income streams separate—and strategically to avoid certain social obligations while fulfilling others—it increasingly began to enable the unimpeded flow of money, from salary or social grant, into the account at month's end and out of it again. Seeing this as an advantage for borrowers, economist James Roth states that wages paid directly into employees' bank accounts provide "a vital link in the township financial service nexus," enabling employees to "borrow without collateral" or "use their expected wages as a collateral substitute" (2004, 78). But the new system had its drawbacks too: it made it impossible to distinguish between different creditors and claimants or to prioritize one over the other.

What, then, of the informal moneylenders with which this chapter began? Alongside the move by the retail sector to formalizing and streamlining credit rather than relying on repossession, and by the banking sector encouraging everyone to open a bank account, the informalization of moneylending practices was proliferating and intensifying. As the furniture business had earlier done, these practices relied on a mixture of bureaucracy with informality, impersonal qualities with social embeddedness. Formalization and informalization inter-penetrate and are mutually constitutive.

Riding the Camel

Informal moneylending has long been practiced in South African township ar-eas and rural villages alike. Not all accounts of this practice depict the lenders (*mashonisas*) as violent loan sharks, however. The structural factors glossed as credit apartheid have limited householders' options to borrow from the formal sector at reasonable rates, inclining them instead toward illegal moneylenders. Such loans may in fact be cheaper than those available from formal lenders who add extra charges to cover their administrative costs and to counteract the risks of non-repayment (Roth 2004, 52). Neighborhood lenders, as shown in a study by Krige (2011), often have a personal connection to borrowers. Indeed, it is often their neighbors' requests to borrow money that are the original prompt for such lenders' to go into business. This community embeddedness effectively plays a role in "capping" the interest rate. Loans, for example, are intended to be repaid at month's end, but lenders often extend the loan without calculating an accompanying escalation of the interest rate. Doing so would make repay-ment increasingly difficult for borrowers, thus giving the lender a reputation for unfairness, increasing the chances that violence be used against him, and prompting complaints to the authorities. "The termination of future contracts" by community members acts to regulate moneylending (Roth 2004, 99). In the "business model" of such moneylenders, community mindedness thus con-verges with careful calculation (Krige 2011, 154–58). In these accounts, which take the perspective of lenders themselves, the local *mashonisa* is far from being the unscrupulous Shylock of literary accounts. The desire of the *mashonisa* to stay in business controls the terms under which repayment is sought.

These smaller lenders thus have means other than the violence of ste-reotypical loan sharks to secure their profits and ways to keep trading—but equally they must stay on the right side of their customers. Some lend only small amounts, and because they are embedded in local neighborhoods, they must adjust their collection arrangements to fit local norms. They often lend amounts of less than R300, charge about 15 percent interest monthly, are relatively flexible in the calculation of interest over time, and have no formal system of collateral. One Impalahoek lender, Samuel Kgore, had a characteris-tically complex package of income sources. He started as a gambler in a dice-board gambling operation and later became its "owner" (see van Wyk 2012);

this is one of a number of microbusinesses that surround the pay point on the day when monthly pensions are distributed. He loaned people money with which to gamble, or when they borrowed from big *mashonisas* to play dice and then were unable to pay the loans back, he lent them small amounts to help get them out of trouble. His clients are pensioners, people with "piecework" (hourly paid) jobs herding cattle for pensioners, and self-employed builders or brick makers. An additional source of income, his monthly state disability grant, further consolidated his complex livelihood strategy. After he receives the grant, Samuel buys chicken feet to barbecue by the roadside, which generates some money for making loans, the interest on which enables him to buy more chicken feet. The dice game both depends on and helps fund these other income streams. There is a certain logic in the way Samuel separates capital from interest: "my gains, I just put in my pocket, and the original money that I lent them, I lend again." Small lenders like Samuel do not compete with larger ones; their products are distinct and aimed at a different market.[20]

A more generalized moneylending, less attached to specific individuals, has become pervasive in urban townships and small towns in the former homelands (see Krige 2011, 136–81; Roth 2004; Siyongwana 2004). Indeed, except perhaps at the extreme ends of the continuum, borrowers and lenders cannot be easily distinguished. Some start as one and later become the other; some are both but at different times and in different registers. Teachers like Lerato Mohale's brother borrow from their colleagues at school. This blurring, somewhat akin to the conversion between longer- and shorter-term registers discussed by Parry and Bloch (1989), is widely recognized in the literature on informal financial arrangements but is often assumed to apply only in rural communities and among the marginalized (Shipton 2007, 2009; Guyer and Stiansen 1999; Guérin, Morvant-Roux, and Servet 2010). In South Africa it prevails increasingly among the upwardly mobile, and among civil servants in particular. The ubiquity of such lending—and its relative invisibility—became evident during a conversation I had with university lecturer Bongile Cengimbo. I had asked whether she might introduce me to one of the many *mashonisas* in Orange Farm. After asking around in the neighborhood, she discovered that her mother—unbeknownst to her—was one of them. (The mother was understandably reluctant to be interviewed, however). Such lenders, operating beyond the system and aware of the illegality of their activities, nonetheless aim at greater economic formality themselves. Ironically, policy makers' attempts to "bank the unbanked" were here at odds with state regulation of illegal moneylending. Small-scale lenders often approached Rebecca Matladi, a teacher of financial literacy, for advice on how to bank their own proceeds and securely store their proceeds without drawing attention to the illicit character of their enterprise.

As moneylending expanded in size and scope, some lenders, modeling their actions on those of retailers in the formal sector, began asking the neighbors of prospective clients to stand surety or started making inventories of clients' assets with a view to repossession in cases of default. Becoming more widespread in the 1980s and particularly the mid-1990s, when credit apartheid was, in theory, coming to an end (Siyongwana 2004), illegal moneylending with interest began to acquire its more financialized techniques, aping or consolidating the techniques of the new microlenders (see the Introduction and Chapter 2) that were to be outlawed at the end of that decade. These arrangements involve a combination of willing engagement and resentment by borrowers. Lenders ask them for their ATM cards as loan security. After withdrawing the money owed to them on payday, lenders return the cards to their owners. Whereas banks and regulated lenders require a "pay slip" before agreeing to offer credit, informal lenders do the equivalent after the event, by taking the borrower's card and withdrawing the money owed to them directly from the bank. (At month's end in Impalahoek, people wanting to use ATM machines often find that they are monopolized by *mashonisas*, who use a succession of cards from several customers to withdraw what is owed to them.) Typically, borrowers, shorter of money than previously, then borrow again, once again voluntarily yielding up their ATM cards. This results in a cycle of debt bondage embodied by the seSotho term *sekôlôtô* ("debt," from the Afrikaans *skuld*). When borrowers nonetheless try to escape this cycle by canceling their ATM cards at the bank and applying for new ones, lenders, aware that it is impossible to get a new ATM card without an ID book, retaliate by asking to keep borrowers' ID books as well.

Such practices escalated from the mid-1990s onward (Barchiesi 2011, 200, 210; Siyongwana 2004). The timeline is corroborated by the following account from Impalahoek, but with an interesting ethnic-racial twist and an account of the spread of financial practices from urban areas to rural ones. Moneylending in and around the village of Impalahoek, Solomon Mahlaba tells me, was initiated by the white farmer Jaap Fourie in the late 1980s (around the same time that Solomon's nephew, Ace, first borrowed from a *mashonisa* in town). Some of Solomon's nieces, who worked on Jaap Fourie's farm, approached their employer to lend them money from their meager wages, in advance of payday. They approached him not directly but, as paternalistic custom dictates, via the farm foreman, or *induna*. Fourie agreed to lend them money, initially without interest. But the *induna* advised Fourie that he could make money by charging interest at the rate of 20 percent per month. This practice, the story goes, had already taken root among township communities, and it was now being exported to the countryside. The foreman's suggestion was not made out of altruism, however: it was a short step toward inserting himself as a broker or agent and charging for the service. "At first they used to pay R20 interest for R100, but when time went on they paid R50 . . . the other R30 was for the agent," Solomon points out. Encompassing this commission, the interest rate went up to 50 percent per month, which is where it remains for larger moneylenders nationwide. The foreman, Nkuna, now an agent, pocketed the difference and gradually started using the proceeds to lend money in his own right, eventually enabling him to leave behind his farm job altogether. He became the preeminent moneylender in the area.[21]

This classically South African story tells of a wily intermediary or agent with little financial muscle of his own who uses his ability to manipulate township practice and dupe his employer, making it the basis of a new autonomy. No longer dependent upon the white farmer, he acquires an entrepreneurial independence that is increasingly validated by—and parallels the liberatory character of—the new democracy. In a manner reminiscent of brokers everywhere, and much like the agents of the furniture stores, this intermediary uses his knowledge and his connection to both worlds to establish the basis for a new realm of illegality. The story describes intricate interrelations of reciprocal interdependency that temper a reenacted and gradually modified racial inequality—a credit apartheid—until it eventually yields the basis of a new unequal dependency: that between the contemporary black moneylender and his or her clientele.

When such agents became moneylenders, they in turn acquired new agents who themselves set up independently. A local air-force employee, Mathebula, was in urgent need of money to pay for a family funeral. The amounts were such that he exhausted his possibilities with one *mashonisa* and was forced to approach Nkuna for a further loan. After borrowing R10,000, it took him six years—from 1999 to 2005—to pay off the loan. During that time he was "working for" Nkuna, who kept his ATM card throughout. At the end of this period he approached Nkuna and asked him for a job, saying, "People know that I'm a regular customer; they know that I owed you a lot of money. There are other people who want to borrow from you but they are scared because you'll think they won't be faithful to you." He assured Nkuna that by having a better connection with these people, he would reassure them of Nkuna's willingness to take them on as clients and would also be in a good position to follow up unpaid loans. Nkuna agreed, gave Mathebula R50,000, and instructed him to lend it to his work colleagues. Unbeknownst to Nkuna, Mathebula, for more than two years, used his knowledge of the way that government salary payments to different types of public servants were staggered, to generate extra profit. He made short-term loans to his fellow employees of the air force from the first of the month until their payday on the fifteenth of the month. Collecting their payments plus interest from the ATM, he then lent money from the sixteenth to the twenty-second of the month to the teachers. Once *they* had been paid, he again collected repayments plus interest from the ATM and lent the money once more, this time to the police, collecting from them in a similar manner at month's end. Upon being discovered and "dismissed" by Nkuna, he set up as a *mashonisa* on his own. The business was so successful that it enabled him to buy a car, to build an expensive house, and to send his children to private schools.

"He started as a borrower, [and] now he is a lender," said Ace Ubisi, who told me this story.[22] The transition from one to the other, or from borrower via agent to lender, involved owing for years and in the process becoming aware how profitable a strategy moneylending can be. Not everyone is in a position to engage in lending on their own account, as did Mathebula. An alternative strategy is to resort, as happened in another case, to "investing" money with the established *mashonisas* who have existing reputations—are better equipped to screen clients, enforce repayment, and the like—and know best how to "make it grow."

Emerging out of these precedents, in Impalahoek, just as in Soweto and in South Africa more widely (Siyongwana 2004), informal moneylending has become pervasive.

Conclusion

What hire purchase and moneylending have in common is an uneven mix of economic formality and reliance on varying bureaucratic technologies, on the one hand, and embeddedness, community connection, and the special knowledge that only those implanted in a local setting can possess, on the other.

With furniture sales on credit, there was a sense of inexorability about the arrival of brown envelopes, a weary resignation coupled with a tendency to deny that reality by throwing the envelopes away or hiding them under the bed. Awareness of this shame and denial led activists with reforming zeal, like Xolela May, to design and facilitate the bringing into law of the National Credit Act. But the highly personalized character of the interactions also meant that agents and the consumers and clients with whom they communicated, and at times colluded, were able to play the system and resist or evade it, even if not for long. These piecemeal forms of illegality, though ultimately not effective, were pervasive.

In what ways does the "new" moneylending draw on and yet differ from the system of hire purchase? The high rates of interest applicable in both often make them virtually indistinguishable to borrowers. Loans from a *mashonisa* may, in effect, be cheaper than those available in the formal sector, given that the administrative costs and risks of non-repayment are considerable, and that "instruments and practices that help reduce the risk premium are frequently either not available, ineffective or costly" (Roth 2004, 52). But the payment of wages and grants into bank accounts has lent a new aspect to informal, illegal moneylending in black township and village areas, in at least some cases. Post-1980 forms of lending have come to rely less heavily on the intervention of the agent as a go-between, a community-embedded character who plays both sides against the middle, sometimes allowing him- or herself to benefit and sometimes the clients, but always to the detriment of the business owner. Many illegal or unregistered moneylenders, reluctant to expose themselves to these risks of non-repayment, now lend only to those who have a regular income—nurses, teachers, police officers, employees of the air force—and from whom they are able to recoup their earnings with minimal effort. As shown earlier, many of the lenders, too, are from those same professions.

We return to the case of Lerato Mohale's indebted brother, who is a schoolteacher. The sense of resignation and of denial that a borrower like him experienced as a result of owing money to a *mashonisa* is as palpable as that experienced by a person buying an appliance on installments, if not more so. The mixture of sentiments—personal gratitude and much-resented enslavement—is also similar. As the arena that was formerly the preserve of credit apartheid has been increasingly subject to state regulation, the informalization of moneylending within the black community has grown apace. Since lenders remain resolutely beyond the realm of regulation, the legislation has even less apparent effect on them than it does on formal lenders. Although the personalized, neighborhood dimension of their business is important, some of them—like their furniture-dealing counterparts before them—have become increasingly socially distant from their clients, necessitating their reliance on intermediaries and agents. But such intermediaries have increasingly fewer opportunities for negotiation, and have indeed become redundant in some cases. The big lenders, for example, have less need for agents since they rely on the even flow of money into borrowers' bank accounts.

Credit apartheid underpinned the particularities of black people's borrowing and lending. "Credit postapartheid," while retaining some of the technologies associated with this, also derives its character from the character of formalized and financialized arrangements. Under these circumstances, "riding the camel" remains a risky experience. Black South Africans, or certain among their number, remain vulnerable to the dangers not only of falling off the camel but also of working for *mashonisa*, that enslavement that *sekôlôtô* implies.

4

"You Don't Keep Money All the Time"

Savings Clubs and Social Mobility

IF THE SOUTH AFRICAN state has a contradictory character, both encouraging free engagement with the market and regulating that in the interests of those unable to participate, it also manifests a further contradiction. There is a strong emphasis on modernity and formalization—an impulse that can be clearly seen in the concerted efforts made to "bank the unbanked," if not in the uneven and sometimes unpredictable results of that initiative—alongside the embracing of attributes considered to be customary. Of these, none has been hailed quite as enthusiastically as the "savings club," or *stokvel*, in its various manifestations.[1] Aimed at pooling funds, whether to pay for the considerable expenses of a funeral, to help taxi owners save the deposit on a new vehicle, to encourage householders to buy big-ticket items, or simply to enable them to stock up on groceries at the end of the year, savings clubs have—albeit belatedly—been fêted by the government and those in the formal world of capitalist enterprise.

The possible benefits savings clubs offer have also been recognized by other sectors of society, all equally dedicated to fostering a culture of thrift to solve problems of indebtedness. This is vividly brought home to me when I visit the offices of the Johannesburg Housing Company (JHC), a social housing provider operating from an office in that city's central business district. The organization is partly modeled on housing associations in the United Kingdom and elsewhere, and its officers are in constant communication with their global counterparts to communicate about international trends. But they have combined these with local cultural mores in their efforts to tackle the problems that afflict their tenants. The JHC prides itself on being different from a run-of-the-mill property rental business. When people fall behind on their rent, instead of simply sending in credit control officers, the company brings in its community development arm, which undertakes activities ranging from running homework clubs and learning centers for children to helping tenants with debt problems. This arrangement has helped the JHC achieve considerable success in reducing rental arrears. The community development officers, a member of the team tells me, are given

> a list of tenants who are defaulting frequently, and we . . . try and assist them to deal with whatever issues they have. We are trying to manage whatever impact people's indebtedness would have on their rentals. So it's a proactive thing—you don't just allow the person to fall into debt this month, and then the following month. . . . [I]nstead we try to . . . flag it and say, "You have had one or two problems . . . can we refer you to this department so that you can try and talk to someone?"

In a manner congruent with this sustainability-focused approach, the aim is to enable the open discussion of problems rather than having clients evade the issue, as they might do with a regular landlord in a capitalist system. Having the Community Development Department in charge is "just another way to encourage the tenant to open up." The aim is also to tackle problems at root, to prevent them from escalating. Given that rental arrears are thought to result from inadequate budgeting skills, from an insufficiently developed culture of savings, and perhaps from anomie and social disconnectedness, members of the department have been discussing the need to encourage savings clubs, especially among their female and young tenants. Such clubs, having "been around for a very long time," are effective. As a JHC officer tells me:

> We have identified that we have many unemployed women. Women usually come together [in clubs]. And we have a lot of single parents. So we are thinking of trying to get more information and help them in terms of starting *stokvels*. And again, we have identified that a lot of young children don't save. And that becomes a cycle. Then they become adults who are not saving. So we have a youth club. . . . [T]hey wanted to start a savings club so each one can contribute R2 per day, and then at the end of the week it's R10. And at the end of the month it's R40. And then they take it to the bank, and at the end of the year they are able to do things for themselves. So we wanted to help to get it going. . . . You know how young people are . . . Whenever they have small change they want to

use it for sweets, so we are trying to encourage them to save this R2. The problem is they only meet on Friday. So already on Friday when they are supposed to meet, they have used the R2. So we want to find a way that the R2 is being collected. . . . We want to encourage saving.[2]

In another innovative move, one of JHC's directors visited India and returned with an idea inspired by a club she'd seen there that aimed to save money for brides' dowries. The idea was that collectors might visit tenants on a daily basis to collect small amounts and pay those into a savings scheme, so that the money "doesn't get used for any other thing except for the need that was actually identified." In this case, however, the idea was abandoned. The impediment was people's lack of trust in any prospective money collector.

Community development officers at JHC also acknowledge the need for alternative and supplementary interventions. Their attempts to encourage a culture of saving by using customary "social" methods are backed up by another, more immediately effective and more recognizably "financial" scheme: that of teaching "budgeting skills." Prospective tenants, with the help of a leasing officer, are obliged to fill out a budget form before they move in to a property, with the aim of establishing whether they can afford the rent. This measure is designed to protect both tenants and the organization itself by ensuring that fewer defaults occur. (It also represents a recognition of the wide ramifications of the National Credit Act—any institution that extends credit to the public, in this case by allowing tenants to live in a building for a month before collecting their rent, might be required to defend its actions by demonstrating that this was not reckless but rather done on considered grounds.) The risk is exacerbated by the fact that certain applicants have been known to provide forged pay slips as proof of income, to be admitted as tenants. To guard against being judged—and prosecuted under the act—as a reckless lender and to protect itself from the problems that arise from the fact that tenants do not "keep money all the time," JHC has resolved to keep records of applicants' budget forms (see Figure 4.1).

The strategy put in place by the community development arm of JHC represents a canny combination of tendencies. Not surprisingly, since all three of the officers I interview are themselves members of multiple savings clubs, they recognize the essence of such arrangements. A savings club, or *stokvel*, marks out a clear distinction between the different uses of a householder's income. To have a tenant save for the monthly rental payment is to make this

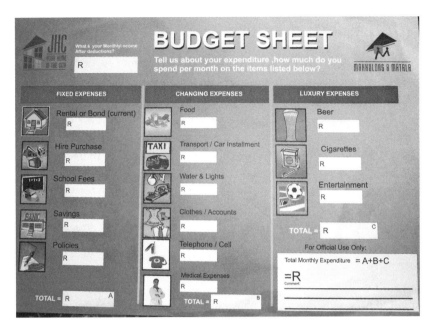

Figure 4.1 JHC budget form
Source: Johannesburg Housing Company. Reprinted with permission.

specific use of their money incommensurable with any other, by putting it in reserve so that it can accumulate as a "lump sum" until its designated use becomes due. But the duration of time, here as with other aspects of credit, can prove problematic. In the case of children—who are preemptively pulled into the very adult notion of saving for rent—the officers recognize that stringent forms of self-discipline are unlikely to work. Getting children to set their pocket money aside requires instead that the collection date be moved to the beginning of the week, when they are first given the money. In the case of adult tenants, the rather misdirected idea of sending a collection agent to gather rent and forestall any other use of the money proved fanciful. That idea foundered on lack of trust: a fundamental issue in all savings clubs, and particularly those in South Africa. Authors have shown how confidence in fellow-members' honesty has here been in short supply (Bähre 2007; Reinke 1998).

The second strand in JHC's comprehensive strategy—the budget exercise—points in a rather different direction. If it proves impossible to inculcate savings behavior by social means, a formalized system of self-discipline must be applied. Both approaches, in different ways, attempt to parcel up a tenant's monthly monies into separate packages. This is something perceived as increasingly necessary, since the linking of salary and grant payrolls to bank accounts has made it more and more difficult to keep money for distinct purposes. Dividing income sources and destinations into discrete amounts, in ways previously practiced (Ferguson 1992), is harder to do than it once was.[3]

The JHC's embracing of the *stokvel* is one instance of a broader trend. During the 2000s *stokvels*, once dismissed as irrational and treated with contempt, were embraced and held up as a solution to many financial problems by the government, the formal financial sector, trade unions, and the South African Communist Party (SACP) (Krige 2012b, 3). In recognition of the particular features of savings clubs, banks have opened special accounts geared to these: it is permitted, for example, for *stokvel* accounts regularly to end up with a zero balance at year-end. (As discussed later, however, some clubs steer clear of the banks to avoid the notoriously high charges they levy in South Africa.) In addition, the many such clubs that engage in lending money for interest are specifically exempted from the obligation to register their activities under the National Credit Act.[4]

Formal recognition of savings clubs has also been reflected in other ways, with the production of a television soap opera called *Stokvel* and a special supplement in the *Daily Sun*, a popular tabloid-style newspaper, which showcases these clubs' activities.[5] Some *stokvels* are members of a national association whose investment arm co-owns a mobile phone business, Nasasa Cellular. The association holds an annual convention at which pleas are regularly made that its affiliates expand their scope beyond merely "supplementing household income."[6] Similarly trying to encourage these associations to expand their activities, SACP chief Blade Nzimande said that they would be more likely to become "a major force in [South Africa's] financial system" if they abandoned their insistence on independence and instead organized themselves into a cooperative bank.[7] Such misgivings aside, the laudatory attitude toward *stokvels* no doubt reflects an aspect of the bottom-of-the-pyramid strategy: it is in the interest of these organizational structures "to try and capture some of the pools of money which continue to circulate outside the formal banking system" (Krige 2012b, 3).

Set against almost a century of longer-term social transformation and the accompanying evolution of what might be called folk finance, this new culture of celebration points to the fact that such clubs are on the increase in both rural and urban settings. Even alerted to this, I am surprised during my fieldwork to discover their sheer number and proliferation. Clubs—whether oriented to the burial expenses of members and their relatives or to buying big-ticket items or day-to-day necessities at year-end—seem to be everywhere. Most were founded in the 1990s or since then. All have the familiar format in which members regularly contribute a set amount of money or goods, yielding a lump sum that is distributed to each member when it is his or her "turn." But there are endless variations on this basic theme: the precise amounts contributed, whether contributions are in cash or kind, whether or not members are required to abide by and endorse a constitution, whether or not they meet face-to-face.

Any given individual may belong to several clubs at once. This point is made in the literature, but there has been more interest in classifying the different "types" according to their functions and in analyzing the separate rationales of these (Verhoef 2001), including the way they "manage risk" (Thomson and Posel 2002), than in exploring why and how a given saver's memberships dovetail and combine. I single out just two examples of club members—one female and one male—by way of demonstration. Both hail from the middle class (new or not-so-new). One is Modiegi Nong, a university administrator. She belongs to a women's tea club that meets monthly; a sisterhood that never meets but has monthly contributions and requires each member in turn to lend the pool out for interest; a family club that collects monthly contributions, meets every other month, and banks its money or invests it in shares and financial products; and a funeral society that meets monthly, requires members to lend the pool for interest, and uses the accumulated interest to buy groceries in bulk at year-end. Thomas Thale is a media consultant who also owns and runs a fleet of minibus taxis. He belongs to three taxi-owner clubs: a banking club whose members take turns to bank the taxi takings at the end of the day; a *stokvel* with weekly contributions that requires members to lend the pool for interest; and a *stokvel* with monthly contributions aimed at securing enough money for each member to put down a deposit on a minibus taxi. He also belongs to the Leoto "burial grocery" club (discussed later), the membership of which he inherited from his sister when she died.

If the intention of various institutions—the state, capitalist corporations, nonprofit housing associations, and even the SACP—is to recognize and celebrate such clubs and even to "capture [their] pools of money" (Krige 2012b, 3), the reality is rather more complex. As the examples here suggest, these clubs coexist with and even embrace, while also sometimes resisting, the formal financial sector of banks and similar institutions. Many clubs take advantage of the fact that they have been granted recognition in the new dispensation. But many evade that recognition and insist on remaining autonomous. They fear that, if their activities become visible to "the government," it might act to curb or restrict them. Their relationship to the formal financial sector and the state is thus far from straightforward.

The ambivalent attitude displayed by club members toward financial formality has been much discussed in the scholarly literature. Famously, scholars have seen savings clubs as a "middle rung" on the ladder to such formality or a means of "financial intermediation" (Besley, Coate, and Loury 1993, 1994; Geertz 1962), although without necessarily assuming that they will disappear when such formality is achieved. Anthropologists studying urbanization and social change in Asia (Geertz 1962) and sub-Saharan Africa (Ardener 2010; Guyer 1995; Kuper and Kaplan 1944; Little 1957) have made the important observation that such clubs have enabled people to adapt to newly transforming circumstances of urban life. They are not, then, survivals of rural custom; they involve "norms and habits [that are] continually adjusted" (Shipton 2007, 14).

Eager to illustrate the essentially rational character of such clubs, writers have often tried to divide their "economic" features from the "social" ones. Apparent deficits in economic rationality are explained by reference to the way they give their members a collective social identity instead, especially in settings of urban disconnect and anomie; but it is also acknowledged that the two aspects are connected: this sociability disciplines people to save money in a manner that might not have been easy for them to do otherwise (Ardener 2010; Geertz 1962; Verhoef 2001). The task of explanation becomes more difficult, however, as the levels of anomie become more pronounced. A study of clubs in Cape Town's townships shows the extremely strenuous efforts made by members to build trust and to offset the considerable risks of default or nonpayment by members who were proving to be far from collegial. Here, the "social" is a means to control what might appear from a strictly "economic" point of view as inordinate risks (Bähre 2007). When such risks are overwhelming despite the social efforts, analysts—reverting to the "economic" view—often find it illogical that members continue to belong to these clubs rather than simply opting to use banks instead.

The recent proliferation of clubs in South Africa, particularly high budget or "investment" clubs among the better-off who might have been expected to invest their money in more "modern" ways (Verhoef 2001; Kibuuka 2006), certainly suggests that communal values and sociability play an important part.

Confirming but qualifying such an impression, this chapter shows how the growth in savings clubs testifies to, and is a response to, the growth of a new middle class. It both encompasses those who belong and enables those who are not quite included to retain some dignity. Savings clubs not only express the common values of the members they include but also tell us something about those who, though aspiring to be upwardly mobile, experience themselves as excluded from that newly affluent class. In the midst of rapid upward swings in wealth and swift descents into impoverishment, clubs provide members with the means to communally identify and engage in reciprocal mutuality, and— guarding against the possible collapse of trust and interchange—to differentiate themselves from those of unequal means who are unable to reciprocate.

The broader backdrop to this is a very particular one (see the Introduction). South Africa has been a country where proletarianization, albeit initially uneven, eventually became widespread. Wage-labor capitalism dominated the economy until recently (Barchiesi 2011, 63; Cooper 2002, 194), but formal employment has since shrunk drastically, and its benefits are denied to many or are available only indirectly. For every person who has benefited from the new democratic order, especially those with some education who have found a place in the public service, there are many who have not been similarly privileged. The result has been high levels of dependency on each source of formal employment: a phenomenon widely documented for blue-collar wage earners but true for white-collar salary earners as well (see Barchiesi 2011, 212; Ndumo 2011, 165; Stauffer 2010). In this setting, savings clubs enable the coexistence of two apparently contradictory trends. Those with good and stable earnings, using the clubs to consolidate their positions and make appropriate investments, also distinguish themselves from those unable to do so. Savings clubs even enable members to "lock away" resources upon which poorer relatives might otherwise have a claim. Simultaneously, however, club membership enables the expression, at least to a point, of an ideology of solidarity, mutuality, and inclusivity.

Husbanding Resources: The Household

It is commonly held to be the case, though inaccurately so, that savings clubs are the preserve of women. Media reports assert this. People I meet in the field invariably do the same and offer a variety of folk explanations for this fact. Women "take care of their families" and "take more responsibility than men," says Abigail Mlate, the single mother mentioned in Chapter 1 who holds a high

position in a government department. "Women are builders, men are occupiers," says Modiegi Nong, the university administrator with the large range
of club memberships. Other, humbler women in village settings make similar
statements. It is a woman's job to care for the household (*go hlôkômêla lapa*),
says Sophie Mahlaba, a clothes peddler in Impalahoek, whereas "men just want
to eat." Indeed, a central intention of savings clubs is to stop the wasteful and
pointless squandering, or "eating," of money (*go ja tšhêlêtê*): something that
men are often accused of doing and that women are thought to be able to prevent. Since men are in any case said to be incapable of cooking and unaware
of what household goods and provisions might be required, there would be
little point in their joining clubs aimed at replenishing such stocks. Women also
point to the cyclical character of the clubs' savings activities and the way this
feature helps mothers who are obliged to meet very particular expenses at year-
end: providing food and drink for Christmas festivities; stocking pantries with
dry goods and cleaning products to last well into the new year; and—when the
school year begins—buying new school uniforms, shoes, books, and stationery
for their children, as well as paying school fees.

Such claims might seem to express feminine ideals of housewifely concern
and thrift that, if somewhat conservative and backward looking, are relatively
universal. They deny what is undoubtedly true: that men do belong to savings clubs, often equally centered on the responsible creation of a sustainable
domestic situation (Krige 2012b), as well as a concern with saving up to pay
bridewealth and/or secure long-term investments. They also deny a reality
that I found in several cases. Men had inherited the membership of a funeral-
oriented grocery club from a mother or sister, thus showing at least as much
concern for thrift, sociable mutuality, and domesticity as that female relative
had done. Finally, the hegemonic female view, by laying the stress on home-
centered domesticity and family orientation, downplays the great proliferation
of investment-style activities in which women's clubs engage, in particular the
way members, in some cases, are obliged to lend out the accumulated pool of
money at interest.

The ideology, if not the practice, of group savings thus stresses such values
of domestic thrift. It makes sense to ask why this might be the case, what is
specific to South Africa about such statements of value and virtue, and why
men and women are seeking to elbow aside one another's claims to own this
terrain of morality. To answer this, we must briefly revisit the discussion in the
Introduction concerning how divergent gendered roles were pivotal in linking

the world of capitalist production (experienced by the proletariat through its payment of wages for labor) to that of reproduction (experienced by workers' fathers, mothers, wives, and sisters using migrant remittances to manage rural homesteads). When 1970s scholars with a Marxist orientation challenged claims that the country's economy was "dual" (Houghton 1976) by emphasizing that capitalism was articulated with and dependent on, yet dominating of, the traditional sphere of subsistence cultivation in which migrants' stay-at-home dependents held sway, anthropologists also recognized that the significant property-owning unit was the "house-property complex" (Gluckman 1950, 195–99; see also Oboler 1994) in which wives were predominant. Separate subfamilies in a polygynous family, each of which owned and held its wealth discretely, were headed by a man's several spouses. This ideology of female domestic control and influence outlasted the decline in and virtual disappearance of polygyny in the latter half of the twentieth century. Although during that century the extent of such a woman's influence varied greatly and depended on outside factors—initially, the regularity of the wage remitted by her husband, and later increasingly its "public" equivalent, the state pension and other social grants (Seekings and Nattrass 2005)—the narrative of a wife's responsibility for the domestic domain retains great force in South Africa (Bank 2011, 165, 182, 237). At the same time, the shrinking wage-labor sector (for those at the proletarian end of the scale) and the declining public influence of all but a small number of black elites (in the case of those better off) have made this very same domestic domain an arena over which men and women increasingly struggle for ownership.

With this in mind, I turn to the world of female-dominated savings clubs in Impalahoek. One day I am sitting in the well-appointed dining room of Sophie Mahlaba, wife of the elder brother of an influential local family. She and her husband make their living from selling fruit and vegetables, primarily at the monthly pension payout, and Sophie also earns money by selling new and secondhand clothes at the same venue. Like many women of some status and influence, Sophie belongs to a number of savings clubs, each differently named and conceptualized, and each with a specific and separate aim (Table 4.1).

What Sophie tells me about her clubs, and what I later observe when attending a club meeting held at her house, echoes what I have heard from other members elsewhere and what the literature emphasizes. In addition to the much-reiterated refrain that these are women's matters, Sophie tells me that the reason for her multiple memberships and for the central role she plays (as

Table 4.1 Sophie Mahlaba's clubs

Name	Date founded	Number of members	Monthly contribution	Bank	Use/ schedule
Tsembanani	1986	15	—	Yes	—
Thušanang club	1989	—	R50	Yes	For bereaved families
Sesebesebe	1994	10	—	—	To "buy presents"
Setokofela	2005	12	R2000	No, stored in safe then given to member	Business, meets December
Grocery group	2010	10	R150/R500	Yes, in husband's name	Groceries, meets year-end

treasurer of one club and a keen and reliable member of the others) is that she is an outsider in the community. She came to the village from Swaziland to marry and has no relatives there. "I am alone," she tells me. "I tried to get other women in a group to be my sisters." This reinforces Shipton's point (2007, 14): such clubs are born of, and facilitate, continual adjustment—they are about flexibility and adaptation rather than custom and fixity. Again reflecting what the literature notes, each club is of a specific "type," distinct from the others in terms of membership, aims, and procedure (Verhoef 2001). Recognition by and coexistence with the formal banking sector is also evident in Sophie's account. An unfortunate incident that she recounts makes it clear that simply banking a club's money to keep it safe does not automatically shore it up against the potential untrustworthiness of members. Tsembanani, by her reckoning the "strongest" and oldest of the clubs, and hence the one in which trust ought to have been most prevalent, has recently been defrauded. In advance of a monthly meeting, the then treasurer visited the bank to make the monthly withdrawal of funds, accompanied by two older members, as the club's constitution dictated. She later made a second visit to the bank, during which she colluded with the bank teller to withdraw a further R3,000, which she arranged to share equally with the teller. Returning to the members, she concealed the second withdrawal by telling them that she had "lost" the bank statement. This aroused members' suspicions, and Sophie telephoned the bank manager, who uncovered the fraud. The club's members changed the bank account and nominated a different group of three to perform deposits and withdrawals in future. They decided to resolve the matter by speaking to the guilty party and insisting that she repay the money. As Sophie is recounting how the treasurer's actions had infringed the club's principles, she lays less stress on the treasurer's thievery than on the way her actions traduced women's proper role: as productive users of money and preventers of waste. "She started to eat [*go ja*] our money. It's not good. It is better if I take the money, go and buy some fruit, and sell it." Money, in other words, ought to be saved and reinvested (*go bea tšhêlêtê*) rather than used up in an unproductive manner (*go ja tšhêlêtê*)—but members cannot always be trusted to do this.

Finally, again echoing what I have read in the literature, Sophie claims that clubs have become more prolific in recent years, even becoming something of a fashion. Their proliferation also reflects personal circumstances in the life of an ordinary member. Her club memberships, starting with those involving small contributions, ratcheted up to those demanding larger amounts as her informal trading activities expanded.[8]

Though I am not able to observe all her clubs in action, I have a chance to see the most recently founded of them, a kind of "superclub," in its full ritualized glory. On this memorable occasion I get a chance to understand the recent consolidation and expansion of club membership in the area. I also learn more about women's stringent efforts to husband resources and prevent them from being "eaten."

I am invited to a meeting at the local community center of a coalition of clubs—known collectively as Kwanang Bana Basehlare—of which Sophie's club Thušanang ("help each other") is a component. The explicit intention of all these subclubs is to help bereaved families. The meeting is held to mark the end of the period of mourning and removal of mourning clothes (*kapolô*) after a death in a club member's family. On this occasion there are two bereaved families, the Mohales and the Maganes, and each of the subclubs is here to hand over a consolidated lump sum to those families' representatives. By way of reciprocity, the families contributed to providing a substantial feast. The reciprocity turns out to involve a chain of gift and countergifts: all club members partake of the feast, and many also helped prepare it. "They buy food for us, and we buy food for them so that by two months' time they will still be eating that food. It is like repayment," the club secretary tells me. "We eat and we pay [*re a ja le re a patêla*]. We exchange [*re a tšintšala*]." Although the function of the meeting is connected to bereavement, this is not strictly speaking the meeting of a "burial" or "funeral" society: rather, the club coexists with such societies, with each of its members belonging to several simultaneously.

That the formation of this superclub was a response to the recently experienced emotional and financial hardships associated with death, and in particular with the HIV epidemic, is clear from what I am told by its chair (*modulasetulô*), Mary Chiloane: "Before, people were not used to death. It was very rare to attend. Now people are dying. From 1990 we tried to do something to improve these arrangements."[9] Several members testify that the club did not simply arise "out of the blue," but was initiated by Mary herself, after she had observed similar groupings when visiting an aunt in the more cosmopolitan setting of Nelspruit (now Mbombela). Mary had been active in the ANC Women's League, had been picked by the ANC for a paid role as education officer just before the first democratic elections, had initiated a local gardening project, and had eventually been rewarded with a stipend-bearing job as cleaner in the local clinic: she is a person of local influence and unusual community mindedness.[10] It is thanks to people like her, bolstered by a resurgence of Africanist confidence in the postelection period, but also prompted by the urgency of the new needs attendant on illness and bereavement, that such large and extensively organized clubs are on the increase (see Krige 2012b).

There was another way this club responded to novel situations. In a setting where incomes were sharply diverging, it espoused an ideology of smoothing out unequal access to resources between different members encountering the substantial costs of bereavement and of postfuneral ceremony. "We welcome everybody, poor or rich," Sophie told me. "Some can't afford to buy bread; others have money." Somewhat against the spirit of this idea, however, the ritualized processes and speeches that take place during the ceremony emphasize that each member—and by extension each group—must make exactly equal contributions. This point is brought home through the use of emphatic phrases, constant repetition, and a call-and-response motif after each section of the proceedings, when Mary Chiloane proclaims "shine"—a term of approbation and acclaim now widely used in rural and township settings—and the audience responds by repeating it enthusiastically:

CALL: Shining, friends [*bangane*].
RESPONSE: Shine.
   We, in our society, when someone takes off her mourning clothes, we help. We go there on Sunday. On Sunday, where we go there contributing R500 as groups, and we read the scripture of Job 2:11. As we go there, we give them the same amount of money. That is why each group contributes R500, while the mourners are wearing black only. . . . That is how our society operates. There are three groups here:

Group number 1 *re* Kwanang (with five subgroups)

Group Number 2 *re* Thušanang (with five subgroups)

Group Number 3 *re* Kogwalepeta/Kgwadithiba (with three subgroups).

They group together to be one group. These are the groups that are going there with the money. . . . . I want to work this way. I need to emphasize [*go balabala*]. We'll put it in the bank. I want to emphasize. . . . It helps us not to eat the money. . . . Now it is better for us, because we have something. And it is equal [*e a lekana*]. It all gets in [to the plate in which the money is presented], from the head to the legs [*nama, e a fella*].

CALL: Shine, friends [*bangane*].[11]

RESPONSE: Shine.

To ensure that each group contributes its allotted amount and to police the parity between groups, the collected offerings of each group are noted in a ledger. The monies, once noted, are then piled together in enamel plates, wrapped in plastic, sprinkled with ash to ensure that no malevolent spiritual forces attempt to interfere or doctor the money with medicine, and finally offered to the bereaved person by club members. The money-offering procession is particularly impressive, as ranks of group members in their uniforms, kneeling, parade forward in serried ranks, interrupting the procession every few "steps" to perform a sideways shoulder roll, to the left and to the right, on the ground (see Figure 4.2). These actions, incorporating domestic enamel plates (see Figure 4.3), show elaborate respect to the recipient of the money, in this case the widower, Mr. Mohale. Although he appears a little daunted as the only man in a huge hall full of women, he responds with a speech of gracious acceptance:

God has watched over us. God was there when this club began. And I hope that you do to others the work that you have done to us. . . . It should not be amongst us only, the Mohales, but you should proceed to do this to others. I don't know how I can thank you, I don't know what to do. I thank you, and all I can say is "Shine." [Applause and ululation.]

I thank you for the work that you have hosted. Please do keep on holding that way, and don't give up or throw it away. Have all the power so that you can hold each other the way you did. Thank you.[12]

The ceremony contains much Christian usage and reference, drawing on the ritualized treatment of money that has long been habitual at meetings of African Independent "Zionist" churches (Kiernan 1988). In a similar spirit to

Figure 4.2 Club members do kneeling dance and shoulder roll (see also facing page)
Source: Deborah James.

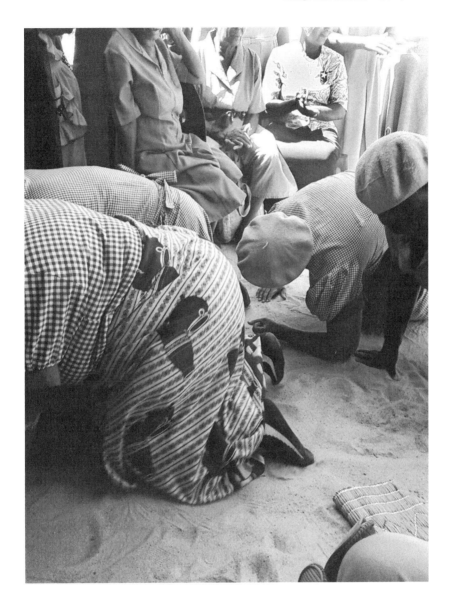

what the JHC was attempting to facilitate, the ritual creates a regulated arena, performatively ring-fencing money through collective action by setting it apart from the flow of everyday use and designating it for only one possible purpose.

But more secular authorities prove necessary when, despite such rituals, systems of mutual responsibility and reciprocity are found to fail. At the

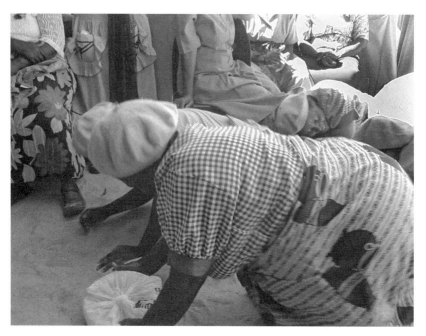

Figure 4.3 Kneeling dance with plateful of money wrapped in plastic
Source: Deborah James.

ceremony, Mary—in similarly impressive performance style—goes on to an-
nounce the recent default of a member. In the process Mary publically exoner-
ates herself from any blame and points out that appropriate steps are being
taken to set the situation right through the consultation of public authorities:

> I am the one who began this, plus Susan Pule. . . . The book here carries every-
> thing. We have given money to a woman but she does not want to pay it back.
> I still remember the Sebothoma family. We gave R14,000 each [to each of the
> two wives]—but they don't show up now. This is why I say I am carrying a lot
> of problems. This is why I cannot carry the burden. The money is not here, and
> people will say it is me. I am responsible for everything, and people think this
> is me.
>
> In our constitution we will take these people to the court—if the *induna*
> [headman] cannot sort it out we will take it to the chief. *Stokvels* must exchange.
> We'll go to the *mošatê* [chief's place], wear black and white, to explain to the
> chief.[13]

The intention, as with the fraudulent treasurer of Sophie's club, was to avoid interacting with the law or the formal authorities. Instead, it was customary leaders who were approached to help arrive at a negotiated solution. I later asked how matters had progressed. The nonpayers had explained, Mary tells me, that the reason they were unable to keep up their contributions was because they were unemployed. Since they had now found jobs on a nearby farm, they had promised to pay what they owed.

Adaptation: Shifting Up and Down the Social Ladder

Self-evidently, then, there is a link between earning a steady income and being able to pay savings club contributions. A person who has no regular source of money will be unable to put any part of it away in savings. In such a club, loss of earnings represents the immovable object that ultimately prevents the high-minded-sounding statements of intended helpfulness and of mutuality from being achieved. If clubs aim to help members collectively husband resources and prevent wastefulness, having members with no resources to husband cannot be sustainable for long, and stories abound of members dropping out or leaving prematurely. (On some occasions, it is just such a loss of earnings that causes the kinds of defaults or fraudulent withdrawals noted earlier.) When this happens, it becomes impossible for all the other members to claim their accumulated pots. The logic of the annual savings cycle is thus destroyed.

Remedies exist to blur social difference and inequality, at least in the short term. Equalizing arrangements are easiest for clubs that contribute in kind, rather than in money, such as the Soweto-based club Leoto ("wheel"), the purpose of which is to buy groceries to help members with the cost of catering on the occasion of a funeral. Similar to many other predominantly women's clubs in that it involves contributions in kind which are intended for use during the large-scale catering that a funeral entails, Leoto differs in one respect. It uses an apparently complex but actually ingeniously simple system to establish equivalence over time, such that no single member will end up paying more even though the price of specific foodstuffs might vary. This is the club of which Thomas Thale inherited his membership on the premature death of his sister. The current treasurer, Michael Hibidu, likewise inherited his position when his mother died. He allows me to copy the diagram, here reconfigured, but only after carefully erasing the names of the members on each spoke or segment of the "wheel" (Figure 4.4). To iron out any differences of cost between members, the club uses an approach of regularly circulating or rotating set obligations.

Figure 4.4 Contribution cycle of Leoto "burial grocery" club

Source: Drawn by Wendy Phillips.

Note: Members' obligations are specified exactly, right down to the level of the produce brand. They are brands well-known and commonly purchased by township dwellers.

When I meet Michael Hibidu and he explains the workings of the club, I am unable at first to understand the logic of the club's system of "rotating credit," but I eventually do so after further explanation. The system operates on the basis of the number thirteen, on two different levels. First, Michael explains to me, the club has thirteen members, each of whom takes a turn to contribute the groceries specified in the relevant spoke of the wheel (see Figure 4.4). Second, each member is asked to nominate twelve relatives as beneficiaries. Added to the member in question, this equates to thirteen people for whose funeral wake assistance will be offered. The costs of catering for such a wake are offset when a member, taking a turn to be placed on one particular spoke of the wheel before moving on to the next, brings the required groceries, specified right down to the brand, on that occasion. A member placed on column 1 when a funeral occurs, for example, must buy and contribute thirty eggs, twelve tins of Koo brand mixed vegetables, and four twin packs of Carlton brand toilet paper.

"That's for the first claim that is put to us, and when the second claim arises we go to the next column. What we are basically doing is to share the costs because some are cheaper, some are expensive. And when there's another claim, we circulate," Michael explains:

> DJ: Has it been worked out that this amount of money here [pointing to spoke number one] costs roughly the same as this [pointing to spoke number two]—so each of these is equivalent to the others in monetary terms?
>
> MH: No. That is why we are circulating. Some are more expensive than the others. For this one here [he points to spoke number five], you just buy Crosse and Blackwell mayonnaise, which is not expensive. It is about R70.[14]

The equalizing and evening out of contributions over time has here been ensured by specifying in detail, down to the number of items and the exact brand, what a member must contribute when positioned on a particular spoke of the wheel. The need for such tactics is, however, perhaps less pressing than it might be in other circumstances. The club's members have broadly similar incomes, Michael points out, since most—other than him and Thomas—are senior women or widows who receive a state pension.

In clubs measuring contributions in money rather than groceries, another equalizing tactic shows a similar preoccupation with numbers. Here, the amounts both of member contributions and of member benefits may be multiplied "times two" or "times three." If a better-off member wants to pay more money into the pot and receive more money when his or her annual turn comes around, he or she is permitted to "join twice" or "three times," or in any other multiple. This serves to recognize discrepancies in income and desired levels of savings and to accommodate these within a single club. In Sophie Mahlaba's grocery club, which runs on an annual cycle from January to October, most members pay R150 per month, but she pays R500; she has joined "times 3.33." She says, "At the end of the year I get R5,000. Others get R1,500."[15] In the taxi owners' weekly *stokvel* to which Thomas Thale belongs, the standard contribution is R1,000 per week, but some members "join four times" and contribute R4,000. Instead of getting R52,000 at year end, those members will recoup R208,000.[16]

What none of these remedies can forestall, however, is the departure of members who have no further income to invest. This was equally or even more important in high-income investment clubs with salaried members that were documented in a study by Kibuuka (2006). Although the members Kibuuka interviewed stressed the importance of interaction, support, solidarity, and friendliness, they also made it clear that employment was a prerequisite—membership would not outlast the loss of a job. Being employed was thus ranked by members alongside "trust" as a factor of key importance. In this respect, the club was not unlike formal financial institutions and banks. As I have heard so often in the course of my fieldwork, "You won't be allowed to have a bank account if you can't show them your pay slip." Some clubs require evidence of members' regular earnings in much the same way.

Unemployment or lack of the regular income from a pension, and the resulting shift down the social ladder, makes for a high dropout rate from some savings clubs. Conversely, acquiring a job (or a better job) and/or a higher income can cause a member to relinquish membership of one club and join—or establish—another. So can aiming at a more expensive purchase: something that of course needs to be squared with one's income. Dinah Zulu, a resident of Sunview, Soweto who works as an informal tailor, belonged to a local club for two years with a monthly contribution of R200, but she left at the end of the second annual cycle to join one with a higher contribution of R1,000. This was less because of a noticeable increase in her earnings than because of a social obligation. She and her husband are expected to buy a fridge as part of her daughter's trousseau. The purchase of furniture here, as with the families described in Chapter 3, was prompted by a daughter's impending marriage. Additionally, householders like Dinah, as I discuss later in this chapter, had started deliberately using savings clubs to avoid the high interest and inflexible repayment terms of furniture retailers. She tells me:

> DZ: I was talking with my friends that we must join a *stokvel* that can pay a bigger amount. So if you want a fridge you can buy it cash instead of paying installments with interest. With this *stokvel* each member is paying R1,000, and then they get R13,000. . . . It's because [retailers'] interest is very high. They don't want six months because the interest is low—they want twelve months then the interest is very high. So if it's R1,000 you pay R2,500.
>
> DJ: You mean the shops won't allow you to take six months [to pay]?
>
> DZ: No. Only twelve months. With Morkels [a prominent retailer], we bought a Hoover, and we wanted to pay over six months. Before they treated six months as cash, but then they say twelve months. I really wanted to buy the Hoover so I took the twelve months.
>
> DJ: How much was the markup on the Hoover?
>
> DZ: From R999 to R2,871.[17]

What prompts people to take up membership of new clubs is a change in economic circumstances. People are easily able to switch from smaller to larger levels of investment in a relatively short time, because clubs operate on an annual cycle and so offer relative flexibility. But people do not necessarily jettison all their earlier clubs and affiliations just because they have become more well-to-do. On the contrary. In many cases, an individual's successively joining different clubs over his or her life course, with substantially different levels of monetary contribution, can map one's upward trajectory without making it necessary to relinquish earlier friendship and savings circles.

If we return to the case of Sophie Mahlaba (see Table 4.1), we can see that her initial memberships, in the 1980s, involved relatively minor sums, but by 2005 she had added to those by joining Setokofela (*stokvel*). This was a group specifically for those who earn a living in the same way as her—by selling clothes on pension day—which had the much more substantial monthly contribution of R2,000.[18] A similar case, but in an urban setting, is that of Modiegi Nong, the university administrator with multiple memberships. Although more like a member of the "old" black middle class in Soweto than a "black diamond"— one of those who have experienced a recent meteoric rise to wealth—Modiegi's club membership profile nonetheless shows considerable social movement (Table 4.2). It expresses her connection to the old life (in the black township of Soweto) and the new one (in the formerly white neighborhood of Leondale to which she recently moved), as well as her diverse obligations, which encompass both local, family-oriented clubs and remoter, more detached ones. In the latter category, her membership of the "sisterhood" of teachers and lecturers tracks

Table 4.2 Modiegi Nong's clubs

Name	Date founded	Membership	Monthly contribution	Bank	Use
Women's Tea Club	1975	Sowetans	R100–R200	No	Help with parties and funerals
Birthday club	—	Sowetans	R400	No	To "buy big-ticket items"
Family club	—	Matilda's family	R50	Yes	To help with food at funerals
Sisterhood	2009	Lecturers and teachers	R400	No	To lend money at interest and "do up my ceiling"
Funeral club	2004	Leondale residents	R50	—	To lend money at interest and buy bulk groceries

her growing sense of self-confident identity as one of a group of professional women with an orientation toward investment coupled with house-proud interior decoration.[19]

Other cases illustrate the situation of those who are less stably part of the "old" middle class. More recently educated and holding salaried positions, many find themselves obliged to attend to the needs and requirements of unemployed family members. Such people's membership of funeral societies is less likely to mark them off from others; instead, membership provides a means to bind them inexorably to their dependents. I ask Impalahoek teacher Lerato Mohale about this, in light of her situation as a widow. In a relatively secure salaried position herself, she occupies the central point in a network of unemployed relatives, both her own and her late husband's. She has taken out a range of different types of funeral cover, of which some are formal policies and others are society memberships. Each is designated as "covering" a different relative or group of relatives (Table 4.3). Her case tersely summarizes the difficulties of "being middle class" where others are less fortunate and where there is multiple reliance on a single source of income.

Lerato's own particular aspirations are more elevated than these, however. They are embodied in her membership—on her own account—of what she regards as the most forward-looking and progressive of all the clubs to which she belongs. The membership of Bohlabela ("those of the East"), yet another "super club" but involving a more educated membership than Kwanang Ba

Table 4.3 Lerato Mohale's funeral investments

Name	Payment	Type	Monthly contribution	Use
Bohlebetho	Pay treasurer	—	R20	Cover grandmother and parents-in-law
Swazi society	Debit orders	Former medical aid	R72	Cover self, husband, children, brother-in-law
Bohlabela Society	Pay into bank	98 educated professionals	R40	Cover children, unemployed uncles/buy Sasol shares
Impalahoek Teachers Burial Society	Pay treasurer	—	R15	Contribute to funeral when a teacher dies
Standard Bank	Debit orders	Formal corporation	—	Cover children
AVBOB Funeral Services	Debit orders	Formal corporation	—	Cover mother
Jimmy club	Pay into bank	In-laws	R200	Cover in-laws

Basehlare, is engaged in discussions about putting its money to more logical use than the usual one of helping members contribute to the expenses of funeral catering. It is a large club with two regional subdivisions and numerous branches, and with well-worked-out contributions at different levels depending on the closeness of one's relationship to the deceased. Although this club will "cover" the funeral expenses of Lerato's children and unemployed uncles as well as of Lerato herself, she is more interested in its aim of investing money than in ensuring that her burial is paid for:

> I want to sell my corpse to the university—they are interested in using a corpse. My family thinks I am joking, but I am not. I hate the way people come to a funeral, to look at whether you are burying the person well—"did they buy a casket?" I don't like this. We have to meet in December, I have to convince them, "when I die, don't bury me. They'll give you my money, you can use it for something else." People don't understand me, they say "what about our ancestors?" I say, "if you are worried about this, take my clothes and bury them." . . . Funerals are too expensive, you spend a lot of money on food.

Lerato disparages the backwardness of her neighbors, maintaining that if they invested wisely by joining clubs like Bohlabela, rather than pooling their money in more backward-looking funeral clubs, they would be able to make real gains.[20] Others share her interest in using money for investment, such as in buying shares in the parastatal petrol company Sasol to secure the education of their children. Lerato's multiple obligations and what might seem like a bewildering array of memberships, policies and contributions, represent a mix of orientations. Determined to remain loyal to villagers' and relatives' obsession with a "good burial," which she has made sure to cover in the case of each relative and of her in-laws, she is equally mindful of the logic of a more forward-looking, less community-embedded approach.

Neither Modiegi nor Lerato is inclined—and it would not make social sense for them—simply to jettison the "social" approach to saving in favor of the seemingly more modern, investment-oriented "economic" one. It is the ambiguity and tension between the two that may help us understand why savings clubs, far from simply "surviving," are on the increase.

The Financialization of Savings Clubs

Given that opportunities to participate in the capitalist-style financial institutions available to others were once so severely curtailed in South Africa, savings clubs doubtless played an "intermediary" role (Besley, Coate, and Loury

1993, 1994) or acted as a "middle rung" in development (Geertz 1962) in that earlier period. But we need a more subtle way to characterize the guise they assume now in the 2000s. They currently exist in complex intersection with more formalized saving institutions, in arrangements that have aptly been termed *portfolios* (Collins et al. 2010). It was in recognition of this coexistence that many of South Africa's banks jumped on the bandwagon by designing special savings accounts for *stokvels*: a sign that the social aspect of saving has imprinted itself on the economic aspect.[21] But the reverse is also true. In Krige's (2012b) account of a men-only *stokvel* in Soweto, given that financialization is now "the only game in town," he has shown how members have reformed their previously rather slapdash arrangements by instigating recognizably formal financial techniques. He thus analyzes the club as engaging in "financialization from below." By doing so, club members, attempting to remake their domestic finances and separate these from the generalized forms of sociability that surround them in Soweto, have tried to draw more definite boundaries between business and pleasure, and between formality and informality.[22]

A similar sign that "finance" has become the aim of and model for what might at first have appeared as "social" arrangements can be seen in the operation of new high-fee, investment-oriented clubs (Kibuuka 2006). In addition to using banks for depositing accumulated funds, the clubs also explicitly mimic banks and the financial sector more broadly. They conduct extensive investigations into the habits and creditworthiness of prospective members, for example (Kibuuka 2006, 44), or employ a financial consultant to manage funds. But this is not merely a mimesis of form. Kibuuka's informants, questioned about their predilection for these clubs, explicitly stated their preference for clubs over banks because of the higher interest rates they offer on savings and the lower rate charged for taking out loans. Showing particular astuteness, they cited the fact that transacting savings and loans through clubs enable members to avoid South Africa's notorious bank charges, the highest in the world (Kibuuka 2006, 51).

Other clubs that take a similar form and work according to similar principles are those designed to enable minibus taxi owners to save money for the deposit on a vehicle. When I meet Thomas Thale in the air-conditioned offices of the media company for which he works, he tells me about the *stokvel* to which he belongs. Alongside his formal employment, he has diversified his sources of income by becoming a taxi owner. I ask him why he prefers using this club to simply taking out a bank loan. He says:

The bank asks a big sum as deposit when buying a taxi-type vehicle. They ask a 70 percent deposit. And interest for taxi operators is fixed at 17 percent, whereas the going rate is 11 percent. The reason for this is that taxis are considered very high risk. . . . For one, I had to put a deposit of R90,000 on a R150,000 vehicle. . . . The advantage is that this [system] offers handsome profits, though no one has actually calculated what these are. The key thing here is that those who are borrowing are also those who are lending. This is a way of getting credit if you cannot get it otherwise.

The levels of canny calculation, unevenly combined with generalized faith in the trustworthiness of the system, are evident.

Even more clearly oriented toward investment are interest-raising clubs, known in the literature as Accumulated Savings and Credit Associations, or ASCRAs (Ardener 2010; Bähre 2007). During fieldwork, I find that these exist in many different guises and a variety of settings. They appear—like other clubs—to be most sustainable when members have a regular income, being commonly, though not uniquely, associated with salaried professionals. In and around Johannesburg and Pretoria, Modiegi Nong's "sisterhood" of teachers, lecturers, and educational administrators is one example. Another is the Dynamic Ladies Social Club, whose members are drawn from the ranks of high-level employees in government. The section of its constitution governing loans stipulates that, with the aim of "accumulating more money for savings," each member is obliged to borrow R500 annually and repay it with 20 percent interest. If they themselves do not need or want to borrow the R500, they are obliged to lend it out to friends at interest (see Figure 4.5).[23]

Equally oriented to making money grow, if relatively humble in monthly contributions, Impalahoek has several such clubs. In those with higher fees, membership is drawn predominantly from among government employees, especially teachers and nurses. Thiakene Machaka ("Build Yourselves, Relatives"), for example, was started by a teacher, Muzila Nkosi. Monies collected on the monthly payday from each member, instead of being simply distributed as a lump sum to each in turn on a rotating basis, are loaned out, either to members or to their friends, colleagues, or relatives. The club has nine members, with each contributing R1,000 a month. Each takes it in turn to borrow the pooled money at 30 percent interest or loan it out, and those failing to do so are simply charged next month as though they had borrowed the outstanding amount. The responsibility for repayment falls on the club member who has been

Figure 4.5 Excerpt from Dynamic Ladies Social Club constitution

10. Loans

10.1 Available savings money may be used to loan club members according to their needs although loan will be determined by how much you have in the savings account.

10.2 Club members are allowed to take loans for outside people however this will be registered in their names, and they will be liable for the payment incase their outside clients fail to pay back loaned money.

10.3 Interest rate is 20%.

10.4 Interest accumulated during the year it shall be shared equally within the club members in the first month of every year.

10.5 All members to take a compulsory R500.00 loan during the year or pay R100.00 this is aimed at accumulating more money for savings.

10.6 Loans are repayable within three months failure to that relevant money owned shall be deducted in your savings account at due time.

approached by or knows a prospective borrower. As Elizabeth Hull, a member of the Popular Economies research team, has elucidated, based on her research on similar clubs in KwaZulu Natal, it is that member's decision to lend, and he or she is obliged to get the money back if the borrower defaults. She shoulders all the risk. Because the organization thus comprises a group of intermediaries who take private responsibility for use of group funds, collateral is built into the structure of the club itself.[24] Such clubs, although lending at interest, were explicitly exempted from the National Credit Act on the grounds of their being embedded in "African tradition," although most were founded only recently.

The Build Yourselves club had started as a pure savings club with no loan facilities. What prompted the move into moneylending was members' keenness to escape from the clutches of stores that sell furniture on hire purchase. Interestingly, they then imitated some of those stores' practices by charging interest to members themselves. "I wanted to prevent members from buying goods on credit. At the end of the year, you can buy what you want with cash," the founder tells me. He considers himself to have been wronged by a furniture store when a garnishee order was placed on his bank account—at significant cost—when he allegedly missed a monthly repayment (see Chapter 2). He contested the order, but his inquiries yielded no results. To avoid such situations in the future, he told me that he and other members aim to put together a sizable cash sum on the annual date when each one's turn comes to receive the accumulated savings and to lend a specified part of it, so as to be able to buy items of furniture, electrical appliances, building materials, or a car—or (in the case of other members, and reflecting the aspirational character of the times) to pay for summer holidays at beach resorts. Having established the club, they first tried a range of banks and later the post office as a means of pursuing their new investment strategy, but they never succeeded in being paid the advertised interest on their savings. It was for this reason that they started lending to members and, in turn, to relatives or friends of those members. The club continues to use its bank account, but as a repository for funds rather than a source of interest.[25] In similar vein, Kibuuka's informants in a high-end credit-granting club used banks selectively and judiciously, but they set great store on being able to make their own autonomous arrangements and to set their own rules rather than abiding by those laid down by formal organizations (2006, 51). In all these cases, independence from the financial sector was explicitly sought where this enabled members to retain their independence and dignity.

This aversion to the worst aspects of the formal lending sector was an outcome of the distorted version of the market rooted in an earlier period, before the advent of democracy or that of the neoliberal moment proper. Some view its shortcomings in specifically racialized terms. Their complaints that banks make no effort to communicate in languages other than English and Afrikaans and that bank clerks show them no "respect" amount, in sum, to a feeling that the institutions have proved themselves incapable of adapting to the needs and requirements of the new black middle class (Kibuuka 2006, 51). Far from abandoning the financial sector, however, they embrace some of its principles while shying away from its exploitative and disrespectful tendencies.

Conclusion

Let us return to Krige's (2012b) findings about the men-only *stokvel* he studied in Soweto. What prompted him to analyze this club as having adopted a "financialized" character was members' determination to establish clear boundaries between ordinary social life and formal financial dealings. Geertz's (1962) article on rotating credit associations makes a similar point. If we set aside the Weberian assumption that peasants need ways of reorienting themselves to become rational traders in a setting where an exchange economy is penetrating an agrarian one, his claims are nonetheless applicable to the South African case. Clubs enable members, first, to "differentiate" as Geertz puts it: to distinguish contexts in which calculation is acceptable from those in which it is not. They then facilitate "reintegration," establishing how and where it is appropriate to connect these separate frameworks once again. Thus, a "commercial ethic" becomes possible, but instead of remaining entirely circumscribed, this ethic can evolve, thereby enabling it to dovetail with the "general value system" of the society overall (1962, 259–61).

Geertz's way of conceptualizing the relationship between these domains is reminiscent of South African debates. It echoes earlier scholarly arguments in which exponents of the dual economy (Houghton 1976) were dismissed by those in favor of an "articulation of modes of production" or "cheap labor" approach in which modern capitalism was seen as having subordinated and subsumed preexisting cultivator or pastoralist arrangements (Wolpe 1972; Beinart 2012, 8–9; see also Feinstein 2005, 245–51). In more recent times, scholars writing on the anthropology of economy have tried to escape from viewing capitalism as automatically dominant, calling for a "human economy" approach (Hart, Laville, and Cattani 2010) that takes seriously how local, "house"-based models of the economy might either underpin or conversely countermand, rather than merely being controlled by, the capitalist sector (Gudeman 2001, 2008; Cameron and Gibson 2005).

If we view savings clubs through this lens, recognizing how they continually adjust to new circumstances and even contribute to forming the landscape that brings those circumstances into being, we can transcend the old "economic" versus "social" terms of engagement. Clubs and their arrangements occupy a point of intersection, similar to Geertz's "reintegration," of two trends. One comprises modern roles within the family, high levels of education, property ownership, and the ability to invest money in a rational manner—all things associated with upward mobility in postdemocratic South Africa. This trend is buttressed by attempts made by both state and nonstate actors to regulate and modernize consumer habits and financial behavior. Informed by this approach, the JHC was doing its careful budget planning with prospective tenants. The other trend is evident in pockets of apparent informality, customary mutuality, and even illogic. In these arenas—which we might call semiautonomous rather than separate (Falk Moore 1973)—housewifely thrift is kept apart from the rapid money flow of the market, valued items tied to the domestic domain are ring-fenced and protected, at least to some degree. Sociability predominates, and egalitarian mutuality is valued. This was the domain upon whose workings the JHC hoped to draw by encouraging children to join savings clubs. The ultimate aim of both, for a social housing company, was not to satisfy the voracious demands of capitalism, as a landlord might do when he demands overdue rent. Rather, it was to ensure a sustainable life, which would perforce need to be lived alongside that world of mainstream capitalism, alternately accommodating and defying its demands.

5

South Africa's Credit Crunch

Narratives and Neighborhoods

WHILE DEBT IS OFTEN viewed in negative terms, credit has an altogether better reputation—but the two ought not to be seen as discrete because they are interdependent, Gustav Peebles reminds us (2010, 226; see also Graeber 2011; Gregory 2012). Whether credit providers are praiseworthy beings who foster economic growth and enable the pursuit of aspirations to upward mobility and consumption, or demonic agents of usury hell-bent on exploiting the poor, is a question that has been hotly contested in South Africa. Similarly disputed is the question of whether debtors are manipulative schemers intent on evading their obligations or poor and ignorant victims of wily microlenders and loan sharks. Bankers and furniture- or clothes-retailing magnates who extend credit argue that doing so constitutes an essential good and that all necessary steps ought to be taken to ensure that the flow of credit does not dry up. A proponent of the liberalized free market will likely agree. The counterargument, made by those borrowing from them, and more vociferously by those who claim to represent these borrowers, concerns the damage to health and well-being that indebtedness can bring.

But the inseparability of debt and credit goes further. It is not only the case that every act of borrowing presupposes one of lending; it is also true that many borrowers are at the same time lenders. Such an observation helps focus attention on this book's primary aim: to view questions of debt in their broader social context. It has particular relevance for the present chapter, which goes beyond the single topics explored in previous parts of the book by illustrating how these different tendencies interrelate. The first part of the chapter explores this interrelation at a particular moment—the period between 2007 and 2008 when South Africans started to be affected by the economic problems blighting other parts of the globe—and in relation to people at either end of the socioeconomic scale. If there have been aspirations among South Africans to get wealthy—as well as incidences of such aspirations having been achieved, particularly but not only among the new black middle class—how far have people been getting into debt to achieve those aspirations, and what effect did the economic slowdown in 2007 and 2008 have on such processes? What belt-tightening arrangements were adopted by householders, rich and poor? In the case of the former, can we find traces in individual lives of the record numbers of repossessions reported during the period—and what were the knock-on effects of those? If, in the case of the latter, it was more a matter of "running to stand still," or getting into trouble despite being less overextended in absolute terms than their better-off counterparts, which factors played a role in such predicaments?

For both wealthier and not-so-wealthy people, it is the interrelation between microlending, hire purchase, the holding of bank accounts, credit and retail store cards, borrowing from unregistered *mashonisas*, and membership in savings clubs that is of interest in this chapter. To look at these practices in context, I explore in the second section how different people in a lower-income township neighborhood make differentiated use of these facilities and, motivated by admiration or opprobrium, how they pass moral judgment on their neighbors and the ways they use their money.

What is at issue here, in particular, is whether the nature of the investment for which the borrowed money was required is considered sufficient to justify the process of that borrowing, or whether, no matter how desirable the things aspired to, people regard it as better (as financial wellness counselors so often advise) to save up and "buy for cash." I consider how the various forms of "social good" in which people invest might interweave or play off one another. Building on the earlier discussion about the contradictory rhetorics (Chapter 1), with some accusing the upwardly mobile of frivolous consumption while others celebrate their culture of sensible savings, I ask what kinds of things represent important investments and which constitutes the proverbial straw that breaks the camel's back.

Economic Slowdown—The Background

In 2008, when recession had taken hold in the United Kingdom, the United States, and elsewhere, and was threatening to cut deeper and last longer than initially supposed, evidence of economic slowdown was clear for South Africa as well. Analyses of its extent differed widely, however. Some claimed that the country's inhabitants, though stretched, were protected from the worst effects of the so-called credit crunch as a result of various measures, especially the National Credit Act, which had come into force a year before. According to this view, government prescience based on a shrewd awareness of consumers' vulnerability to indebtedness through spending on items like furniture, cars, clothing, and the like, had ultimately helped guard against a more profound vulnerability: the overextension of credit for houses, and in turn the reposses-sion of those. Forewarned as a result of earlier "reckless lending" to the poor, the country was said to have averted a much larger crisis: a crisis like the one that affected the United States when "subprime" mortgages were freely granted to all and sundry. "South African banks remain relatively unharmed amid the global economic crisis, thanks largely to the strict regulations that govern credit extension," said Fred Steffers, managing director of the Consumer Pro-file Bureau. In the introduction to a journal special issue "Popular Economies in South Africa," Elizabeth Hull and I showed how other commentators con-curred: the worst effects of the crisis had allegedly been avoided "due to the introduction of these regulations, [which provided] banks with some degree of protection from external pressures" (Hull and James 2012, 6).[1] Government spokespeople understandably propagated this view, countering evidence of low consumer spending by pointing to positive prognoses. The Treasury's director-general disputed negative views: "You cannot have this economy going into re-cession if at the same time you are predicting the economy will grow by 3.2% this year."[2]

Other voices contested this, pointing to evidence of a "marked economic slowdown."[3] Broadly concurring that such a slowdown was under way, analysts nonetheless had divergent views on the role played by the problem of indebt-edness and by South Africa's unique way of dealing with it. It was clear that rich and poor alike were affected by the global rise in food and fuel prices, and the local rise in inflation and in the interest rate (the prime rate had risen four points from June 2006, to 14.5 percent in February 2008, reaching 15.5 per-cent by August).[4] These factors, in combination, caused "growth in consumer spending, the economy's main engine . . . to slow sharply," according to the Reserve Bank. But in the same statement the bank argued that its policy of sta-bilizing interest rates had already proved successful in reducing householders' debt for the first time in five years.[5]

For radical free marketers, such as Free Market Foundation director Leon Louw, it was government interference that was to blame. Interference had forced "our market to deny credit to creditworthy people" and had thus "caused or contributed to a collapse in our credit-intense sectors (vehicles, housing, furniture, clothing, and so on) by as much as or more than the collapse in America's sub-prime housing sector."[6] Others, while not necessarily agreeing with this overall analysis, nonetheless pointed to how the effect of the National Credit Act had been to make banks and other lenders, fearful of the effects of the new regulation, more cautious in extending loans, thus affecting the ability of consumers to borrow, which in turn contributed to the slowdown. "When the NCA came it shut the gate on easy credit," according to one report, "and people found they could no longer finance themselves."[7] However, some predicted the cautiousness of lenders to be a short-term thing, taking around a year to work through the system.

That South Africa around that time had a R1.1 trillion credit market and that nearly half its 17.56 million credit-active consumers had "impaired records" by June 2008 were among the findings of the National Credit Regulator's "maiden" report, issued in 2009. Fulfilling its aim of giving a comprehensive report, the regulator also pointed to reductions in the ready availability of credit. By June 2008, the number of applications and the value of credit agreements had declined (the latter by 4.6 percent to R76.9 billion from R80.7 billion) in the previous quarter: about half the amount was for property mortgages, which themselves had declined by 4.3 percent (see Chapter 6). Around 30 percent of agreements were with banks, and the remaining 13 percent were with "micro-lenders, clothing retailers and specialist vehicle financiers."[8] Differentiated approaches between the latter two subsectors are significant. Given that an estimated "80% of smaller loan applications" were being "turned away by the big four banks," which had been warned off lending to poorer people, micro-lenders and other smaller credit providers, having "picked up the slack" were "reporting record growth."[9]

Pointing the finger most unambiguously at the indebtedness itself, rather than at attempts to regulate it, was an analysis by Carel van Aardt, of the Bureau of Market Research. Debt, he said, was a "shocking burden" and ultimately unsustainable. One reason for this was its "direct effect on households, many of which will have to sell valued assets to pay off debts," another—here he concurred with the previous analyses—was that the resulting "lack of spending power is reducing economic growth." He analyzed the situation as owing itself not to the *lack* of credit offered to consumers in the current period but to the *extent* of it offered during an earlier one.[10]

What is of interest for this chapter is the way in which these circumstances, however analyzed, were affecting household economies, ideas and practices regarding appropriate investment, and householders' resultant choices. Some impressions are given by newspaper articles with a more detailed and fine-grained focus and with a specific emphasis on credit-based purchases. Reporting on such phenomena as the default on house and vehicle repayments, resulting repossessions, and the resulting need to apply for debt counseling and debt review, many of these accounts are written in the spirit of the market-savvy living standards measure (LSM) to emphasize lifestyle choices and characteristics, rather than foregrounding race as apartheid analyses might have done. The inevitable inclusion of racial categories made it clear, however, that white consumers owed more than black ones; and that "richer" rather than "poorer" people were most in debt.[11]

Reading between the lines, the racial and ethnic background of consumers were evident from their names and different lifestyles. In two 2008 newspaper reports illustrating the plight of overindebted people, for example, there was significant divergence. One report concerns a young white man, the other a young black woman. The former, Kuisie Kramer, was twenty-three years old and lived with his mother in the suburb of Pretoria East. He had obtained his first store card, from clothing retailer Edgars, to buy the requisite smart clothes to work in the restaurant job he had started straight after finishing school. He had procured a credit card to fund a trip to Thailand, later persuaded his mother to apply for vehicle finance on his behalf to buy a car, and later still had taken out a personal bank loan to fund repairs to that car. Earning a monthly salary of R11,000 (R132,000 annually), he now had debts of more than R100,000 and would need R4,000 monthly to pay off his debts.[12] The latter, twenty-nine-year-old Kay Moyo, was a married woman with two children. While her first line of credit was also a store card (in this case from Truworths) to purchase clothing, her second, a store card from Ackerman's, was taken out to help her buy clothes for her children. Shortly thereafter she found permanent employment—ironically, as credit checker of a company's prospective clients. She used her pay slip as the basis for a hire-purchase agreement for a sofa with furniture retailer Morkels. She then acquired a credit card from First National Bank (FNB). A vehicle finance agreement with Wesbank made it possible for her to buy a car so that she could travel more easily to visit her mother in another town, who was caring for her children during the week, and a personal bank loan enabled her to start paying for repairs to her mother's house. After separating from her husband, who had been paying the rent on their home in Johannesburg's high-density Hillbrow district, she found herself in trouble. Creditors "were calling me each day: Nedbank, FNB—'When are you coming to pay?' I didn't have money to pay." Clearing a lower monthly salary than Kruisie of R6,400 (R76,800 annually), she, like him, had managed to acquire debts worth R100,000. As a married woman with children, significant commuter costs, and obligations to other family members, her monthly repayments were higher than his, at R5,188, and her household commitments, including rent (which he as a single man living with his mother was not paying), amounted to R4,800.[13]

As reported in the press, and later displayed prominently on the websites of the National Credit Regulator, many such overindebted people had sought, and were receiving, debt counseling: about six thousand people, nationwide, at the time. In Kay Moyo's case, her plight was "despite her working as a credit vetting officer," but it was also through that work that she had found out about the remedy. Both people had one significant asset for which they had borrowed money—a car—but neither is reported as having had to give it up. Instead, the remedy sought would be to negotiate with creditors—providing agreement could be reached to do so—to "extend the period for repayment," probably by a year.[14]

What stands out in many reports at the time, however, was that large numbers of vehicles were indeed being repossessed, using the tried and tested methods of the furniture sector. What emerges equally clearly was the sheer number of vehicle loans, mostly to people in an income bracket considerably higher than that of Kruisie Kramer or Kay Moyo. Those suffering 85 percent of the vehicle repossessions were earning R240,000 a year.[15] Other sources, focusing attention on how "black diamonds" were experiencing the credit crunch, were more specific about the income bracket and socioeconomic and racial profile of those most indebted and most vulnerable. The "biggest losers," according to Cas Coovadia, chief executive of the South African Banking Association, came from this group and included "those trying to secure a foothold at the top," and in particular those "with home loans from R2 million to R5 million."[16] Bearing out van Aardt's prediction about people being forced to sell off "valued assets to pay off debts," a Johannesburg-based property investor, Sean Wheller, was reported as "seeing more and more people who wanted help selling their homes." Largely because of the sheer size of the new property-owning class, "the volume was more than he could handle." "Many people failed to heed the warning signs that have been there for the past three years and they now find themselves in a critical situation," he explained. "It looks scarier now because unlike in the [19]80s we are now talking about millions of people who are running scared of the banks."[17]

Richer and Poorer Indebted

Bearing out these wider trends, press reports give some insight into the nature of hardships being borne, savings undertaken, and investments aimed at or forgone by consumers affected by South Africa's version of the credit crunch. Sales of "interest rate sensitive categories, such as clothing, furniture, appliances and electronic equipment," were reported to have "deteriorated . . . but the sales of basic necessities [such as food] held up well."[18] Those expenses not obviously related to the interest rate were also affected: parents from all walks of life started defaulting on school fees, and schools began doing "asset checks" to ensure that debtors were not keeping parts of their savings aside to dodge what they owed.[19]

Reports also indicate that price and interest rate hikes were having an impact on some of the customs and practices, described in previous chapters, which are specific to black communities, and in particular to "the black emerging market." A sales representative from Benoni had, with his friends, left it too late to propose to his sweetheart. Initially having planned to pay *lobola* (bridewealth) at the end of the year, members of this cohort presumed they would no longer be able to afford it (see Chapter 1). About half of those questioned said that "members in their *stokvels* are beginning to miss payments, which in turn impacts on their group's savings scheme." (This was happening in rural savings clubs as well: an Impalahoek club had started to founder after having kept going for two years.)[20] One Soweto man had decided to quit his *stokvel*, instead investing with the Johannesburg Stock Exchange, "because he knows he can sell his shares anytime he wants" rather than being constrained by the *stokvel*'s annual cycle. People were starting to switch to less expensive or known brands, prepared to settle for "anything that looks good on me," and opting to take shoes to the menders rather than buying new ones.[21]

Giving further insight into what cutting back entailed for different sectors of society, the "Verbatim" column in Johannesburg's *Saturday Star* of 19 July 2008 displays divergences that almost embarrassingly reveal the extreme inequality for which South Africa is infamous. These are all the more powerful for being starkly presented, without further comment. Its statements by individual consumers also reveal how even people on low incomes had become used to consuming things that might, two decades earlier, have been regarded as unaffordable luxuries. On one end of the scale, an unemployed person making a living by recycling refuse reported that he had been reduced, because of rising transport, electricity and food costs, to living on *pap* (maize porridge) alone. No longer able to afford to buy new clothes "once a month," he and his wife were able to do so only "at the end of the year." One step better off, a security officer on a monthly salary of R1,650, whose wife earned R10,000, reported that, having previously been able to afford eggs, meat, muesli, and hot chocolate, he now "just shops for the basics" and was no longer able to afford to rent DVDs or go to the movies. His statements reveal the rising price of borrowing because of the rising interest rate: "we haven't got a lot of debt, only our rent, a bank loan and a furniture account." But where he formerly repaid R350 monthly, the cost had now risen to R560. Still higher up the earning ladder, a journalist spoke of the need strictly to plan his weekly menu "so that I'm not tempted to rush off to Woolies [Woolworths, an upmarket retailer] when I'm too tired to think"; he also reported having canceled his Internet and satellite television subscriptions.[22] Finally, revealingly indicating what hardship entailed at the higher end of the scale, a "government employee" talked of rather different changes. Both buying food to cook and eating out were expensive, but she had cut down on the latter: "I go to restaurants three times a week maximum." Also, she was eating seafood only once a week. Her facials were once instead of twice or three times a month, and she was shopping around to get a better deal on car insurance and a housing mortgage—which was "up by R2,000 a month since two months ago."[23] The column, appropriately, offers no comment on these glaring discrepancies: the facts speak for themselves.

Accounts of the "average" debtor, figures correlating income with debt vulnerability, and impressionistic and journalistic reports are certainly helpful in the overall trends they depict. They can be misleading, though, in that they conceal the particular ways that householders at either end of a wide spectrum had invested their borrowed money and their reactions when their choices proved unsustainable. Given that indebtedness is a sensitive subject, it is difficult to probe the details of people's income, expenditure, and owings, but facts and figures provided by debt counselors go some way toward filling this gap. Those hailing from the wealthier strata of society were showing up in large numbers to seek such counseling, as mentioned earlier. The stories of debt counseling in

Chapter 2, collected in 2008, illustrate this. In the case of the new elites, the stories tell a perhaps somewhat predictable tale of flashy expenditure, accompanied in some cases by a marked unwillingness to take the necessary steps to cut back. In the case of the multiple card-holding suburbanite recounted in Chapter 2, her debts amounted to R485,000 and her monthly salary was R19,000; she had been paying her monthly living expenses, estimated at R53,000, by "living on credit." Having "rotated the money" for some time, taking "the Absa Credit Card to pay Nedbank, take Nedbank Credit Card to pay the Standard Bank, and so on," "she got to a point where she realized this was not going to work any more."[24]

Those from society's poorest segments—whose plight had been of more long-standing concern to policy makers—are far less well represented among the clients of debt counselors. In lower-income neighborhoods, such counseling is something of which the people I meet have barely heard. Very few have used it. I find myself able to fill in some of the details in the patchy story of the poorer indebted, however, when I am introduced to a man of very slender means, Richard Madihlaba, who sought advice on his debt problems from Mareesa Erasmus in the Pretoria University Law Clinic.[25]

The details of his financial profile reveal a tale of almost unimaginable exposure to consumer credit for one with so few resources. Mareesa had meticulously documented his "lines of credit." As I listen to his distressing account, I can discern the outlines of a list—of those items in which a young male migrant, however poor, ought to invest. Richard is a sePedi speaker whose home is in GaNchabeleng, in Limpopo Province. He first came to Pretoria in January 2007 and started working as a security guard: a low-paid sector in which increasing numbers of men, particularly migrants, find employment as inequality increases, crime rises, and suburbanites attempt to protect their assets from theft. His first venture into retail credit—not unlike that of Kuisie Kramer, mentioned earlier—was to get a store card with Jet (Figure 5.1), so that he could buy clothes on credit. Jet is a clothing retailer aimed at those in a lower income bracket than the Edgars chain, to which Kuisie was indebted, but owned by the same corporation, Edcon. In Richard's case, however, the clothes he bought were for his children.

Having fathered three children with a woman from his home village, Richard had come under pressure from his mother "to pay *lobola* before she died." With the aim of fulfilling his promise to her that he would do so, his second undertaking was to take out a loan from African Bank for "more than R5,000,"

Figure 5.1 Jet store branch with advertisement for store card
Source: Deborah James.

which—he tells me—he is still paying off. Another important investment he made was in education, taking out a study loan. For the repayment of that loan, fortunately, he will be liable only when he earns more than R23,000, which does not look likely in the near future.

Richard then incurred further debts: one from a registered microlender, OneCorps, which he paid off within three months. He borrowed a further R2,800 from the same lender to buy a DVD player for himself. Later, to buy a second DVD player for his family back home, he was given a loan by RCS (Retail Credit Solutions—a credit company providing "flexible and creative payment terms").[26] In this and similar instances, what Cohen (2004, 18) called the "traditional business model" of selling furniture on credit, with the "risk of non-payment" borne by the retailer, has been displaced. More recently, retailers have started branching out into microlending as an equally or even more profitable business, and consumers have tended to borrow money from microlenders to buy goods rather than getting credit from the furniture stores themselves via the hire purchase system.[27] In Richard's case, then, there had been no repossession agents knocking at the door. What there was, instead, was endless phone calls, as one can see from the next part of the story.

Richard has paid back dutifully, which brings its own problems. As soon as he repaid his loan to Jet, his credit limit was automatically increased. By the time I meet him, he owes the company R6,000. What tipped the balance for him, making such repayment impossible, was a sustained period of loss of earnings (see Hurwitz and Luis 2007), when the employees of the security firm for which he worked went on strike. He went three months without pay and then was laid off. During that period he received numerous phone calls from RCS "to say 'when are you coming to pay us?'" This drove him to borrow from a further microlender, SA Loans, "to get money to pay them." That unwelcome reminders of this kind have become a daily affair is the first thing Richard mentions at his meeting with Mareesa. He is continually receiving telephone calls and text messages from his creditors. "They are trying to find out when I am going to pay," he says. At one point during our interview his mobile phone rings and he puts it on speaker, to demonstrate to Mareesa the kinds of messages he receives. As it happens, and barely less intrusively, it is someone offering him a R50,000 comprehensive cancer insurance package. "Isn't this wonderful news, sir?" the caller asks. Richard switches the phone off. Even low wage earners now have mobile phones, which makes them easy targets for advertisers, and companies are reported to have little compunction about giving out information to other marketers (see Breckenridge 2005).

Finally, Richard has a bank account with Standard, with an overdraft facility. By the time he approached Mareesa, he thus had a large number of debts, including an instance of the much-warned-against situation of "borrowing from Peter to pay Paul." As Mareesa pointed out later, he was "borrowing money from someone—SA Loans—who charges 360% interest, to pay back someone—RCS—who charges 100%," so was getting "much deeper into a hole."[28]

I later hear more from Mareesa about her dealings with the various creditors: the details substantiate claims made that credit had been extended in a "reckless" manner and they support the suggestion that some form of regulation was overdue. While these details are more germane to my discussion of regulation in Chapter 2, they are worth a brief discussion here. Mareesa, having started debt counseling with Richard and demanded statements from his various creditors, is most critical of the microlenders. Her disapproval is clear from what she says about OneCorps:

He took a loan on the 2nd October and by the 7th October they charged him a month's interest (R840 for five days)—that is 30 percent per month. They phoned him up, and on the 7th of every month, they add a month's interest. We took them on about that, told them to recalculate the account, and they ended up paying back my client R200. We had a few clients from OneCorps. With one, she actually got back R2,000 that they'd overcharged her.

Richard's repayments to this company were being made by a debit order on his account. After being laid off from the security firm, he got a job at a firm called Pick and Pack, and the first month he worked there, says Mareesa:

They had not been able to get the debit order on his account honored, so the next month they [OneCorps] took off a double debit order. Which took his whole salary. So he came to me one day, saying, "I have no money, I can't even get back home. I am here. I have got two feet and the clothes on my back and that's all." So I took it up with OneCorps, saying "reimburse this," and they blatantly refused, saying, "We approached the client to pay last month, he didn't, and in terms of the contract we're allowed to take off this money." So we couldn't do much. But eventually we did get them to write off his debts.

Getting creditors to "write off" the debts ended up being Mareesa's solution to Richard's woes. By the time of the interview she has managed to achieve this with most of his creditors, pointing out to them that he simply does not have enough of his salary left to live on (the point raised by Xolela May in Chapter 2). What Mareesa tells me, however, substantiates the impression that even those lenders officially registered with the regulator were disinclined to comply with best practice—except when, approached by a lawyer, they get "a bit of a fright." They'll "cheat a client until he becomes aware of it," says Mareesa. "When we take it up with them, they go, 'Oh, OK.' So I think they know about the problems. But they won't do anything unless it is brought to their attention."

Unlike many people in similar circumstances, Richard benefited from expert legal knowledge and advice under the new terms set by the National Credit Act, and from the hard-nosed and uncompromising approach of his particular debt counselor, who gave him free and well-informed advice. He also derived some advantage from retailers' willingness, albeit reluctantly, to honor the spirit of the act even if its prohibition on "reckless lending" had taken effect in June 2007, only after Richard's debts had already been incurred. Although bankruptcy or insolvency is common in South Africa, it is, paradoxically, unaffordable for those owing amounts under R50,000 (Boraine and Roestoff 2002, 4). (It was for precisely such people that debt counseling had been explicitly designed.)

While Richard is in this sense "luckier" than others who share his plight, what is less clear is the effect of his many loans, and the investments for which he'd used them, on his broader life prospects and long-term future. It was to procure the basis of household stability that he took out a loan to pay *lobola*, to further his own and his children's education, and to buy clothes and material goods for the household. He was also sending money home for building supplies, hoping to start building his own house on his residential stand in his home village. His profile, then, is very much that of the frugal individual—the opposite of the profligate consumer often profiled by news reports. Broader conditions, however, seem to be blocking his life chances. His wife, he tells me, is spending the money he sends back on things other than those he had envisaged and has absented herself, leaving the children to be cared for by her mother. "She is working, but I don't know where," he says. On his last visit, the children were unwashed and poorly clad, and their schoolwork was being affected.

I ask him whether it was debt that caused the problem with his wife. He agrees: "Somehow, somewhere . . . the problem of my financial situation" had a bearing. His wife's family had expectations he was failing to meet. "You must pull up your socks," his mother-in-law admonished him on a recent visit:

> Then I thought maybe she thought I was being irresponsible in supporting the kids, or something. But to be honest with you, I have been trying. Buying food, clothes. Mareesa has also helped me with food parcels, clothes. So I cannot really see that that would be the reason. . . . I once brought my wife my bank statement, telling her, "I have a problem. People are debiting the money from my account. That is why I am not getting that much money. I have been working in security. And I have to pay some of the accounts, like Jet, and those accounts that I have to pay by hand. So the money that I send you is the money you can use to buy food and other things. You mustn't . . . hurry me." I remember the other time she needed me to move away from where we were staying at my mother's house, to my [own residential] stand. I must build. But building costs a lot of money. Maybe she is angry because I am not meeting her expectations. Maybe she was expecting me to be a rich man, buying her expensive clothes.

Still committed to the institution of conjugality, in this case by helping pay for the substantial costs of a wedding beyond the *lobola*, Richard and his cohort of men from the same area formed a savings club, Rekgonne ("we can"), in the autumn of 2008, the aims of which were to pay for the wedding of each member in turn. Contributions or subscriptions are R100 monthly, he tells me, with a larger amount of R1,000 payable when a member has his wedding party. So far the club has funded the celebrations of two of its members. The initiative is viewed as positive by Mareesa, who says, "I encourage *stokvels*. . . . They are helpful." It is undeniable, however, that the monthly contribution, plus the extra R2,000 that he was obliged to pay for the two members married off thus far, constitute a further drain on Richard's uncertain and vulnerable finances. Echoed here, we hear familiar themes about the unsustainability of marrying. Doing so is considered the first and necessary step on the path to "building" and securing a rural homestead, yet it incurs so much expense that it threatens to undermine that very security—and indeed the conjugal arrangements on which it is supposed to be based.

Richard's circumstances, as a migrant from the rural areas and member of an unstable and low-paid sector of the workforce, is somewhat typical of those whose lives are most frequently documented by anthropologists in South Africa (White 2010, 2012a, 2012b). His case is of particular interest since it provides details and demonstrates aspects of the broader context, which are difficult to find in official statistics and press reports. What marks Richard off as particular—different from the suburban house owners more often revealed in statistics and surveys, and distinct from the township house owners to be discussed in Chapter 6—is that he has no fixed property to repossess. His not-yet-built house, on a stand that will have been allocated by a system of chiefly authority, still falls outside the ambit of attempts to create a single economy of property ownership in South Africa—of which more later.

Neighbor Profiles in Tembisa

In a continuing bid to overcome the problems of finding out details about personal finance without being intrusive, I resolve to use the neighborhood connections and the knowledge of one of my research assistants, Daphney Shiba, who lives in the township of Tembisa, near Kempton Park, northeast of Johannesburg. I first ask Daphney to conduct a short, structured, questionnaire-based survey on people's financial arrangements, and she later tells me more about the people concerned (for a summary of the results, see Table 5.1). This proves a useful way of getting at information about the extent of formal and informal borrowing and lending in a particular neighborhood. Anonymity is

Table 5.1 Tembisa neighborhood survey

		Employment	Bank accounts	Bank loan	Store card	Friends	Savings clubs	Mashonisa
A	Woman	Unemployed, formerly worked for insurance company	FNB, Standard	African Bank, loan for study	Truworths, Lewis	Yes	Stokvel, insurance	No
B	Man	Middle management	Absa, Standard	No	Beares, RCS	Yes	Credit-granting club	No
C	Woman	Cleaner	Standard	No	Legit	Yes	No	No
D	Man	Pensioner	Nedbank	No	Jet	Yes	Insurance	No
E	Man	Self-employed, builder	Standard	3 loans, for marrying	No	Yes	Insurance	Yes, 40% interest monthly
F	Woman	Cleaner	Standard	Loan for study	Jet, Miladys	Yes	No	Yes
G	Woman	Pensioner	Absa	No	No	No	Stokvel	No
H	Woman	Part-time, Game	Nedbank	National Student Financial Aid Scheme loan for study	Truworths, Mr Price, Foschini	Yes	Burial society	Yes, 30% interest monthly
I	Man	Retrenched	Standard	Loan for phone bill	Truworths, Woolworths	Yes	No	No
J	Woman "money-lender"	Never worked	Standard	No	No	Yes	No	No
K	Woman "inveterate borrower"	Unemployed, formerly worked at Jet, Woolworths	Standard	Loan	Unspecified	No	No	Yes
L	Woman	Works at a printer's office	FNB	No	Foschini, Jet, Milady	Yes	Credit-granting club	No
M	Man	Unemployed	No	No	—	Yes	No	No
N	Woman	Unemployed, formerly worked as a nurse	Absa	No	Donna Claire, Woolworths	Yes	No	No
O	Woman	Works at university dining hall	Capitec	First Choice, to pay off store card	Woolworths	Yes	No	Yes, 25% interest monthly

guaranteed and hence the approach of survey plus insider knowledge satisfies the demands of research ethics, much as a market research survey might do, but yields extra nuance.

While this method cannot be relied on to provide statistical data, it gives some insight into the highly differentiated character of credit practices within a neighborhood. Some of these—tentatively—can be correlated with gender, age, employment or unemployment, and the like. But others simply give one a sense that here, as in any community, there are contested moral dimensions, debates, and arguments that emerge between and among people—partly in response to and in passing judgment on one another's behavior.

The survey covers fifteen householders: ten women and five men. All but one have bank accounts, and three hold separate accounts for salary or transmission and for saving, respectively.

Formal Bank Loans

Five householders had taken out a loan from a formal bank, something that became much more difficult after the National Credit Act was passed into law (Ndumo 2011, 139). Of these, one—a man (E)—had, like Richard, borrowed money to pay *lobola*, and again to pay *ukuhlambisa*, a practice in which the prospective bride's family states what they want to buy: blankets for the mother, a suit for the father, and shoes for all the siblings. About to get married, he was about to take out a further loan to fund the wedding ceremony itself. Self-employed as a builder, he indicated that he had been able to pay off the loans, but he also revealed that he periodically borrows from friends and family "for household emergency," and indeed—intermittently—from an informal lender at a rate of 40 percent per month. The one outstanding debt he specifically named was his tax bill, which, he said, "I always make sure to pay with at least what I have." He held no store cards, saying, "I don't see the need," but he did have an insurance policy.

Of the remaining four bank loans, one was taken out by a man (I) to pay a phone bill for his father, and the other three were for educational purposes. All had been or were being paid back. All but one of the borrowers reported positive outcomes and felt that borrowing from a formal institution was advantageous (comments included "I could afford it," and "[it removes] worry about where I would get the money from"), and the anonymity and formality were appreciated ("they do not know you"). One woman (A) took out a loan for the higher education of siblings (who she reported had finished their degrees); a second (F) borrowed to cover children's school fees (as a result, they were "no longer bothered [by the authorities] at school"). On a more negative note, the third (H) borrowed from the government's National Student Financial Aid Scheme (NSFAS) student loan service "to further my studies," but this had resulted in neither the completion of the course of study nor in the borrower's finding employment in a related or relevant field. In an increasingly prevalent pattern, this thirty-year-old woman was working instead as a part-time employee of the large retailer Game, and she was obliged to repay the loan out of her earnings.

Store Cards

Of the fifteen people surveyed, ten held store cards. Five held two cards each, and two held three each. Confirming the general trend noted earlier in the case of Richard Madihlaba, away from buying furniture on hire purchase (Cohen 2004, 18), only two of the nineteen cards—from Beares and Lewis—were for such items. Fourteen were for clothes, and three (I, N, O) were with Woolworths (Figure 5.2). Woolworths has a twofold attraction. Formerly thought of as so elite as to be beyond the reach of the average township dweller, it now allows both the display of status and enables people to buy groceries on credit, making it possible, in the words of Mrs. Ngunyula, to "swipe the card, even for bread" (see Chapter 1). Of the remaining four who did not hold store cards, one of two pensioners in the survey—the woman (G)—stated her opposition to the practice. "I prefer to buy cash rather than creating debts," she said, affirming an ethic of old-fashioned frugality that echoes what has become prevalent for the members of savings clubs (see Chapter 4). Her preference for cash reflects, in addition, her regular access to it as a pensioner. The other pensioner—a man (D)—had a Jet store card, but he too stated the virtues of buying without credit. "I got my house, cash; I got my Geen and Richards [furniture and appliances], cash; I bought two cars, cash," he affirmed. A disabled person, he had also paid for his prosthetic leg with "cash." Those less convinced that cash is the best way and have positive attitudes about credit tend to be younger holders of store cards who, although owing, manage to pay off their debts with regularity. They speak of credit as "helpful"; and of "accessible usage without cash"; and appreciate being able to "buy anytime." They also mention the "reasonable terms and low interest rates."

Figure 5.2 Woolworths branch with advertisement for store card
Source: Deborah James.

Informal Moneylending and Borrowing

It was at this point that Daphney Shiba's background knowledge became particularly useful, since it illuminated the sometimes awkward question of loans
from unregistered lenders or *mashonisas*, and of how these interact with other
credit sources. Within this area it is not always easy to distinguish friends and
neighbors (who might or might not charge interest) at one end of the spectrum from more professionalized unregistered lenders who invariably do
charge interest and from "formal" (registered) microlenders of the kind whose
expansion and subsequent regulation was discussed in Chapter 2: the term
mashonisa can be used for all three (see Chapter 2). While twelve of the fifteen
respondents were in the habit of borrowing money from "friends," five of those
were doing so with interest. One, the self-employed builder mentioned earlier
(E), was happy to concede that he regularly borrows money from an informal
lender or *mashonisa*, who he described as "good" and whose monthly interest
rate of 40 percent is seen—rather shockingly—as "reasonable and understand-

able." A second, the part-time employee at Game with the student loan (H), concurred. *Mashonisas* often come to her workplace—a widespread practice—and she borrows from them at the somewhat lower monthly rate of 30 percent. She too mentioned their "reasonableness," as well as the fact that "they understand."

A third, the female cleaner who took out a bank loan to pay her children's school fees and had store cards from Jet and Miladys (F), denied borrowing informally. Admitting to having trouble with outstanding debts, she was repaying her bank loan and her store cards "with what I have," prompted by the stores' insistent communications: "they were bothering me by calling." Of her monthly salary of R1,900, she was paying R700 to Jet, but she was once obliged to pay R1,200 because she had skipped a month. She denied taking out loans from informal lenders, but others claimed that she was known to be repaying one, a member of her local church, who lends money to her wider family as well. Most recently, she borrowed R1,000 from the lender to fund a ritual visit to the church headquarters in KwaZulu Natal.

A fourth respondent (O) both admitted to borrowing in this way and had a much more jaundiced view of it. She described herself as having "been through" the *mashonisa* experience, but it turned out that the loan she took out was from a formal (registered) microlender, one of those that requires the prospective borrower to bring her "ID original, pay slip, bank card." A worker in the university residence dining hall, what prompted her to approach the lender was that she owed money on her Woolworths store card and had been blacklisted by the credit bureau as a result. Keeping her actions secret from other household members, she then approached registered microlender First Choice for a loan, at a monthly interest rate of 25 percent. She ended up, she said, "working for the person, because all my money was taken by the person . . . You pay more and it never finishes." In line with widespread local practice, she used the colloquial *garnish* (from *garnishee order*) to describe the lender's reclaiming practices, equating it with the way that formal retailers acquire direct access to their customers' bank accounts, and saying that such lenders "take money the way they want."[29] She asserted her preference for borrowing from the bank—but in her case this was impossible given her blacklisted status.

What all these informal borrowers have in common is a general profile. Their attempts to save and to invest in securing a future for their relatives and/or children sometimes bring them of necessity into the ambit of moneylenders (called *mashonisa*, but in reality encompassing both registered and unregistered lenders and charging a fairly broad spread of interest rates). Only one person in the survey, the fifth of its "informal borrowers" (K), admitted to being—and was thought of in the neighborhood as—a person of spendthrift tendencies. She approximates the kind of borrower, often highlighted in the literature, for whom living beyond her means has led to the unsustainable borrowing arrangements that proliferate where loan sharks are present.

This person, who I will call the "inveterate borrower," formerly had a job at clothes retailer Jet, where her boyfriend was a manager, and later worked at Woolworths, but at the time of the survey she was unemployed. She had a bank account, but it was dormant since she had "no money to save." She held store cards; had taken out a bank loan; and was frequently borrowing from neighbors and *mashonisas*, whom she described as "convenient and always willing to help," and who charge 30 percent interest. Her debts to all three were outstanding, and as a result, she had found herself paying "a lot more than expected." She was widely known in the neighborhood as a gambler in casinos and in the Chinese numbers game *fahfee* (see Krige 2011, 190); sometimes she would go into the nearby shack settlement in search of more gambling opportunities. When asked by formal creditors for repayment, her way of dealing with this was to "negotiate with the stores and the bank that I will pay when I get a job." When asked by friends, relatives, and moneylenders, she is claimed to say, "I'll give it to you sometime next week"—after which she then departs for the weekend. With surprising frankness, she herself admitted that her borrowings had negatively affected her household members and neighbors. After being interviewed for the survey, she said, "It was awkward and stressing because it reminded me of all the mistakes I have done in my life."

Finally, one of the respondents in the survey was widely known as a person who practices *ukushonisa* (informal moneylending). A forty-five-year-old woman (J), she was unemployed and living with her niece and the niece's grandchildren. She reported making some money gambling on *fahfee* and acting as a *fahfee* runner. She extended loans to old people, or to "drunkards," sometimes taking advantage of their inebriation by telling them that they had taken out loans out when they were drunk and then demanding repayment. She uses the system of loan repayment documented in Chapter 3 that involves confiscating ATM cards, thereby securing immediate repayment once payday arrives.

Savings Clubs

Of the fourteen respondents, five reported belonging to savings clubs (see Chapter 4). One—the part-time Game employee with the outstanding student loan (H)—belonged to a burial society. She explicitly attributed her membership to the well-known forced savings that such clubs achieve: a burial society is "better [than bank saving] because I am not really good with money—I use it anytime." A second respondent—an unemployed woman who formerly worked for an insurance company (A)—reported having multiple memberships. She belonged to three clubs, one of which was a burial society. She expressed her enthusiasm for the clubs in similar terms: the "interest grows faster and money grows quicker than with individual savings." She also had an insurance policy. A third—the female pensioner who preferred buying everything for cash (G)— was a committed member of a *stokvel* "to make extra money." Members "contribute R50 to save," the host sells food and alcohol when it is her turn to have a party, "and anyone else is welcome to support by buying. It assists in that you can see what you can buy with the accumulations, because it is too much [plentiful]." The fourth and fifth (B, L) reported belonging to credit-granting savings clubs or Accumulated Savings and Credit Associations (ASCRAs).

One of these, a middle-aged woman who worked in a printer's office (L), was a member of several savings clubs: one of which, "for the growth of the savings," lends money to its members at 40 percent interest. (The idiom of "growing" money was common in the survey, perhaps reflecting the wide spread of financial discourses). Her savings strategies are thought of by herself and others as successful: she was intending to buy a house, and for cash if possible. The other, a man with a good job in middle management (B), belonged to a *stokvel* that hosts parties and lends the resulting pool of money to members at 25 percent. While enthusiastic about the club in principle—"the accumulation is good, it is yours [the host's] and you can see it, people support you"—he had in fact discontinued his membership. For one thing, he said that one of the members, in a practice that is a well-documented problem with such clubs, "ate [stole or wasted] the money." For another, given that he was provided with housing benefits by his new employer, he had left his old house and his old neighborhood behind. "With the difference of class," Daphney told me, "he has now moved from the working to the middle class."

The remaining nine respondents had no membership in savings clubs. One younger woman (N) said she hoped to belong to one in the future; another

(C) said she was covered by her mother's membership. Reasons for not belonging ranged from "I never believed in them" or "I don't see the necessity" to a
preference for formal insurance. Finally, the "inveterate borrower" (K), somewhat revealingly, said, "I cannot afford the payments."

* * *

What this neighborhood survey contributes to our understanding of indebtedness in the period of South Africa's credit crunch is encouraging in some ways
but distressing in others. On the positive side, it suggests that people were making investments in future well-being and security, as well as attempting to guard
against the shocks that might obstruct them. Bridewealth and wedding festivities, as well as education, were seen as sufficiently important to merit borrowing
money. Death and the need for burial were being provided for with both savings
clubs and insurance. More discouraging, however, is the fact that little of the
education thus invested in had opened the way to job opportunities (see de Wet
2013). Indeed, little education had even been completed. On a similar note, the
country's alarming unemployment figures were reflected in survey participants'
stories. Alongside two pensioners, one casual and four permanent employees,
and a self-employed person, the survey featured four newly unemployed people
and three who had never worked. Only one of the employees had become a
member of the "new middle class" and had moved out of the neighborhood.
Unlike some of the people discussed in Chapter 4 who had kept up with former
friends and acquaintances despite upward mobility, he had abandoned his earlier savings club when forging upward into a higher income bracket.

Usefully, the survey puts some of the more obviously usurious practices
discussed earlier in this book into context. From some of these discussions one
might have gained the impression that a household plagued by a combination
of debts—to clothing retailers, furniture stores, banks, and the like, but particularly to unregistered moneylenders that charge high-interest loans—would
soon find itself in an insupportable situation. If everyone were borrowing at
such rates, their monthly earnings would quickly diminish and disappear. It is
exactly this kind of worry that is often expressed in popular street talk, and by
those who write about such things in the press and in the pages where readers'
letters are published. Most recently this came into view in discussions about
the miners of Marikana, whose strike was still under way as I was writing this
in November 2012, and whose borrowing of "unsecured loans" from usurious
microlenders is reported to have been disastrously high (see Chapter 2). While

such worries are certainly well founded, my survey shows that not everyone in a township neighborhood was consistently borrowing on such terms. Rather, loans of this kind coexist with a range of diverse financial arrangements in a "portfolio" (Collins 2008; Guérin 2014). At the same time, it is notable that ten of the fifteen survey respondents discussed in this chapter held store cards, and many seem to have had their indebtedness problems compounded by them—perhaps a case of supply creating its own demand. Alongside the cards, which charge exorbitant interest, some respondents were short-term money borrowers at a rate of 30 percent per month, but only one was getting into trouble by doing this habitually. One was herself an informal lender who made use of the ATM card-confiscation technique, but she was a small-time *mashonisa* and did not approximate the "big" moneylending arrangement at its most extreme. At the same time, two *stokvels* were lending—to members and beyond—at rates of interest that varied between clubs but were relatively high. All in all, the levels of borrowing, both formal and informal, indicate a local economy based to an alarming and unhealthy extent on forms of activity that might be described as making "money from nothing," and that Krige (2012b) typifies as "financialization from below."

Displaying a wide range of divergent experiences, and recording some widely felt neighborhood prejudices, moral judgments and habituated sentiments, the survey also shows how the behavior of neighbors and friends can generate, or reaffirm, ideas about appropriate conduct in response. Viewing and experiencing the borrowing of some elicits from others a range of reactions: from sympathy through mild embarrassment to strong condemnation. Held up as particularly desirable by some is that old-fashioned sounding, yet newly revived, virtue: "buying for cash."

Conclusion

In a setting of economic slowdown, this chapter has demonstrated how newly straitened circumstances affect people's consumption and investment, and how different types of expenditure and investment interact. The expense that emerges as most necessary and valuable—and given its magnitude, the one for which credit was hence a necessity—is education, especially at a tertiary level. Higher education has become a necessity rather than a luxury. But massively expanded demand for it, coupled with an absence of state funding or bursaries, in some cases was causing a severe drain on households' resources, especially in those families in which none of the previous generation was educated to higher level but in which all of the next one have come to expect it. That which people most value is also that which costs most and hence requires borrowing speculative resources from the future (Peebles 2010, 226), with all the attendant unsustainability that entails.

Marriage, and the obligatory wedding party that accompanies it, was also considered an important expense—especially by men, their parents, and the in-laws to whom they owed money. Although, as I showed in Chapter 1, many upwardly mobile people were resigning themselves to doing without the formalities of marriage, those lower down the scale were perhaps less able to flout social convention and felt obliged to get themselves in hock to afford it.

Across the board, belt tightening was being practiced and forms of self-denial put in place—though what counted as austerity varied so widely as to sound, at times, ridiculous. School fees, incurred one rung up the social ladder from what might have been comfortable, suddenly became unaffordable. The transport costs involved in getting to school were likewise too steep. People were reverting to less expensive kinds of food, buying cheaper and nonbranded clothes, and/or buying them less often. What led to such cutbacks was, as Van Aardt had predicted, not just higher prices but also the need to repay earlier debts.[30] For low-paid security guard Richard, for example, it was his commitment to keep up his newly restructured repayments to clothes retailers and microlenders that was driving his newfound austerity measures: so determined was he to repay his store cards and other debts that he was starving himself. Mercifully, sense prevailed when his adviser, spotting the unsustainability of the situation, insisted to his creditors—backed up by the moral authority of the new legislation—that they "write off the debts." But this possibility was available only to those few fortunate enough to come within the ambit of the new regulations or (as in his case) to find a funded counselor for whose services he was not obliged to pay.

Household planning in the domestic domain—concerning payment for food, school uniforms, and the like—was still possible. This was especially so for savings clubs members with a strictly conceptualized annual or cyclical arrangement structuring their savings contributions. Going beyond mere frugality, some of these clubs were turning themselves into "investment vehicles" by having members borrow at interest and/or having them lend that money out to friends in turn. But a number of clubs were, according to anecdotal evidence and to newspaper reports, experiencing defaults. Throwing out the calculation of the entire cycle and its sustainability, these defaults exposed the vulnerabilities of the savings club system to precisely those contingencies against which they were intended to guard.

Indeed, savings clubs and *stokvels* aimed at enabling members to accomplish important social life-course status rituals like weddings were, in the case of Richard, foundering on the sheer expense of such events, especially at a time when the price of consumables was rising. Trusting to more formal channels, the self-employed builder from Tembisa had already borrowed and was expecting to be able to use his steady earnings as the basis to borrow again, from a formal bank for this same purpose—seemingly irrespective of the rising interest rate. He was planning to be able to do this while simultaneously making the necessary repayments of yet another "debt"—taxes. The delayed *lobola* payers reported on in the lifestyle column, presumably likewise borrowing at interest but more upwardly mobile and with more expensive lifestyles overall, were—in contrast—being affected by the interest rate hikes. The important social investment of marriage was, in all cases, requiring that men get into debt. But whether repaying such debts was sustainable depended on the income of the person concerned, and—less predictably—on fluctuations in the official interest rate.

At the same time, people were continuing to trust in the ubiquitous funeral societies to hedge against shocks, often using complex arrangements with different societies to cover different relatives, and/or pairing these up with formal insurance. Skillfully "juggling" their finances (Guérin 2014; Guérin, Morvant-Roux, and Villarreal 2013), they were alternately using their bank accounts and letting them become dormant, alternately repaying or avoiding their obligations to retailers, sometimes taking out more expensive loans to pay off cheaper ones, and borrowing from informal lenders or becoming lenders in their turn—sometimes all at once.

Some of the areas of value, investment, and future orientation described here, often described as customary (although they have been much reinvented), sound quintessentially "black" or "township-like" in character. They are practices that might be thought to reinforce or perpetuate a dual economy of credit and the credit apartheid in which that dual economy had its roots (see Chapter 3). Set off against these, however, are a set of arrangements that appear more oriented to integration within the "single economy." Vehicle purchase was one of these. Cars have been briefly referred to in the current chapter as much-valued items for which large amounts of money had been borrowed and that were being repossessed in record numbers (though, in the case of the two "debt-counseling recipients," Kruisie Kramer and Kay Moyo, their counselor-aided debt restructuring was helping them avoid this drastic solution).

Most important among these, however, in a modern capitalist society built upon the institution of private property, is the buying of houses, usually with mortgage bonds. In the following chapter, I explore how the dual economy of property—alongside difficulties in making a living if one is not a member of the black empowerment elite—is perhaps the single most important thing that stands in the way of establishing a single economy of credit.

6 "The History of That House Keeps You Out"

Property and the New Entrepreneur

ALONGSIDE FRUGALITY and belt tightening, a central rhetoric advocated in South Africa as a means to avoid indebtedness—and hence one way through which credit "demand" is tackled—has been that people should earn their own money through individual initiative and enterprise and become productive members of society independent of the state (see Barchiesi 2011, 162, 166; Marais 2011, 223; Neves and du Toit 2012, 130). This tacitly denies, but is perhaps also aimed at transforming, the crucial fact that many of the people in this upwardly mobile group are in fact public servants, employees in state-owned enterprises, or recipients of black economic empowerment (BEE) "tenders," typically offered to those with political connections, and much criticized for their nepotistic character (see Atkinson 2007; Johnson 2009; McNeill 2012; Southall 2007, 2012). But there are obstacles to becoming an entrepreneur outside this system. Seemingly promising business opportunities are undermined, in particular, by the endurance of a dual economy in the realm of property. With prospective fortunes in this arena scuppered, some have turned to other enterprises, many of which involve rent seeking rather than productive industry. Moneylending can appear as one such alternative. More reliable in the short term, it further increases the sense that when all else fails, people, trapped in what remains a second economy, revert to making "money from nothing." Difficulties in moving upward thus seem almost overdetermined.

This brings us to a topic that has been missing from this book's accounts of credit so far: fixed property, the extension of credit by way of mortgage bonds, the repossession of such property, and the role it plays both in underpinning the continued flow of credit and in facilitating the livelihood strategies of the new middle class. Complementing the question, explored in Chapter 5 and elsewhere, of how people invest the money they have borrowed, this chapter asks about the importance of "real estate": something widely assumed to lie at the basis of an integrated system of market relations and economic growth (Anders 2009, 55–59; Department of Trade and Industry 2004, 16–17) and, in turn, of the formation of a self-confident bourgeoisie.[1] In South Africa, secure residence has also been considered important to the establishment of a new democratic order more generally. Given how severely the right to territory and tenure were undermined by the forced removals of apartheid, its reestablishment was one of the key promises of the constitution.

With the advent of democracy, as aspirant homeowners scrambled to get on the property ladder (after having previously restricted their borrowing to lesser items such as furniture), involvement in market relations was sudden, precipitous, and in some cases uneven. The results could be difficult for those trying to make a living in property sales, as the story of Frank Pule illustrates. When I meet him, Frank is an aspirant entrepreneur in Soweto who started doing property speculation in 2004 after his previous business, truck transportation, began to flounder. His parents' preference was that he work for a regular wage, as his father had done, but jobs of that kind are scarce, and he, as the father of two children being schooled in the formerly white suburbs, has expenses far greater than those of his parents' generation had ever been (see Steinberg 2008, 104–5). His new business venture has been to buy houses on auction in formerly white areas, where townhouses in clusters were being sold off in the early 2000s, especially in areas south of Johannesburg close to Soweto, or in newly developed areas like Midrand, between Johannesburg and Pretoria. The availability of such houses he puts down to the aspirations—sometimes unrealistic—of the newly salaried classes who had recently moved out of Soweto and into these suburbs.[2] They have "got in over their heads," he says. It was not simply deciding to buy a house on mortgage that was rash, he explained. Rather, it was adding to the newly acquired expense of such loans with extra purchases—furniture, luxury cars, and the like:

> Property . . . is a necessity, it is very important. But "we'd like to fill it up with expensive furniture, and you must see that we are from such and such an area." Then people will say, "Oh, you say you are from such and such an area, but you don't have a car."

Many of these recently purchased townhouses, having been repossessed, are being resold at auction. "People don't know what it is like buying a house. They think, 'Because I am working at SABC [South African Broadcasting Corporation], I will afford this house.'" The sudden availability of credit just after democracy—that accompanied political and economic freedom—has been a factor inclining people to engage in consumption without giving it much thought, Frank tells me.

His buying and selling of the repossessed townhouses originally seemed to have considerable promise. The indebtedness of an initial swathe of house buyers had originally meant the ready availability of such properties. A second factor underpinning the flood of repossessions lay in men's reluctance to endow their estranged wives with a share in the property in cases of marital breakdown:

> Some of them would just stop paying those bonds [mortgages]. . . . The husband—maybe they are divorcing, and now they are fighting—would stop paying those houses just like that. They would not be having a problem in repaying, but now that they are fighting, "What's the point of me repaying this house?" Because I know if I am paying this bond . . . and I divorce from my wife, we are going 50–50.

Frank has been buying such properties, whose availability after repossession is announced each month in the *Government Gazette*, to resell to other buyers. But he, in turn, has encountered problems—indebtedness has started to work its way through the system. There are fewer potential buyers in a second wave looking for townhouses, and he has been stuck with several that he is unable to sell. Black buyers, because of the steep rise in interest rates in 2007 and 2008 and the new restrictions imposed by the National Credit Act, have no further lines of credit—"You don't get people qualifying to buy," said Frank—while those white buyers who do qualify for housing loans no longer want to live in these "blackening" townhouse areas. These broader factors have intersected with domestic struggles, explained Frank:

> There's girlfriends and boyfriends. I would be married to [my wife] and if I have got extra money on the side, I would even buy my girlfriend a house. . . . At first, when I started in this business, teachers could afford to buy two or three houses at the same time with the amount of money which they were earning—because of the lower interest rates.

> . . . That's when a man could still buy himself and the wife a house, and then a girlfriend, on a joint bond . . . still afford to buy a second house. Once they start fighting, they would stop paying for that other house. But now because the interest rates have gone so much higher, they can hardly afford one house.

After the slowdown in 2007 and 2008 that was affecting the estate agent business, the option of turning instead to buying and selling "old township" houses (also known as "family houses" in the literature) in Soweto might have seemed an attractive one. But Frank has been warned off. Memories of family entitlement during apartheid spurred popular opposition to any attempt to commoditize these township or family houses.[3] People trying to buy or sell them face vigilante action. What had made some families newly vulnerable to having these houses repossessed was the use of such houses as surety when taking out subsequent mortgages to build extensions and then defaulting on them. Frank told me:

> There might be a four-roomed house, a kitchen dining room and two bedrooms. What would happen, at home, when one starts working, then when the banks were still light on giving money . . . a son would say, "Ma, I have started working, the bank can offer me R80,000 or so. Can we build two rooms and a garage here outside?"[4] And then they build this. As soon as he cannot afford [the repayments], the bank comes and attaches everything. They sell the whole house.

While this sounds potentially traumatic for the occupants of such a house in Frank's example, it was even more likely to spell disaster for an entrepreneur, such as Frank, who was trying to profit from the entry of such property onto the open market. He and others in a similar position quickly learned the error of trying to sell a repossessed township house: "The history of that house keeps you out. The family won't want to leave." Neighbors will know the house as having belonged to its occupants over several generations, and the owner, sensitive to matters of status and competition, will have been secretive about having borrowed money from the bank to do alterations. "Now if the bank comes and says, 'We're taking the house,' people look and say, 'Hey, we know the great-grandmother, et cetera, and now this is the fourth, fifth generation, there is no way these people can owe money.'" To attempt to sell such a repossessed house is to invite the wrath of local vigilantes. In one such case, community activists had registered their displeasure by dancing the *toyi-toyi* (an antiapartheid activist dance) outside the door, the owners had refused to move, and the sale had been aborted because the property had turned out to be, in effect, inalienable.[5] Frustrated by the failure of his new real estate endeavor, and searching for alternatives, Frank had recently resorted to lending money at interest.

Rights Versus Property

The interrelations between property and credit in the context of this rapidly changing economy have been of concern to the judiciary and to policy makers. Shaping the deliberations are two predominant considerations. One is the assertion that, for the true potential for an inclusive credit landscape to be unlocked, free market conditions must prevail. That is, the investment potential of buying and selling fixed property can be fully achieved only if there are no restrictions on their dealings. Where that market is restricted, and in particular where the resale of such property is difficult to realize, the possibilities for credit will also be skewed. Underpinning this idea, even if not overt, is the assumption at the heart of "secured lending": that the repossession of such property for resale must be the ultimate option open to the lender. In other words, access to credit would be nearly impossible if creditors were to experience insuperable difficulties in confiscating and reselling the property by which their loans were secured. (Chapter 3 showed how, in a period when fixed property was not available to black buyers as a means to achieve such "security," a business model involving repossession nonetheless applied in the case of movable property: of white goods, appliances, and furniture.)

The second assertion is that citizens have the right to be protected from summary removal. The eviction of a person who has no alternative and is financially bereft is in conflict with the rights established at the advent of South Africa's new democracy. The South African Constitution states, "Everyone has the right to have access to adequate housing."[6] No one should be summarily stripped of his or her basic needs for survival—shelter and secure residence are principal among these—and repossession would represent a fundamental threat to them.

The tension between these approaches, centered on "property" and "rights" (James 2007), has run as a constant thread through South Africa's transition. The former is motivated by a conviction that a single economy of credit is essential—in part to enable the "democratizing of finance": an aim undertaken by Finmark Trust with the aid of the United Kingdom's Department for International Development (DFID) (Porteous with Hazelhurst 2004).[7] The latter entails an equally strong conviction that the poor and marginal require protection from that very same single economy in cases where it threatens their well-being. Although the two stand in an apparently dichotomous relation as ideologically opposed positions, circumstances and pragmatic realities have forced their proponents to give way to each other in recognition of on-the-ground realities. And although, in their stripped-down form, they appear to apply only to "the poor," as do so many development policy debates, they have knock-on effects as well for those further up the scale, including those who aspire to belong to South Africa's new middle class.

Those in favor of "democratizing finance," for example, have recognized that a free market in property is very far from being realized. Initially motivated by de Soto's (2002) assertion that granting freehold title over land to its informal occupiers will enable the unleashing of credit, especially for investment in small enterprise, extensive research was conducted in South African urban and peri-urban areas to explore its applicability in South Africa. Researchers concluded that in only one of the four types of township housing identified—that which is "privately developed" (owner built)—was the market functioning, and then only poorly. Researchers identified the other types of housing in formerly black areas as "informal" (usually meaning shack style), "old township" (those built by the township municipal authorities and known locally as "family houses"), and "incremental" (involving later additions to a shack style or municipal-built house). (See Table 6.1 on page 184.) People were distinctly *not* using their houses as "assets" to unleash capital for other ventures. Nor were they using their property as collateral. Instead, especially in the case of "old township" houses, occupants tended to be very cautious and conservative, viewing their residences as the inalienable property of the family and seeing them in terms of "use" rather than "exchange value" (Shisaka Development Management Services [SDMS] 2003, 35). In these sectors, as a result, conditions governing resale in the former townships were said to be "swamp like" (Porteous with Hazelhurst 2004, 136), thus inhibiting the growth of a secondary housing market in such areas.[8]

If such a market *were* to exist, banks then would be persuaded to lend money more readily to people living there, knowing that the property would be able to be repossessed in cases of loan default and sold on in their turn. But market forces on their own were unlikely to be able to encourage such lending (Porteous with Hazelhurst 2004, 136–37). The government after 1994 had already made extensive efforts to encourage the emergence of such a market by providing a variety of new home-loan arrangements, but those had largely foundered because of "cash flow" problems. Extensive public-private partnerships would be required in the future, and research done and efforts made in specific local contexts, to unleash the market potential of houses in those contexts. "As house value is unlocked in an area . . . and residents experience the benefits, so the demonstration effect should encourage other areas to participate" (Porteous with Hazelhurst 2004, 137).

Confidence in the ultimate triumph of these forces continues to be expressed, but concessions are made to the need for regulation alongside market forces. Those in favor of protecting the rights of the vulnerable and opposed to letting the market reign have similarly qualified their position, recognizing that certain limitations might be necessary to the ring-fencing of property. Limitations might be especially required in the interests of respecting the law of contract, not only where banks are the lenders but also where those extending credit (and using fixed property to secure such credit) are lenders of a lesser, smaller kind. The debate between these positions came into its sharpest focus with a celebrated judgment in the Constitutional Court. The judgment set the terms of discussion and dispute for a number that followed it and laid the grounds for an amendment to the existing legislation while also acknowledging the need to temper full-blown protection. The case was that of *Jaftha v. Schoeman and Others/Van Rooyen v. Stoltz and Others*,[9] heard on appeal in the Constitutional Court in 2004. It came to light that two very poor women living on the fringes of the small town of Prince Albert in the Western Cape, owing debts of R250 and R190, respectively, had had their homes repossessed, or "attached," by a local firm of attorneys acting for the women's creditors, and then the houses were sold in execution to recover the debts. Both women were unemployed and uneducated. Both had bought their meager houses using one of the state housing subsidies made available after 1994 but had been forced in 2001 to vacate the houses following their sale in execution. The legislation enabling this had been the Magistrates' Court Act of 1944, section 66 of which enables a sheriff to attach the debtor's movable property but, if none such exists, to issue a "warrant of execution against the immovable property" (9).

Overturning the High Court judgment that had upheld the sale in execution, the Constitutional Court judge ruled that the matter—since it concerned "the right to have access to adequate housing" (14), which ought to be unassailable—was indeed a matter of constitutional importance. How, he asked, could "the collection of trifling debts" be "sufficiently compelling to allow existing access to adequate housing to be totally eradicated" (27)? The minister of justice and constitutional development, one of the original respondents, had stated the importance of debt recovery for the "the administration of justice." She reiterated the mantra, reminiscent of de Soto's (2002) idea, that "for poor people with few assets [other] than low-cost housing, often the only way to raise capital to improve their living conditions is to take out loans against security in the form of their homes." She also pointed out that "not all creditors are themselves wealthy and that there might be circumstances in which creditors deprived of the execution procedure would be left in a difficult financial situation because of outstanding debts which they might otherwise be unable to recover" (25–26). In recognition of this point, the judge acknowledged that "the interests of creditors must not be overlooked" (28) and ruled against the "blanket prohibition against sales in execution of a house below a certain value" (31), which the appellants had requested, since doing so would make it difficult for creditors to recover debts owed to them by the owners of the properties in question. In effect, his ruling prohibited those sales in execution if these would be likely to lead to indigence and destitution. Despite the minister's reminder that those selling on credit need the ultimate security of knowing they might have recourse to confiscation (a widely practiced option, as this book has shown), the judge stood firm.

Restrictive clauses discouraging the sale of state-provided housing built as part of Nelson Mandela's government's Reconstruction and Development Programme (RDP) had already been put in place by the time of this case, under the Housing Act 107 of 1997. A further preemptive clause, extending the protection of state-provided property, later prohibited such sale for eight years following the acquisition of such a house—though ineffectively so: many were being sold illegally.[10] The *Jaftha* Constitutional Court judgment was generally acknowledged, in subsequent court cases, as having influenced *all* possible repossessions and executions of property. Intended to ring-fence the housing rights of the very poor, the case—along with the National Credit Act—nonetheless had an effect on those in the higher, or "suburban," housing market segment, often in areas formerly reserved for whites. This became evident when the banks attempted to repossess the properties of clients who had defaulted on their mortgage payments. "In the Cape, matters have all but ground to a halt,"[11] said one judge, suggesting that excessive "protection" was being extended to all and sundry because of that original judgment. Clarifying matters, the judge ruled that only in cases where the loan in question had been taken out to pay off the house (not the case with *Jaftha*) might the house be seized to defray expenses.

In a second case, the First Rand Bank took two defendants to court for failing to continue payments on their outstanding mortgage loan of R940,095.[12] The defendants had approached a debt counselor to undergo debt review, after which no further attempt had been made either to restructure or resume payment to the bank. Echoing what had become a familiar complaint, the judgment in this case made it clear that using debt counseling as a stalling tactic to delay repayments indefinitely would not be tolerated. He deplored the way that the National Credit Act, with its debt counseling arrangements, had provided debtors with the means to escape all their obligations, seemingly in perpetuity, and he ruled that such payments must be resumed within three months. Underpinned by such rulings, obstacles to the repossession and execution of property due to loan defaults became less insuperable than they had seemed to be after the initial judgment in the Constitutional Court.

The reassertion of such rights in these subsequent court cases seemed to espouse the same spirit as that which the minister advocated in the original hearing, with her wish to ensure that creditors not be deprived of the right to repossess property. But these latter cases were reasserting such rights in respect of large banks rather than the small-scale lenders she had invoked: those who might be "left in a difficult financial situation because of outstanding debts." Ultimately, then, while the need for the protection of poor people's property was asserted, concessions were made to the necessity of maintaining the property regime and the continued right of lenders—of whatever kind—to stay in business and collect the monies owed to them. In much the same spirit as that recounted in Chapter 2, a balance was here being attempted between keeping open opportunities for small-scale sellers, agents, and intermediaries, and curbing their excessive enrichment at the expense of the very poor.

The rise in townhouse repossessions that had initially enabled Frank Pule's business to take off had been underpinned by a long-standing principle in South African law and reemphasized in recent hearings: attaching property is legitimate in cases where people have stopped repaying loans. Without this, the flow of credit might cease. But there were other things stymying Frank's enterprise. Besides the rising interest rate, a further impediment derived from recent state regulation. Influenced by the National Credit Act, mortgage lenders were no longer willing to extend bonds to all and sundry, whereas they had readily done so in the early 1990s. As Chapter 5 shows, the number of loans granted had declined in 2008. Albeit less effective in other respects, the one area on which the act had an impact was on the provision of housing loans. This was why Frank was stuck with two houses, bought at auction, that no one was in a position to buy.

The other factor—Frank's unwillingness to get into buying and selling of "old township" housing stock because "the history of that house keeps you out"—owed itself to a longer-lasting situation: that of state involvement during the apartheid period. This was the process through which the apartheid government municipalities had originally provided subsidized housing, on a leased basis, to township residents in their separated spatial zones. These were signed over to sitting tenants in the dying days of apartheid. For families formerly holding council-built and council-owned "family houses" on the basis of a ninety-nine-year lease, the state transferred title deeds into the hands of tenants, beginning in the late 1980s and accelerating in the post-1994 period, with very uneven results. On the one hand, the transfer of property from the local state into householders' hands, coupled with the propensity of many such householders, particularly those in the new middle classes, to forsake their property in these areas by moving out of townships into the "white suburbs," (Steinberg 2008, 104–7) led to a new market in real estate and a reported property boom. This has happened both in township areas—Soweto house prices had tripled between 2001 and 2010 (Krige 2011, 130)—and in the suburbs. On the other hand, however, there are factors that have served to render such property unsalable. In the late 1980s and early 1990s, banks, "lacking confidence in township dwellers' ability to repay loans," were said to be stifling the market in real estate by refusing to grant mortgages to those wanting to buy houses in these poorer areas, in an exclusionary process that came to be known locally as "red-lining" (Krige 2011, 130; Porteous with Hazelhurst 2004, 121). The banks displayed a similar reluctance in formerly white zones that have newly "blackened." This reluctance has knock-on effects for residents: when these houses *have* been purchased, often for cash, frequently better-off families have bought them. Conversely, poorer families are often driven to sell them—not because of missing mortgage repayments (they now "own" their houses), but because they are unable to meet the payments for municipal services (von Schnitzler 2008). Driven into debt because they cannot pay the municipality, they have had little option but to sell their houses (Krige 2011, 130–31), a trend that has been similarly noted in the newer areas of the government-funded RDP houses provided during the Mandela presidency (SDMS 2003, 35; Payne et al. 2008, 31). It is somewhat ironic that the *Jaftha* judgment upheld the right to housing as a fundamental one that, in that particular case, trumped the entitlement of small-scale creditors from low-income neighborhoods to be repaid. The right to housing has been, in effect, less secure in those cases where the local state, as provider of municipal services, is also creditor where bills remain unpaid.

What neither the proponents of rights nor those advocating the primacy of property acknowledge, but what Frank was all too aware of, is that the fierce and bitter conflicts in families occasioned by the transfer of "old township" houses into private hands are related to the instability of marriage arrangements. These former council houses have come to be viewed as communally owned family property, and the right of any single individual in such a family to "own" a house is a matter of great dispute (Krige 2011, 130–31; Robins 2002; Porteous with Hazelhurst 2004, 121)—in one notorious case the conflict even ended in murder (Krige 2011, 130–31). Beyond this, Frank's remarks about divorcing couples and two-timing husbands, quoted earlier, indicate that these disputes—and the resulting nonpayment of mortgage bonds—relate, in turn, to marital breakdown and conjugal instability.

"Going Home"

The relationship of marriage, property, and inheritance is an anthropological commonplace, but it is one that has been more thoroughly explored in relation to classic African systems of rural cultivation and landholding, most memorably by Jack Goody (1971, 1976), than modern urban ones. It remains of key importance for our understanding of the topic of this chapter. As was indicated by Frank's discussion of marital strife and of men buying multiple houses for multiple partners, broader structural factors have intersected with household conflicts (see the Introduction) to produce particular kinds of conflicts over property ownership. These tensions have been intense when daughters return "home" to their natal houses—what residents call "family houses," but what the housing policy literature dubs "old township" houses—after conjugal breakdown. During my fieldwork, it became apparent that women's place as nurturing householders—attempting to secure the domestic domain (see Chapter 4) and often solely responsible for their children, and with high ambitions for them (see Chapter 1)—is significantly affected by their ability or inability to hold secure access to property. I explore this in relation to cases of women living in the different "housing types" mentioned earlier, and summarized in Table 6.1.

Table 6.1 Housing types and forms of title

House type	Built or subsidized by	Title	Case studies
Informal	Owner	No	—
Incremental (RDP)	Government	Yes, but restrictions on sale	—
Old township "family"	Government	Yes (former leasehold)	Sara Leroke, Dora Usinga
Privately developed			
• "White" suburb	Owner or private developer	Yes	Lerato and Jimmy Mohale
• Township	Owner or private developer	Yes	—
• Former homeland	Owner or private developer	"Permission to occupy"/ customary tenure	Alice Mokgope, Joanna Chiloane

"Family Houses" in the Township

For a woman who separates from her partner or divorces her husband, opportunities to secure access to the house in which she previously lived, while married, are limited. Her husband, after remarrying or setting up house with a new partner, often finds ways to transfer such rights to that partner. The original wife is thus reliant on being able to return, for her ultimate security, to the "family house" where she grew up. This, however, has the potential to lead her into conflict with her brothers, sisters, and other family members, who might equally be counting on that house for security: communal property access here trumps the rights of any individual member and can threaten to extinguish the latter.[13]

The importance of this factor becomes clear when I talk to the ebullient and cheerfully upbeat Sara Leroke, a Soweto resident to whom Detlev Krige introduces me. Her account tells of a complex and interrelated chain of property rights and entitlements, in which her marital connections and disconnections are balanced against the obligations and entrustments associated with her family of birth. They sound every bit as interconnected and convoluted as the classic mortgage "chain" in a modern property purchase.

I meet Sara in the back room of the Soweto house where she lives: her siblings occupy the main house (for genealogy, see Figure 6.1). It is one of those "two rooms and a garage" extensions much beloved of Sowetan families: a way of enlarging their houses to accommodate the expanded family as siblings marry and have children, to let to tenants, or, as in Sara's case, to accommodate a daughter who returns there after divorcing. These same extensions are the

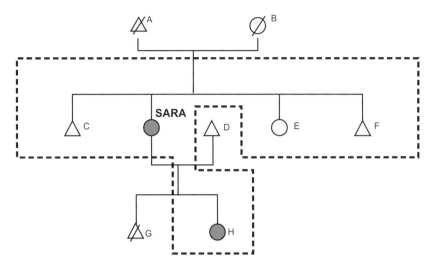

Figure 6.1 Sara Leroke's household
Source: Drawn by Wendy Phillips.

ones of which Frank told me. Some householders borrowing money to fund such extensions, after defaulting on payments, have their houses repossessed. But in Sara's case, the building loan she and her father took out was paid off in full during the 1990s.

Sara is very aware, however, of the phenomenon Frank described. "You know how people often lose their houses because of these garage and two rooms?" she asks me. She tells me of a personal experience of this threat when, in 2003, her then husband (D) was forced to step in and rescue his own father from the repossession of the "family house," which had been extended using a loan from the bank, and where the couple was living at the time: "Because the father couldn't keep up the payments, the bank sent people to come and evaluate the house. So they could get back their money. . . . They evaluated the house at R70,000. They were going to sell it to recoup their money." Her then husband took out a loan for R70,000 "to save the house": a loan that he is continuing to pay back.

Sara, however, no longer lives in her husband's family house. After divorcing, she returned to live in her own one. The "garage" where she lives—part of the upgrade—is small and modest but has been attractively furnished by its house-proud occupant. She tells me about the various moves by which she returned to live here in her natal home. After separating from her husband, she moved away with her two children (G and H). First, she rented a similar back room, and later a house, in an area near the hospital where she worked as a nurse. Some time after the death of her aged father (A), and following the sudden and tragic death of her son (G), she was summoned by her mother (B) to "come home" and live in the family house. Her agreement to return was not motivated by need, since she was earning a good income at the time, but by her mother's injunction to return and assume the status of chief household nurturer:

> She used to mention often "I know Sara will stay here, I know Sara will look after them, I know Sara won't cause problems, I know Sara will do the right thing to keep the peace." I think she depended on me. I was seen as the traditional mother, so I cannot abandon the sheep. So I had to stay with my two brothers [C and F] and sister [E] because they were the unmarried ones.

Given her status as the second-born child, oldest daughter, and hence family "mother," she says, her parents gave her the right to put the house in her name. But she is aware that sensitivity is necessary when it comes to individual ownership of what is considered a family asset. Given that it can create "some animosity between the children," she says, she prefers to leave the matter vague and undefined rather than specifying ownership. "Because you don't want to fight with them. They will say, 'Yes we give you the house,' and when you starting making things they will say, 'You think you own it.'" Ultimately, with family houses, she tells me, "You never get to own them."

It was this need for sensitivity that made it necessary for her, although acting as "mother," to move into the garage with her daughter. In the complex of dwellings of which this family house consists, she explains:

> There are rooms where my brothers stay. My sister stays in the house with her son. And me and my daughter stay here. Actually I have detached myself from the house, although I am still looking after the house. I don't want to give them the feeling that I am owning the house. So I stay here in the garage. I think it's fine. It's convenient for me. And they can be free to move in and out as much as they want to. I don't want to be a thorn to them.

When I ask why she might be a "thorn," she refers to the murder case I mentioned earlier:

> I have read it in the papers, and you will see it in courts or on TV that two sisters hired somebody to kill a brother—fighting over these houses. You have to

come to a point where you make room so that you all feel comfortable staying in a place. I love my privacy in here because I read a lot and I study a lot, and I read the Bible. They are there in the house. They are looking after the house. I go there to cook and, with us, we take turns to cook. So I switch with my sister. But you will find yourself cooking three days in a row because you don't mind. And we pray together every [evening at] half past seven.

Such arrangements seem to represent a reasonable and altogether necessary, if perhaps ultimately unsustainable, compromise between the competing interests of an ever-increasing population of inheritors.

I gain more insight into the possible permutations, variations on this theme, and linkages when I talk to Dora Usinga, a grandmother caring for her grandchildren, a resident of Sunview, a nearby neighborhood in Soweto (for genealogy, see Figure 6.2). Her housing situation illustrates the factors that have rendered single female household heads doubly dependent on access to their natal "family houses," thus making these houses even less likely to enter the

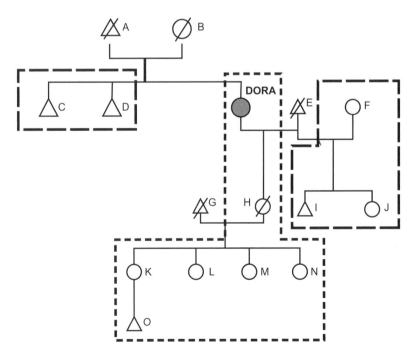

Figure 6.2 Dora Usinga's household
Source: Drawn by Wendy Phillips.

"secondary housing market" (Porteous with Hazelhurst 2004, 136) than they might otherwise have been. Dora lives in a sparsely furnished house that, as with most residents in the area, was bought with the help of a housing subsidy from the employers of her daughter, the parastatal Transnet (see Barchiesi 2011, 220). In her case, the situation is exacerbated because of the prevalence of HIV/AIDS for which South Africa became notorious when the epidemic peaked and before the government began to fund antiretrovirals. She was called to care for her four granddaughters after the death of their parents—that is, her daughter and son-in-law.

Earlier on in her life, Dora, like Sara, had returned as a single mother, separated from her husband, from her marital to her natal home in the "family house." Her husband (E) had left her for another woman (F). Dora, as a permanent resident of Johannesburg, had the appropriate rights—under apartheid legislation section 10(1)B—whereas her husband had come from the former homeland of Gazankulu. As a result, the couple's municipal-built house in Diepkloof, Soweto, had been in Dora's name rather than her husband's, and she understood herself as having an entitlement to it in the longer term. "I had children so I thought the children would be able to live there," she says. The second wife, however, allegedly by bribing officials, was able secretly to sell the house soon after the council had transferred it into the couple's hands in the late 1980s. "I wanted my house," Dora tells me, "but they would not give it back to me." Unable to assert her rights, she returned with her children to her parents' family home in Meadowlands, a Soweto neighborhood some distance away. There she stayed until her daughter (H) asked her to come and live with her in Sunview, to help her care for her sick husband (G). After both the daughter and her husband died, Dora remained in the Sunview house, caring for her grandchildren (K, L, M, and N) on her own. But she has no right to reside there except as their guardian. She still has claims on her original, natal "family house" in Meadowlands: she needed to activate these once her claims to the marital house in Diepkloof had been extinguished as a result of its fraudulent sale by the second wife. But great uncertainty prevails over how such claims might be realized. Her brother (C) lives there with his family, and he and her other brother (D) all have claims on the house that are equal to hers.

The communality of the "family house" thus has complex effects. Returning to the story of Frank Pule, one of these effects is that they are not salable, and so would-be property speculation as a mode of livelihood is not viable. This is something that owes itself to domestic circumstances as well as to the apartheid legacy, to arrangements of mutuality as well as to those of the free market.

Beyond the Township: The Former Homelands

In what ways do these "swamp like" (Porteous with Hazelhurst 2004, 136) housing market conditions exist beyond the townships, especially among public servants? And what implications do they have for wider questions of credit, investment, and aspiration? Among the salaried teachers and other civil servants living in Impalahoek, households headed by divorced women were common (see Chapter 1). The status of individual plots remained indeterminate, since all land was held under communal "customary tenure"—a system that had become entrenched under apartheid—under the custodianship of the chief, who allocated plots by issuing permission-to-occupy (PTO) certificates. But it was nonetheless common for individual householders to invest in building and improving their homes. Some had started applying for mortgages to buy houses in formerly white areas.

For such women, investment in property interwove with wider strategies for securing a middle-class future. Teacher Joanna Chiloane, a single parent, is a great believer in modern financial investments offered via formal institutions. As is common in the village, however, she made no use of mortgage finance. Instead, she has engaged in a self-build arrangement common in South Africa's former homelands. Advised by her uncle, a headmaster nearby, she "borrowed" money from a unit trust that she had bought for her two children. She tells me: "When I started to build this house it was 1999. And then each child had R11,000. So I took that R11,000 from my daughter because she was still very young, and I used that R11,000 to get the house." Later, with the aid of the "thirteenth check" birthday bonus, Joanna paid the money back into the unit trust account intended for her daughter's education. That trust was later put to its intended use: her daughter studied at the University of Johannesburg, and her son studied at the Technikon in Pretoria and was working as an engineer. Overall, Joanna's package of investment priorities has worked according to plan. Embracing financial formality, she distinguishes her approach from those followed by her fellow teachers who put their faith in *stokvels* and savings clubs, of which she is intolerant. She tells me that she gained some insight into the retrograde character of group savings arrangements when she was quizzed about "what we black people do" by a white colleague, who suggested that individual insurance or funeral policies were preferable. Her fellow teachers, more inclined to group savings strategies and "clubs," found it puzzling that Joanna's strategy has paid off, she tells me: "If a person becomes successful, they question how."

The story of a second teacher in the village, Alice Mokgope, reveals the existence of a local market in real estate, despite the lack of formal title and again making no use of mortgage loans, interest rates, or estate agents. Alice had lived in one section of the village, but when she divorced her husband, she needed a new place of residence. Through a kind of domino effect, a five-room house became available in a different area when the man who built the house got divorced in turn. He sold it to her for R10,000. She put down a deposit of R5,000 and arranged repayments of R500 until she had paid him the full amount. In parallel, she committed herself to investing in the further education of her son, paying out of her salary to put him through a teaching course. "He went in 2004, 2005, 2006—but he didn't finish. In 2007 he was staying there but he wasn't attending classes. I discovered it only at the end of the year." He had high hopes of further study and aimed to do electrical engineering, but his aspirations were as yet unrealized. She, like Joanna, is a single mother operating with relative autonomy. But in this case, unfortunately, her private property dealings were not accompanied by the educational success of her offspring: her son's educational trajectory has been disappointing to her.[14]

Following the transition to democracy, more ambitious public servants had started investing in titled property in formerly white areas. But such investments could end disastrously. In the case of Impalahoek teacher Jimmy Mohale, whose story Isak Niehaus has grippingly documented, aspiration outstripped capacity to pay. Together with his then wife Lerato, also a teacher, Jimmy "purchased a plot in a comfortable middle-class residential suburb" in a nearby town and later decided to build there. The couple "took out a loan of R40,000 from Standard Bank," with each owing R20,000. "To pay back the loan the bank would deduct R900 from our monthly salaries. We also added our savings," Jimmy said. At the same time, the couple decided to invest in educating their children privately, distrusting the state schools (in which they themselves were teachers) (Niehaus 2013, 104). But dissent later split the household. The marriage broke up, and disagreement about appropriate expenditure followed. Jimmy complained that his wife was failing to keep up her repayments. She took him to court, where he was ordered by the magistrate to pay R1,500 monthly in child maintenance by debit order; he was unable to finish building the house or to sell it on the open market, yet he faced possible repossession by the municipality, which was owed R16,000 in unpaid rates (Niehaus 2013, 113). The problem of selling houses for less than their value or having them repossessed to meet debts to municipal service providers has, then, proved more widespread than among owners of low-cost housing (see Krige 2011, 130–31; SDMS 2003, 35; Payne et al. 2008, 31). These troubles were compounded by disappointments on other levels. The couple's earlier intention to educate their children privately had borne fruit, in that the children had completed their schooling. But their subsequent education was not all the parents had hoped for: their daughter, instead of attending one of the country's premier universities, had settled for a course on financial management at the local technical college. The couple's aspirations on both the housing and the educational front foundered because of marital strife, among other things.

Houses, Women, and Mobility

This story of depressingly dysfunctional conjugality reiterates some of the themes of domestic discord identified by Frank Pule as originally underlying the wave of house repossessions and hence the instability of property ownership. The cases of female teachers who bought their own houses and planned their children's education independently, however, give a more positive view. Domestic circumstances intersect with property ownership to play out in rather different ways.

Arrangements such as those concerning the "family house"—which constrained Sara and Dora, earlier—represent a hybrid of contradictory elements. They combine the advantages of nonpartible inheritance, by which property remains undivided and devolves to a single heir, with those of its partible variant, which gives all children an equal stake in their parents' property. But the situation is in dispute and seems ultimately unsustainable. It represents one instance of the uneasy combination in South Africa between the egalitarian "rights" discourse and the more hierarchical "property" one, here refracted through the lens of changing gender roles and marriage patterns. Underpinned by a spirit similar to that which prevailed in the *Jaftha* judgment, the "rights" discourse maintains that houses are communal and ought to be protected from the broader market rather than being alienated for private gain. Underlying that cozy-sounding communality, however, run currents of gender inequity and conflict.

Those keen to establish a single property market maintain that such houses would be better used as saleable commodities. Although this position sounds almost stereotypical in its free market presumptions, it does carry potential benefits, even if these are framed in somewhat utopian terms. Being able to unambiguously "own" a family house might have benefited both Sara and Dora, for example. While their cases sound very different—Sara enjoyed some stability, whereas Dora was living on the edge of vulnerability and depriva-tion—both were swept up into the world of aspiration, with its considerable costs, which this book has described as ubiquitous. Sara was pursuing her own higher education, in part with government study loans. In Dora's case, the chief expenses, for which she was relying on her pension plus a grant from Transnet, were for the education of her grandchildren, one of whom was attending a local further education college and one of whom was aiming to go to university after secondary school. Having definite assets would have been useful for both. The literature affirms, though, that mortgaging houses using property as collateral is rare, not only in South Africa, where banks are nervous about the possibili-ties for repossession that ultimately underpin this (Porteous with Hazelhurst 2004), but also in other developing contexts (Payne et al. 2008, 39).

In the setting of the former homeland, where property title is allegedly less certain, the rights of single or divorced women seem, ironically, marginally more secure.[15] The contrast cannot be comprehensively drawn, however. This is because the house owners, in the case of the three Impalahoek teachers, have the security of a monthly salary underpinning their independence (Niehaus 2012, 334). (Neither of the township dwellers, Dora and Sara, enjoys such se-curity.) These teachers' investment in house building or house purchase—rea-sonably modest in two cases—looks set to provide them with some long-term stability and their children with at least a measure of a basis for upward mobil-ity. (Evidence of such aspired-for mobility is common to all the cases discussed here, irrespective of the means for achieving it.)

Secure housing finance and definite title—in the case of the Impalahoek couple that bought the house in a formerly white town (Niehaus 2013, 104)—did not on its own improve matters. Conjugal disagreement meant that this case resulted in non-repayment and eventual repossession. The secure title much lauded by adherents of de Soto's (2002) doctrine, then, is not all it is cracked up to be. Qualifying that doctrine, it has been claimed that "formaliza-tion may be appropriate to the upwardly mobile but less so for the unemployed and marginal" (Kingwill et al., cited in Payne et al. 2008, 8). But its appropriate-ness, and the implications for property ownership, resale, and establishment of a housing market, will depend on circumstances. It will be contingent less on formality of title as such, and more—as Goody (1971, 1976) points out in his anthropological classics—on the complex interrelations of marriage, income, and inheritance.

Making Money from Nothing

As the case of Frank Pule demonstrates, there are several obstacles to making a living as an entrepreneur—especially as a member of the "new middle class"—in the economic landscape of present-day South Africa. While the uncertainty and inalienability of property play their part, the wider context is also important. An important historical legacy concerns the way in which state regulation before, but especially during, apartheid limited entrepreneurial activities by blacks (Cobley 1990, 141–48; Crankshaw 2005; Hull and James 2012, 7). The stunting of such activities was inevitable given the pervasiveness of state planning; the fact that few Africans were granted trading licenses, especially in racially segregated areas; and the fact that shop owners from other ethnic minorities benefited from restrictions on black Africans' business and (in the case of Gujarati-speaking South Asians) from the racial legislation that prevented penetration by white businesspeople (Cobley 1990, 143; Hart and Padayachee 2000; Kuper 1965, 76, 261–89; Seekings and Nattrass 2005, 142). Although some black merchants profited from the lifting of these restrictions and transformed their approach to business, the uneven or dualistic legacy of apartheid remains (Hull and James 2012, 7).[16]

Pertaining specifically to the post-1994 era, a problem of which some aspirant entrepreneurs complain—and that some nonetheless overcome—is the fact of needing to be "connected" to get one's enterprise off the ground. This has been most notoriously documented in the story of the government's infamous tender system. "A recently enriched upwardly mobile class of politically connected 'tenderpreneurs,'" as Fraser McNeill, a member of the Popular Economies research team, observed, "form companies, and make bids—in which they succeed because of their longstanding links to political elites—to provide goods and services to the government, ranging from housing to hospital equipment." They then use their wealth to engage in "conspicuous patterns of consumption, leading lavish lifestyles" (McNeill 2012, 91). Although elite engagement in this practice has received most critical attention, there are many humbler individuals who similarly strive to procure such tenders.[17] Those unable to cultivate or benefit from such connections complain of exclusion, but those who do succeed often end up disappointed when the promised work fails to materialize (see Hull 2012, 170–72), or—even worse—when they win the tender and undertake the job but are never paid.[18] Aspirant businesspeople also complain of difficulties in getting bank loans. Despite injunctions for blacks to engage in self-started enterprise, and despite initiatives to democratize finance and enable equal access to banking in order to facilitate such enterprise, such difficulties and forms of exclusion have been remarkably similar at different ends of the scale, as the following cases demonstrate.

In and around Impalahoek, complaints about the need for "connections" are rife. I am introduced to one aspirant businessman, Milton, in a roundabout manner, via Ace Ubisi. Milton's story illustrates how each small business enterprise relies on each other one, like the components in a house of cards. It also shows how small-scale businesspeople in a local setting, as in the *Jaftha* case, can hardly survive without exploiting their neighbors to some degree.

Ace Ubisi is himself an aspirant entrepreneur. Hoping to earn some money taking photographs at weddings, funerals, and other events, he put a down payment of R2,000 on the secondhand computer he needed to download the photographs and burn them onto CD. Known as a "lay-by," this notorious and ubiquitous system involves making a deposit on an item in the expectation of paying the rest of the price within a set period or forfeiting the deposit (Roth 2004, 72; see also Chapter 3). But in Ace's case—as in many—the period of three months expired before he managed to settle the outstanding amount of R1,100.

So that Ace can plead for leniency with the salesman in person, I am using my hire car to give him a lift to the nearby town of Bushbuckridge. When we arrive, however, the premises are no longer occupied by the computer shop—it has been replaced by another small business. Anxiously fearing the worst, Ace dials the mobile phone number of the computer salesman, Milton. Milton answers, assuring his customer that he is still in business. Ace gives him an elaborate excuse that is somewhat economical with the truth and persuades Milton to reinstate his lay-by. We drive to a nearby settlement and meet Milton at a house where he is visiting. He says the computer will be ready the following day at five o'clock and will come with a six-month guarantee.

Feeling skeptical about the apparently peripatetic and fly-by-night character of these arrangements, I nonetheless agree to drive Ace to Milton's home to fetch the computer the next day, which involves a half-hour drive over rutted gravel roads and turn-offs along a series of subsidiary tracks, after which we end up in what looks like a typically rural homestead. There are maize plants and mango trees growing in the yard, and Milton's elderly mother is sitting out-side on a grass mat, taking a rest from crushing maize with a wooden stamper. The rooms of the homestead are mud-walled and thatch roofed: Milton's com-puter stock is stored, anomalously, in one of these. We go inside and find him installing a copy of Office 2007 on the computer intended for Ace. After Ace pays the outstanding money, he takes possession of the computer, and we drive back toward the main road, giving Milton a lift. On the way, Milton tells us about how his computer operation came to be evicted from its former business premises outside Bushbuckridge. The landlord had someone coming in who had promised to pay him double the rent. He spun Milton and his partner a yarn about wanting to use the premises for his own small loans business, but they heard from a friend that this was simply a cover. They consulted a lawyer and were told that the action was legal provided the landlord had given them the requisite amount of notice. Alongside the higher rental, connections are what really count here, Milton says. Connections—or the lack of them—have also made a difference to his employment prospects. Most jobs are taken up before they are even advertised, and it is widely believed that they go to people with links to local political figures. Before deciding to start a business, Milton had applied for an information technology job in the municipality—but the job had been given to a well-connected person, he claims, before it was even advertised. Perhaps equally or more telling for the needs of the small business, securing finance likewise depends on "who one knows." Despite having a well-worked-out business plan, he has not been granted any of the several loans for which he has applied, whereas a friend of his with no business plan at all but the right connections was successful in his loan application.

Milton, despite these setbacks, has kept his business afloat and is remark-ably upbeat. I find myself marveling at his resilience and at the anomalously low-tech character of the premises to which he has been forced to relocate, with his mother's maize-stamping hand mill just outside the window. I also have to revise my tendency to jump to conclusions about the exploitative tendencies of small-scale entrepreneurs who operate a "lay-by" system, as Milton did in the case of Ace. It is through such techniques that small business owners keep their enterprises afloat—and even then only with extreme difficulty.

Like Milton, but much further up the ladder of success, there are stories of self-made men who celebrate the fact that they have managed to make great strides, despite their lack of BEE connections, patrons, tenders, or bank loans. In one case reported in the press, Ndaba Ntsele and his partner started small and then expanded from construction to jewelry importing, selling Krugerrands and importing car radios. They eventually "won the licence from Portland, Oregon–based Nike to run operations in SA for the sports clothing company, which was re-establishing itself in the country" after the lifting of apartheid-era sanctions. Unable to procure loans from South African banks, they were eventually "lent the necessary money by global titan Citibank."[19]

Similar stories abound. Underlying a sense of pride in having "made it" unaided, the protagonists express scorn for those who rely on patronage and connections, and annoyance at the banks for their failure to loan them money.[20] Such entrepreneurs emphasize thrift and the need to live a simple life while benefiting from those who are more extravagant. Frank Pule himself opted to continue living in Soweto rather than moving to the suburbs like the aspirant suburbanites from whose aspirations—at least for a while—he benefited. He and his wife, perhaps learning from the mistakes of a relative who bought a house in a formerly white area that was later repossessed, restricted their participation in the suburban lifestyle to sending their children to school in those suburbs while remaining resident in the township of Soweto.

Those who, unlike Frank, did manage to succeed in becoming wealthy on the basis of property deals, nonetheless emphasize how they secured the future by restricting lavish expenditure. One report recounts the remarkable business acumen of "property queen" Phemelo Ngcobo. Admittedly, she was not completely "self-starting." She earned a good income from her appearance on one of South Africa's soap operas, *Generations*. She then invested her earnings in a one-bedroom flat in Sandton, which she rented out to cover the bond—"The value of my first flat went up R200,000 in six months," she said:

> But the two-bedroom flats next door were selling for twice as much. At 24, I realized it was time to get serious about my business decisions. I swapped my 4x4 and Civic for a Corsa Lite and began learning about financing from banks and lawyers. I put every cent I could raise into property.[21]

She is praised in the report for having "geared her speculations for long-term returns and not a fast buck," which she did by deciding to rent out her "multimillion-rand homes in prime locations . . . to the corporate market at up to R50,000 a month on long-term contracts." Having initially been tempted by the flashy lifestyle of the "black diamond," what she notes as key to her success is her decision *not* to live in the manner favored by those in that category—or by her clients.[22]

Such accounts of success based on shrewd enterprise and sound investment, beyond the world of the newly wealthy salaried civil servants and politically well-connected "tenderpreneurs," give insight into the factors that constrain such self-made businesspeople. In all the accounts, newfound wealth depends, in some sense, on "gathering people"—renters, recipients of state salaries, or even neighbors and locals with not much of an income. As Detlev Krige, a member of the Popular Economies research team, points out to me one day in 2009 when we meet to discuss the project, these entrepreneurs have little option but to recruit participants, to get access to people's salaries or income. This is an unusual permutation of the characteristically African tendency to gather "wealth in people" (Guyer 1993; see also James 2012, 35). Thus, in arrangements resembling a giant "pyramid scheme," cash is circulated and redistributed, and money is made "from nothing."

By way of illustration, Detlev tells me about a Sowetan friend of his who had recently moved "up market" to the suburb of Four Ways. The friend is trying to put together a property development in Soweto. He says there is plenty of money around, but general reluctance—even from the banks—to start spending. Each person is watching everyone else to see who will take the plunge. Despairing of any movement, Detlev's friend recognizes that the only actor who is able or prepared to spend is the government, so heading back in the "tenderpreneur" direction, he got busy arranging a partnership that involves applying for government funding.

Some of the features of this system, we agree, give it a character not unlike that of financialization everywhere (see Krige 2012). Gaining access to the money of the people at the bottom of the pyramid is essential to generate profit, as banks did in the case of the United States subprime mortgage market. But in other respects, we conclude, it is quintessentially South African. Given the significance of redistribution in the country's economy—largely of state funds but not only so (Bähre 2011)—and the efforts made by so many to gain access to those funds by one means or another, South Africa's regime has been characterized as "distributional" rather than "neoliberal" (Seekings and Nattrass 2005)—or as stated earlier, it is one in which "neoliberal means interweave with and facilitate redistributive ends" (Hull and James 2012, 16).

This reliance on "recruiting people," in South Africa's version of financialization, can run into problems. Some forms of the new enterprise, in particular, rely on the sale of, and the willingness of other upwardly mobile to buy, precisely those financial products that became the rage after the birth of South

Africa's new democracy. But such enterprise is vulnerable when mobility is stalled and the wealth of the recruited people runs dry. The case of insurance salespeople and brokers discussed by member of the Popular Economies research team Erik Bähre is a good illustration. While many township dwellers have been ready to buy insurance policies, they are also notoriously likely to cancel these when times are tough, as when they need a lump sum, or during the recession of the late 2000s (Bähre 2012, 150).[23]

This inconstancy, while financially unsustainable for these purchasers in the long term, has particularly disastrous effects on the economic situation in the shorter term of the intermediaries or brokers who sold them their policies. Debt counselor Rethabile Tlou tells me that several people who have approached her for advice, having found themselves in debt, are insurance salesmen. When their clients cancel policies, these brokers fall into arrears with their payments on cars, houses, and the like.[24] Through a bizarre circularity, individuals facing the insecurity of their new livelihood strategies—like these salespeople, or indeed like Frank Pule—might then find themselves with little choice but to *borrow* from informal moneylenders. This is becoming difficult, since the bigger moneylenders increasingly lend only to those with regular incomes (James 2012, 35; see also Chapter 3). Alternatively, or intermittently, they might turn as Frank did to *lending* money to those in dire financial straits. We are reminded of the point made by anthropologists writing on credit and debt: the two ought not to be seen as discrete because they are interdependent (Gregory 2012; Peebles 2010, 226). It is not merely the case that every act of borrowing presupposes one of lending; many borrowers are, at the same time, lenders as well.

Conclusion

This chapter has explored how residential property intersects with the other elements in which a household invests its income and from which its members might secure their future. Demonstrating some of the complex interrelations of credit and property as they play out in everyday life, the chapter shows how these situations not only are influenced by, but also affect, the broader world of policy, politics, and economy. The policy literature, which advocates fixed property as underpinning a free market, suggests that secure title, combined with readily available mortgage finance, might help bring an end to South Africa's dual economy. It would give owners collateral which they might use in order to gain access to credit. Speaking against the "advantage to creditor principle" that dominates laws concerning indebtedness (Boraine and Roestoff 2002, 4),

the view from a social justice perspective instead has stressed the need to protect inalienable rights. That perspective advocates that those rights be protected
from the arbitrariness of the market, especially where creditors threatened confiscation. (Interestingly, as the law developed, it ended up protecting the rights
of the banks and large-scale mortgage lenders to repossess property rather than
those of the small-scale neighborhood—often "illegal"—lenders that had featured in the Constitutional Court judgment. But some of these lenders, as we
saw in Chapters 2 and 3, had "other means" of securing their loans, by recoup-
ing them from borrowers' bank accounts.)

The hybrid compromise between the two approaches has had complex
ramifications. Some householders, enticed by the promises of the market, responded to its call. In the initial honeymoon period, when loans—for example,
to fund garage-and-two-rooms extensions—had been easy to get, they had
used their township or family houses for collateral. What had made repossess-
sion difficult was not simply the strong sense of family ownership. Nor was it
only the resistance mind-set, of the apartheid struggle, which drove neighbors
onto the street to dance the *toyi-toyi* when house owners were threatened with
eviction by the banks. A further factor was the instability of conjugal arrangements and the need to "return home" after a marriage breakup. The net effect
was that many householders were keeping rather than selling the family houses
with which they had initially been provided by apartheid's peculiarly skewed
version of welfarism. This lack of individual ownership—in combination with
other factors like irregular income—seemed to be inhibiting the abilities of
single women, whether mothers or grandmothers, to improve their lot and
that of their children. The conditions that prevented the growth of a secondary
housing market, then, have complex determinants (and effects), ranging from
domestic struggles at the intimate level of the household all the way to state
policy and the law.

Further ingredients were stirred into the mixing pot of property, investment, and livelihood arrangements: the reliance of the black middle class—
both new and not so new—on state employment, and the domestic struggles
that occurred as female public servants strove for greater autonomy. Some
single female teachers in the former homelands, pursuing modern and individualistic rather than customary or communal approaches, were securing a
foothold on the property ladder and procuring a good education for their children, despite the insecurity of tenure and lack of title in those areas (Niehaus
2012, 334). Others, attempting to move into the modern property regime and

leave behind the uncertainty of the homeland system, found their strategies foundering when the acrimony of divorce came into play.

All these complex factors, in turn, have affected small-scale entrepreneurs' opportunities to grow their businesses and to climb the ladder of social mobility. Such individuals—some unqualified, some lacking connections, some unable to secure loans or finance—have nonetheless tried to overcome the odds. And many have succeeded. But their moneymaking activities are hemmed in by South Africa's continuingly "dual economy." Rather than being able to engage in untrammeled property deals, it is by "recruiting people"—one means to participate in redistribution (Bähre 2011)—that they are able to pursue their objectives.

Many who have achieved rapid mobility (and many who have not) have a sober and prudent attitude to matters of investment and are all too aware of the need to secure the future by becoming property owners and educating their children. They know what is likely to bring a return in the longer term. At the same time, however, considerable obstacles exist to moving up the ladder at a slow and steady pace, since it is difficult to earn a living except by trying to make "money from nothing."

7 New Subjectivities

Advice, Aspiration, and Prosperity

> The Lord's standing order for your life is like a debit order. . . . [I]t must
> go at the end of the month—the bank must obey your instructions . . .
> the moment you sign, from this account to that account. . . . The standing
> order is a debt that God owes you. . . . He was forced to make a statement
> of debt—*sekôlôtô*.
>
> **—Pastor Mohau Rammile, "God's standing orders"**

ALTHOUGH INITIALLY there were signs that the South African state was inclined
to deal harshly with "reckless lenders," the emphasis soon shifted—as Chapter 2 shows—to borrowers instead. Replacing the earlier calls for those lending money to exercise caution, the message became that borrowers ought to
develop self-control. Numerous education programs and techniques aimed
at reforming financial habits were planned and rolled out. These ranged from
preventative measures (such as the teaching of budgeting skills initiated by the
Johannesburg Housing Company, or JHC), to ways of helping "after the event"
(such as the restructuring of debt obligations offered by debt counselors).

Exploring these kinds of interventions in more detail, I discovered during
my fieldwork that it is necessary to look beyond the explicit "financial advice"
offered to the newly upwardly mobile and those with similar aspirations by
nongovernmental organizations (NGOs) and other well-intentioned advisers.
Attempts made to influence the behavior of people in this group also include
religious injunctions like the one in the sermon that opens this chapter. South
Africa has its fair share of counsel offered by both secular and religious authorities and institutions. Churches have long been important in shaping behavior
change and instilling values. Christian ideas and practices were foundational
in the formation of the "old" black middle class, later taking hold more widely
with the proliferation of African Independent Churches.[1] Most recently, members of the "new" black middle class have started flocking to neo-charismatic
or Pentecostal churches (Schlemmer 2008; Bernstein 2008; Bernstein and Rule

2011). Philanthropic and humanitarian organizations, likewise offering counsel and trying to effect transformation, abound. Originally serving to complement state functions, they have more recently morphed, merging and becoming hybridized with both state- and market-oriented institutions (see Fisher 1997). Advice about self-help, empowerment, and the like, though having roots in the NGO sector and to some extent in the churches as well, has started to permeate society at large, being offered through government channels, by larger and smaller businesses, and by self-help books.

If the suggestions of self-help counselors appear to have little in common with the admonitions of fire-and-brimstone pastors, there are some grounds for viewing them in the same frame. While both NGOs and Pentecostal churches encourage participants to aspire to economic betterment, churches, argues Dena Freeman (2012), can be even more effective than their secular counterparts in inculcating new ways of behaving, since religious discourses are aimed at reshaping subjective experience in a more holistic and experiential way than simply giving tips for how to save money or invest it more rationally.[2] But both types of institutions with their associated rhetoric have relevance, in different ways, for the changing personal trajectories described in this book.

Pentecostalism and the New Subject

Pentecostal Christianity—particularly that of the recent efflorescence of churches classified in the literature as "neo-charismatic"—has been a key arena for the reshaping of subjective values and orientations (Anderson 2004), but in South Africa their role in implanting values has been understood in contrasting ways. One, primarily sociological, searches for policy solutions. Following the Weberian approach of Peter Berger, who saw neo-charismatic churches in Latin America as enabling the development of rationally calculative modernity and economic growth, policy-oriented studies explored the potential of these churches as models of democratic organization and accountability that might be usefully tapped into for matters of broader political organization (Bernstein and Rule 2011, 124–25). Writing of Africa more broadly, however, Jean Comaroff (2012) complicates the Weberian model with its posited relationship between religious values and economic behavior. In a setting of neoliberal late modernity, in which the state has waned in significance and the market is predominant, these churches tend to dissolve the boundaries between rationality and quasi-magical ritualized religiosity. A third perspective, attempting to pinpoint something about Pentecostalism that is distinctive to twenty-first-century South Africa, diverges from the view that it is quintessentially neoliberal. Erik Bähre (2011) views these churches as similar to areas of practice with which they are not normally compared—social grants and insurances. What they have in common is to facilitate the redistribution of income.

These positions are not necessarily mutually incompatible, however. In combination, they help bring home the point of the next section of this chapter: the churches create a separate redistributive world of taxation and welfare (Bähre 2011) while simultaneously inducing expectations, in line with neoliberalism and market-oriented excess, of miraculous return. Although they orient themselves away from the world of public political engagement and engagement with the state, as Jean Comaroff (2012) suggests, they also—as she similarly notes and commensurate with what the policy authors maintain (Bernstein and Rule 2011)—provide a language of conscious and engaged citizenship that is otherwise difficult to articulate in the wider domain, and even enable self-aware recognition of the role that the state has played in their new status.

Abundance, Calculation, and Redistribution

Neo-charismatic churches have often appeared to be focused on members' prospects of prosperity and wealth, while also insisting that those congregants pay generously—that is, tithe—into church coffers. These practices have been roundly criticized by Bähre (2011), who points out that pastors have a habit of disappearing with the money. Although sharing that skepticism, van Wyk (2014) takes a somewhat more sympathetic approach, recognizing the sincerity of congregants' belief that riches will be forthcoming after regular contributions have been paid. But there are also analyses indicating that the money derives from worldly sources and serves useful purposes. Tithing, they show, makes it possible to create an autonomous community of citizens with its own property portfolio and welfare system; it also helps inculcate notions of self-control, financial planning, and saving (Bernstein and Rule 2011; Freeman 2012; Comaroff 2012).

Purchasing real estate and building up a portfolio of church property is an important way in which congregations establish their economic viability. Many churches aim to own their own designated places of worship rather than holding meetings in temporary accommodation like marquees, cinemas, and the like. Information technology salesman Sello Morake tells me that the Assemblies of God church to which his father belongs, in the Mpumalanga capital Nelspruit (now Mbombela), bought its own plot, for a church building, in 2009. Having previously been a small congregation that met in rented premises, the church members later procured and are repaying a mortgage for R700,000. My field-work visits to other churches, of different sizes and with vastly discrepant levels of ambition, confirms this commitment to bricks and mortar. At a meeting of the Living Word Church, with its rudimentary meeting venue of a marquee on an empty plot in Soweto, its pastor urges congregants to help meet the savings target of R60,000 so they too might move into more permanent premises. At a meeting of the His People Church in Pretoria, held in a theater, the treasurer uses graphs and PowerPoint presentations in his yearly financial statement to show how close the congregation is to reaching its goal. It aims to buy a city apartment block that will serve as a headquarters and in which members might live as a community or from which they might generate rental income.

Besides the aim of investing in fixed property, there is also a strong em-phasis on self-help twinned with the need to aid the less well-off. In one Soweto church, a pastor interviewed by Bernstein and Rule (2011) outlined the contributions made by his church to congregants' school and university fees, their outreach activities with those suffering from HIV/AIDS, and their help to the poor. Tithing—which might at first seem irrational for people on low incomes—serves a redistributive function. Where black South Africans formerly relied on close ties to members of the extended family, Erik Bähre (2011) claims, they are now seeking to replace these reciprocal obligations with less personalized arrangements. Given the rate of unemployment, which means that only a few will benefit from the individualized benefits that come from inclusion in the market, congregants pin their hopes on a new kind of sharing, seeking prosperity "through large-scale redistributive arrangements" (Bähre 2011, 373). Tithing, through which monies are collected centrally in a fund and then dispersed by impersonal means such as debit orders, provide one such ar-rangement. It allows intimate face-to-face reciprocity to be replaced with this more formal and institutionalized system of redistribution.

Less concrete and more focused on the attempted shaping of behavior and attitudes, tithing is linked to calculation, budgeting, and saving. It goes along with and encourages a measured approach to using money, as I learn when talking to Kopano Twala, a young university lecturer who belongs to the His People Church. "Good stewardship is key," she tells me. "One must tithe, one cannot just spend as one wants to." An important means to encourage this, she says, is through church mentoring programs, which have older men giving younger ones advice on how to use money. Similarly making the claim that a sage and rational approach to savings and investment can buttress rather than contradict the tithing system, ultimately facilitating redistribution and sharing, is Pastor Rethabile Matome of the Living Word International Church. Leading a service I attend at one of the church's Soweto branches, Matome is part of a husband-and-wife team of pastors. She tells me:

> Personally, as a minister, I have a couple of ways I combine—I have more than one property, and secondly I have some savings which I invest in. I try not to spend more than 70 percent of my income on myself. I share, and spread the rest to the church, and on my savings and investments.[3]

She decries the lack of financial education more generally and speaks of the need for congregants to recognize that you ought to "structure your income in a way that you will always come out earning more." Having them do so, she says, will benefit both themselves and the church. If they have sustainable finances they will be able to contribute to church finances as well. As she explains:

> That is why—in assisting towards the church—there's a lot of development we would like to do. If you are not financially strong you will not be able to assist as you would like to do. So teaching people about finance and how to take care of their finances, becomes an advantage to us as well—so that we can continue to do the things we want to do.

Summing up the educative potentials of this approach from a policy-oriented perspective, Laurence Schlemmer (2008) of the Centre for Development Enterprise (CDE) spoke of Pentecostals' approach to money matters:

> [They exhibit] a kind of quasi-Calvinist pattern of deferred gratification. In other words, don't spend all your money now. Rather, invest it wisely. Marshal your energies so that you can do things better and have more effect. . . . Tithing enters into this because people felt that tithing was a spiritual investment. But it provided them with a model of saving in other respects, as well. In other words, it's almost as if tithing gave it a greater impact—to putting money aside for larger purposes, for constructive purposes.

One must perhaps be wary of taking this account at face value, since the CDE research was conducted by policy makers setting out to find evidence of the churches' more rational or Protestant dimensions rather than their more magical or affective ones. But it is certainly buttressed by what I established in my discussions with pastors and congregants.

Contrasting markedly with such claims about rational planning, the sermons seem to invoke a world of abundant return based on faith alone. They vividly evoke the expectation of future plenty. Seemingly paradoxically, however, this discourse is interspersed with language drawn from banking. In a "Financial Seminar," Pastor Mohau Rammile of the Global Reconciliation Church in Bloemfontein, Free State Province, speaks of "the Lord's standing order for your life." It is like "a debit order . . . it must go at the end of the month—the bank must obey your instructions. . . . The moment you sign, from this account to that account." He goes on to use further imagery from the world of finance:

> The standing order is a debt that God owes you . . . He was forced to make a statement of debt—*sekôlôtô*. . . . From tonight, when you pray, you are going to invoke a standing order. Look at that house. That furniture. That car. Say "tomorrow I am going to drive you."[4]

As the pastor gets more excited, he begins to speak with greater passion:

> In your business, in your studies. God has unfinished business with you. There is an outstanding amount of money coming your way. There is an outstanding amount of cars, and marriages, and relationships. God is going to settle some scores with the devil in your life. We are reversing every curse, we speak restoration of everything that has been taken from you. I decree finances, not just a six figure, but a seven figure. I force it upon your spirit, upon your life and family.[5]

In this "Financial Seminar," widely available on CD, like other sermons by well-known preachers, imminent good fortune arises without congregants needing to take any practical steps. Similarly expressing expectations of unworked-for abundance is a CD by Pastor Matome, husband of Pastor Rethabile, of Living Word International Church, temporarily housed in its marquee in Soweto. In his discussion of the "two financial systems," there is the "world's system" of poverty in which there is "not enough," and there is "God's system" of "more than enough." He encourages his congregants to switch to God's system, based in a world before the fall. Before Adam was condemned to live "by the sweat of his brow," the benefits of harvest were distributed without toil, and we should revert to this arrangement once again.

These millenarian expectations of plentiful harvest are not, however, the only theme of the sermon. Underlying them, and encompassing both global and national aspects, is a trenchant critique of the new order. Pastor Matome, employed in a bank like his wife and fellow pastor, clearly has an acute awareness of the weaknesses of the global financial system. He uses this skillfully to strengthen the message that only "God's system" is enduring. Countering a statement by an imaginary protagonist who says, "No, I'm not poor, I've got R30,000 in the bank," the pastor says:

> You cannot bank on your bank. Just because your bank has never gone broke, you think it's not possible. . . . Who has studied economics here? If you study economics you will realize this whole system is a gamble. Nobody knows when it will break down. They are riding on it as long as it lasts, until it breaks down. That's what happened in America. South Africa didn't tell you, if the bank goes bankrupt you might lose your money. If Standard Bank says "I'm bankrupt" and you say "you owe me," how can they pay you if they are bankrupt?

He expands his critique of the "world's system" to encompass those who, although thinking they have benefited from it, remain in bondage to it: "Right now, less than 10% of the world holds the riches of all the world. The business world keeps you stupid: earn a stupid degree, do a stupid job, for a rich guy." He is speaking in apparent repudiation of the accomplishments and practices of his congregants, many of whom although of humble means are studying at university or paying for their children to do so:

> I want to dash this degree thing. People think it's the hope of the world. "Man, you must get a degree." Get a degree if you want. But get a degree with a smarter mind. The business world says "we need engineers," so they promote engineering at university. Who needs them? The rich guys. We are short of scientists. Who needs scientists? The rich guys.

He nevertheless assures his congregants that he is not recommending they skip work. Like him, they will be going back to their day jobs on Monday morning. Critical of the high levels of unemployment, he speaks with approval of the empowering character of work:

> People are sitting at home because they are waiting for jobs for money. Work gives you benefits, you have a positive mind, you wake up early. When you work, there are other benefits than money. When a person has no work, he frustrates his woman, frustrates the whole family.

The pastor then slips seamlessly into a condemnation of the circumstances of those who have benefited unduly from the government's strategies of black economic empowerment (BEE) strategies, in which privileges have been doled

out to those with connections, while leaving many in their wake without equivalent advantages. He speaks scornfully of the cars, pay-TV subscriptions, and
other outward and visible signs of wealth while criticizing the fact that these
are the fruits of affirmative action and its associated cronyism. "Have you ever
seen someone throwing food to hungry dogs?" he asks. "People are fighting for
this cake, fighting to bring in their cousins and their uncles, fighting to bring
in their friends."

Completing the impression that his sermon represents a strong critique of
the post-1994 South African social order, with its disparaging references to "the
rich guys," the pastor draws on a section of the Old Testament that has long
been a favorite with church pastors ministering to South Africa's dispossessed:
the slavery of the Israelites at the hands of the Egyptians. Having stored "the
riches for the righteous in the hands of the wicked," he said, "God promises he
will restore them to us."[6] Evoking the same episode in his CD sermon, Pastor
Mohau Rammile says:

> Your descendants will be strangers in a foreign land; they will be slaves there
> and will be treated cruelly for four hundred years. But I will punish the nation
> that enslaves them, and when they leave that foreign land, they will take great
> wealth with them.[7]

This trenchant reference to the Israelites' promised restitution following their
years of oppression in Egypt echoes countless others, in South Africa and
beyond. The episode is commonly evoked in defense of beleaguered and oppressed people far from home (Genovese 1976) or in support of identities
newly created in the wake of catastrophic transformations (Schama 1987, 93–
125; James with Nkadimeng 2003a, 2003b).[8] Mixed in alongside multiple references to wealth, consumption, and profligacy, evocative images like this enable
sermons to engage in complex ways with the desires and conflicts discussed in
this book so far. Pastors speak with admiration of those who get rich quick, yet
they express profound mistrust in banks and politicians, aware that the roof
might come down at any time. They also scorn those who succeed too easily.

In sum, these churches combine a variety of features. Demonstrating
that they epitomize South Africa's new redistributive approach to economic
arrangements, they are concerned with securing a separate and internally
coherent system of taxation and welfare (Bähre 2011). Suggesting that they encourage a more classically "Protestant ethic" (Bernstein and Rule 2011), they

simultaneously nurture a capitalist-style interest in property investment and an inculcation of rational approaches to the allocation of income. And the expectation of abundant wealth that transcends this world's preoccupation with work and monthly payment supports the analysis of these churches as quasi-magical, "late modern," and neoliberal in their orientation (Comaroff 2012). But alongside these there is also a biting critique of the rising inequalities of twenty-first-century South African life and a critical allusion to the role of state patronage in putting this in place.

It is this latter feature that will be pursued in the following section. Whatever role these churches play in fostering the entrepreneurial mind-set that goes with the emergence of a middle class, the additional circumstances that have conspired to bring that class into being and have bolstered it must also be acknowledged. And among some of their members, who are pursuing the classic middle-class goals of a higher education and who have acquired the detached self-reflection that such an education can bring, this acknowledgment has indeed taken place.

Self-Reflection and Critical Citizenship

"The key to the new middle classes is the Bible churches," I am told by a young woman, Kopano Twala, who lectures at the University of Johannesburg. Her view of the situation combines detached analysis with personal involvement. When we meet one day, she tells me that her own sister spends inordinate amounts of money on transport to travel to the huge Rhema Bible Church every weekend with her friends to listen to the sermons of Pastor Ray McCauley. When Kopano queried this expenditure, her sister replied that she and her friends were convinced their church membership would ensure their future wealth. On a subsequent occasion I learn that Kopano herself is a member of such a church, as is her partner, Sello Morake. Although their church, His People, is very much less oriented to the get-rich-quick culture than are the huge churches such as Rhema and its offshoot, the Grace Bible Church, they tell me that it nonetheless has some of the same characteristics. I find myself wondering how Kopano's analytical perspective squares with her own involvement.[9]

From subsequent conversations it becomes clear that Kopano and Sello have the kind of self-reflective view that is not often conveyed in scholarly or policy-related accounts of the churches. The analysts already mentioned in this chapter—whether following the Weberian line of argument, highlighting neoliberalism, or pointing to the significance of redistribution—occasionally sound somewhat patronizing. In suggesting what functions the churches play for their adherents, the analysts seem to hail from a walk of life very different from that occupied by rank-and-file church members. For Kopano and Sello, however, committed involvement combines with dispassionate observation to yield an unusual perspective.

Reflecting a broader experience across the board in South Africa, with its predominantly Christian culture, an important point they make is that neither of them experienced "conversion" into Pentecostal adherence, since both were brought up as church members. Instead, joining the church enabled a reconfiguration, or shift, into a zone of experience more attuned to their new material and moral world of experience. In the case of Kopano, whose family had been stalwarts of the black middle class and members of a mainstream "mission church" for generations, she had a Lutheran background. In Sello's case, his family had experienced upward class mobility only in his parents' generation. Paralleling this, the family had made a series of moves: from the older Pentecostal Apostolic Faith Mission church, very populous in rural areas of the former Transvaal, to a newer, independent church founded by his father. Finally, the father switched to a larger church—the Assemblies of God—of which his wife was a member.

I meet with Sello at a coffee shop in an upmarket shopping mall, after going with him to attend a meeting of his church. He draws my attention to how different our surroundings are from the ones in which he grew up. The vivid picture he paints, of the contrasts between his provincial upbringing and the slick urban setting where we find ourselves, seems equally indicative of another important disconnect: between what an upwardly mobile person might have aspired to one generation back and what he or she can achieve in the 2000s. While acknowledging the full extent of the change undergone by his father, Sello also points to the subsequent gap—between the class to which his father had aspired and that in which he, Sello, has found himself.

His parents lived in a village (near Impalahoek, as it happens) before moving to the then small and sleepy provincial town of Nelspruit (now Mbombela), which has since 1994 grown rapidly to become the capital of the new province of Mpumalanga. Their relocation to Nelspruit, itself involving considerable social and psychic dislocation, was paralleled by the role of Christian conversion in reshaping value orientations and aspirations. He tells me:

My father came from a working-class family, but his conversion is what pro-
pelled him to change. He is now a teacher of maths and science. He had a big
desire to study, and went to school. But once he was at school, it was seeing this
singing done by the church members that drew him—along with the message of
hope and a better life. He was looking for something better, but could not quite
define it. The church became a vehicle.

It was alongside his newfound motivation and professional status that Sello's
father's religious leadership evolved. When he first joined the Assemblies of
God, in which he is a pastor at the time Sello and I meet:

> The members were mostly domestics, working-class people, even the grounds-
> man was a pastor at the Afrikaans school in Nelspruit where we used to hold the
> services. Now, with the influence of my father and other teacher/professionals,
> the regional leadership had to get a pastor who was more educated.

In a growing alignment between what were previously distinctly "rural" and
"urban" churches, both have come to share a new business orientation and interest in property and share investment. "Assemblies of God, Nelspruit Branch,"
he tells me, "has also now bought shares in Telkom [the parastatal telephone
company]."

Aside from this evidence of a new church "culture of business"—echoing
national and indeed global trends—what strikes me about Sello's account is
the relatively gradual process, over at least a couple of generations, that eventually led to his current situation. Although already a smart and sophisticated
young information technology salesman, he is not yet satisfied with what he
has achieved and has yet further ambitions, including starting his own business. The step-by-step alteration of style and orientation across the generations
that occurred with his parents is at odds with Sello's wish to "make a break" that
is more complete. He feels that his parents' existing church affiliations, fervent
and committed though they were, do not mirror or express his own new situation. It was this feeling that underpinned his choice of His People, which he
joined while at university: "I feel that this church speaks to me, to where I am,
to where I want to be. I am the person I want to be."

When I ask what the precise differences are between His People and the
earlier-established Pentecostal churches in which he was raised, his answer gives
a subtle and self-reflective insight into the complex modalities of rapid class

mobility—and the conundrum faced by successful people concerning those who are "left behind":

> The difference is that in a more traditional church, working-class people tend to set the aspirations. It is hard for one to translate these into one's own aspirations—you do not share things with those around you. You are either trying to bring people up with you, or otherwise you are talking down to them. It is about class aspiration. But, from another angle, you get upper middle class people who take up a sort of missionary role in relation to those of the working class. They feel that they need to serve those in this lower class—not necessarily to "bring them up." If you look at the thread of discussion during the service this morning, this is a church in an urban setting. Because of the class of people represented there, their visions and goals are all about importing their vision of society into all spheres—government, the corporate sector, etc. Here, they can have a bigger impact as a church. Now, if you are in a rural area, such ideals are rather too high-flying. There it is issues of subsistence that concern them—they are at the bottom of the hierarchy.

This account provides reflection on whether a person who has moved up through the ranks must necessarily regard himself as connected and accountable to those who share his background, or whether that person will feel more comfortable being "the person [he wants] to be." Stating individual feelings in a characteristically middle-class manner, it contains reflections both on the importance of being connected to others that share these orientations and on the inevitability of disconnectedness from those left behind with whom little is now shared.

Kopano gives further insight when I later talk to her about similar matters. For her, church membership enabled breaking away from family expectations that were themselves implanted in middle-class ideals, but those of a previous generation. She was coming under pressure from her mother and other family members to go along an expected route: to complete the studies that she had begun and for which she had been given a bursary. Her mother could not countenance the possibility that Kopano might not complete the degree. But Kopano received support from the pastor, who emphasized the need for her to find her own route, realize her own talents, and build upon those, rather than following an established path laid out by others. This individualist-sounding advice proved to be valuable since it encouraged her in her decision to discontinue her studies in management and pursue instead a career in the humanities.

The discrepancy between the aspirations of the individual and the fate of the broader community is something to which Kopano has given much thought. How do upwardly mobile church members square their success with the failure of so many? And how and why have they retreated from what she notes was their earlier tendency to engage more publically with social inequalities? It is a withdrawal that, she says, is mediated by the notion of an individualized purpose, calling, or discovering of one's own route:

> In the early 1990s the church became involved in the struggle against apartheid. Even Rhema Bible Church opened up its doors to all at a time when the nature of politics and the economy was changing. It provided a perfect opportunity for people. Being in a context where the message corresponds to the broader situation, this offers an explanation to people. But it also gives people an explanation for gross inequality. If you're able to earn R100,000 per month and others have nothing, you feel there is a destiny and purpose. And so you don't have to struggle to reconcile this with the existence of inequality. You'd feel guilty if you used it all yourself, but here you are giving some of your money away. It is the church that uses it. The middle class are removed from their own societies—or the societies to which they formerly belonged—and are not aware of the extent of poverty and marginalization out there, or of the scale of injustice. Certainly very few of my students know about this, so one can assume that the people at church are similar.

Kopano, having developed a sophisticated insight into her own situation and that of the new black middle class in general, goes on to reflect on some of the complex relationships between the ideology the churches propagate and the actuality of their members' situations. The disconnect between the church's attitudes toward gender relationships, on the one hand, and the actuality of their members' lives, on the other hand, is one of the things with which she finds it difficult to come to terms. Her account reveals the extensive interventions made by churches in members' lives—part of their welfare and outreach activities—through a series of home-study groups and counseling arrangements, as well as by distributing advice and sermons on CDs. In line with the conservative-style family values propagated by the US churches on which the South African ones model themselves, these groups and sermons celebrate and try to propagate the idea of the submissive religious wife, obedient to her husband. They attribute many of society's ills to the absence of father figures in modern families and provide intensive mentoring to men as a means to counter this. The church endorses patriarchy in all its senses, Kopano tells me, thus legitimating the idea that the man is the image of the Christian God. Women in the church participate in and endorse this position, by taking their sons off to "men camps," for example. But there is a disconnect here. Many of the people who consume these CDs and partake of the advice are young professional women—as she is. "I try to be open with my friends," she says, "challenging the women who are consuming all this stuff on CDs about how to be a prayerful wife."

Her account reminds me of the many women—business professionals, graduate students, lecturers, and people in important government positions, as well as the rural schoolteachers or more modest NGO volunteers in Impalahoek—that I have met in the course of my fieldwork. These are people who not only earn their own living and support their children but are also, in many cases, single or divorced. Ongoing and stable conjugal arrangements seem to have been in the minority. Is it possible, I ask myself, that the efforts of the church represent a rear-guard action to stave off further such domestic struggle and schism, and to restore the sanctity of marriage? Doing so in frank contradiction of the socioeconomic circumstances in which these struggles arise perhaps suggests a measure of desperation. But it is also possible for value orientations to affect material and social contexts, as Weber suggested: perhaps the sermons, mentoring sessions and "men camps" will make, and have made, a palpable difference.

There is a further aspect of critical self-reflection in Kopano's account of the church and its relation to the new black middle class. "There is a coincidence," she explains, "in the Protestant ethic being preached among people where the structural nature of the South African economy is advantaging entrepreneurs." She continues:

> The higher education system is more advantageous to black men and women than before. Now, not many are turned away. There is funding available if you are black—government loans and the like. People find more and more opportunities, because of the transition—and this dovetails with the church's message of destiny, of calling. This somehow gives testimony that what they have heard at church is true—that this is the real church. They are not aware that the context is what is making this possible—especially during the Mbeki years. During these years, policies were geared towards producing a black middle class, a big white-collar sector. This was a key invention of Mbeki. All this coincided with the great influx of new churches in post-1994 South Africa.

Besides the members in the church who benefited from active strategies to foster the growth of this sector, many people in the church work directly for the government, writing speeches for ministers, and the like. They are part of a larger phenomenon of class mobility in black society post-1994. In addition to being the beneficiaries of the particular strategy to enlarge the middle class that was one legacy of the post-1999 presidency of Thabo Mbeki, their story is also that of a broader process with "political" dimensions linked to those of "race." It is the story of what Roger Southall calls the "substantial upward mobility of significant segments of the ANC's constituency," including not only a "party-state bourgeoisie" but also a "middle class strongly dependent on the state" (2012, 10, 1).

It is the apparent disregard for these political factors in church members' own class formation and identity, linked to their tendency to focus on that specific identity at the expense of broader social conditions, that some of the more self-reflective congregants like Kopano and Sello noted. At the same time, they provide insightful and plausible reasons why this should be so and why the church appeals to them. But the broader literature on these churches in South Africa, as well as the speeches by pastors discussed here, reveals that both members and pastors are critical of the fact that the government's affirmative action program has reached so few people. The churches are said to have made up for this by empowering more people, from more diverse walks of life, than the state's policy of black economic empowerment (Schlemmer 2008). Politicians interviewed by researchers in the CDE project said they knew that this policy was resented for benefiting only a few: the churches could help by explaining how ordinary people might also derive advantages (Bernstein and Rule 2011, 107). Pastor Matome's cynical statements about the dogs fighting over food in a feeding frenzy induced by affirmative action, and his disparagement of those aspects of worldly wealth that such an advantage can bring, reveals a similarly critical stance.

Let us return to the question of whether and how the neo-charismatic churches in general, and in Africa more specifically, transform value orientations and subjectivities. The particularities of the South African case make it necessary to qualify broader assertions about this. There is certainly some truth in the claim that such churches blur modernist-style boundaries between religion and the secular, as one can see from Sello's claim about "importing their vision of society into all spheres—government, the corporate sector." It is true, too, that they take charge of responsibility for members' welfare, education, and the like by ensuring some redistribution. The churches' orientation also dove-tails with and promotes a neoliberal subjectivity to some degree. But where it might be the case, for other parts of Africa, that the market has supplanted the state in importance (Comaroff 2012), this is less so for South Africa. The rise and enrichment of its new middle class has not in all cases been an overnight sensation. In many cases there has been a more gradual emergence, over a num-ber of generations, of affluence with its accompanying mentality privileging individualized advancement. And the eventual emergence of that new class, accompanying political liberation and democracy after 1994, owed itself not simply—indeed, not primarily—to the impetus of purely market forces. It was a "middle class strongly dependent on the state": whether through employ-ment in the civil service, the government's explicit focus on black economic empowerment, or the system of public procurement with its notorious "ten-derpreneurs" (Southall 2012, 13; McNeill 2012; see also Chapter 6). If it is a class whose formation depended on the interweaving of neoliberal means with redistributive ends (Hull and James 2012, 16), the accompanying subjectivities similarly combine these apparently unlike tendencies.

Financial Advice and Financial Well-Being

While the churches express and enable rapid social transformation and upward mobility, those who work in the area of advice or self-help have focused in on one particular facet of that change: the problem of debt and the need for self-discipline and the reform of the individual needed to tackle it.

Some organizations offering financial advice approximate the classic NGO model: they raise funds from donors to enable their not-for-profit activities centered on self-help and empowerment. The Black Sash is perhaps the best known of these. As mentioned in Chapter 2, although the Black Sash continues to focus on how to access rights within the law, its advice no longer centers on how to cope with the exclusionary effects of race-based legislation—such as the infamous "pass laws" of apartheid. Instead, a large part of its efforts are directed at helping those who have become indebted, that is, aiding those ex-cluded on economic rather than racial grounds. It does so by offering email and telephone advice, distributing copies of a handbook that offers budgeting skills (Figure 7.1), and advocating on behalf of the consumer.

Illustrating how the giving of advice has infiltrated the world of corporate capitalism with its new emphasis on corporate social responsibility, a series of similar organizations offer similar services. One of these, You and Your Money,

Figure 7.1 Cover of the Black Sash's reference guide *Debt and Credit*
Source: The Black Sash. Reprinted with permission.

receives some of its funding from donors to teach people "financial literacy," supplementing those funds by running workshops for a wide range of firms and companies keen to acquaint their employees with such literacy. In similar vein, and mindful of the destructive effects of indebtedness on "employee financial well-being," companies such as BMW have benefited from funding by the German foreign-aid agency Deutsche Gesellschaft für Internationale Zusammenarbeit (GTZ), which paid for an investigation into the destructive effects of garnishee orders (see Chapter 2). The intention to inculcate sound financial practice and adequate budgeting skills animates a vast number of other organizations. Those concerning themselves with social housing, like the JHC, are among them. In the interests of collecting rent from tenants to ensure a viable future for the organization and those who benefit from it, they communicate with prospective tenants or have their "community development" arm contact those who are in default, to give them advice on how to budget (see Chapter 4).

Self-help discourses of this kind have, as mentioned earlier, permeated the marketplace and society at large. Started by enterprising individuals, many advice organizations operate as small businesses and are obliged to ensure their own financial sustainability rather than relying on donor funding. Indeed, it was the expectation of this same phenomenon that animated how debt counseling was conceived in the National Credit Act. Envisaged as a "business opportunity" for potential counselors as well as a service provided to those in need, debt counseling was explicitly framed in the act, and endorsed by policy makers, as a means for small entrepreneurs to make a living. It thus specifically excluded from its official definition of debt counselor those, like church pastors or the Black Sash, that had previously been offering advice on a charitable basis.

Two such businesses, both run by women, deserve mention here. Thuthuka SA was started by Phumelele Ndumo. She wrote the book *From Debt to Riches: Steps to Financial Success* (2011), which by December 2012 had sold 3,500 copies: a substantial number in South Africa's relatively undeveloped publishing world. Written in an accessible style, incorporating many case studies from real life, and aimed at the lower but upwardly aspirant middle class, the book's approach is that of telling its readers "things that credit providers don't want you to know." While speaking to and acknowledging the concerns of those whose origins she shares (she puts herself into the narrative as a person from humble beginnings who has managed to succeed in business), Ndumo gives advice to help readers to come to terms with their material situation while also focusing on realizable future goals. She also offers talks at "power breakfasts" to companies who deem their employees to be in need of budgeting and financial skills. Her approach provides an antidote to unrealistic aspiration while endorsing its more modest variant.

Rather more upmarket in focus, Wealthy Money was started by Vangile Makwakwa. She, too, has written a book, *Heart, Mind and Money: Using Emotional Intelligence for Financial Success* (2013); does motivational speeches; and speaks on radio phone-in shows. (It is while listening to one of these, on Radio 2000, that I first hear her speak.) Having worked as an analyst in the mining and energy industry and later studied for an MBA in the United States, as her slightly American accent testifies, she comes from, and aims her message at those in, a higher salary bracket but with equally acute financial problems.

A prominent theme concerns the complex relationship between present and future that is highlighted by many who write about debt. Delayed gratification is necessary for those seeking to budget sensibly. In trying to teach people about this, Ndumo criticizes some of the shallow aspirations thought to be widespread among the upwardly mobile. Engaging with attitudes similar to those discussed in Chapter 1—"people cannot wait and budget, they are in a hurry for everything"; "credit means you can immediately get what you need without any delays" but "you are working backward instead of progressing. . . . People are just quick to get things without calculating the cost"—Ndumo explicitly addresses the contradictions between living well in the present and doing so in the longer term. Asking people, "How do you want your kids to remember you?" she gives examples of two contrasting types of parents. One type of parent spends money on "nice clothes and cellphones on credit"; the other sacrifices those expenditures to give their children "a good education," ultimately ensuring them an adult life as professionals (2011, 186). The latter approach reflects how two of my informants, Abigail Mlate and Thandi Thobela, expressed the need to "talk to" their children, stressing the need to work hard and resist pressure to buy things that cannot be afforded. The emphasis, then, is not simply on self-sacrifice, but on delaying the present gratification of one's children's desires for the sake of their future well-being. Ndumo advises people to "sacrifice what you want now for what you want later" (2011, 165). Hammering home the point, she points out that the only way people can acquire "everything they ever wanted" at this moment, and all at once, is on credit. She brings home the time dimension in vivid detail, showing how failure to save in advance, rather than paying excessive interest after the event, means that there is "no end in sight as to when the debt will finally be paid" (2011, 3).

Here emerges the second key theme. It is being trapped in this latter state, Ndumo says, that leads to the "pain of debt" (2011, 3). The term echoes, but is more vivid than, the medicalized discourses used by the GTZ in its publications on the need for "employee financial wellness" (Crous 2008) in the BMW factory (see Chapter 2). Vangile Makwakwa is equally concerned with well-being: she claims to have coached a Catholic bishop on the link between "health, spirituality and emotions."[10] But her emphasis, in line with the more middle-class character of her target audience, is on the importance of such practices as yoga and meditation. When I hear her on the phone-in show, she has recently returned from a month of meditative retreat, which she strongly advocates for those seeking the "emotional intelligence" essential to managing finances effectively.

One ought to be open with family members about how much one owes one's creditors, says Makwakwa. She equates this with the need to be honest about sex. There is an important parallel here between the self-help discourse used in relation to illness and that which concerns indebtedness. A range of donor-funded programs addressing the South Africa's HIV/AIDS epidemic were centrally concerned with getting patients to recognize their status. This was seen as a first step to coming to terms with that status by "living positively," and likewise having the wider community acknowledge that status rather than stigmatizing its sufferers. In the world of financial advice, there are similar injunctions to come to terms with what one is. Warnings are issued against excessive attention to what one's neighbors might think, since this can ultimately inhibit one's broader well-being. Do not live in fear, says Vangile on the phone-in show, that others will find out you are less wealthy than you want, or have claimed, to be.

These observations point to the third, and perhaps most important, theme emphasized by these writers and others in the world of self-help. This is the need for self-disclosure and self-knowledge as an individual, and its corollary, the need to withstand pressures from wider family and society. Encapsulating this approach, Ndumo's book (2011) advocates the need for open and honest self-reflection and self-knowledge to become aware of and to value one's "self." To this end, she echoes the recommendations of many debt advice givers by offering suggestions on how to document monthly expenditure. It was a similarly "open" approach that the JHC adopted when considering how to deal with recalcitrant tenants: the aim was "to encourage the tenant to open up" to enable the up-front discussion—rather than the evasion—of problems (see Chapter 4). Likewise, the explicit aim of the Black Sash was to get people thinking about and confronting their debts rather than, as in the past, being in denial: "if it's in a brown envelope with a window don't give it to me" (see Chapter 2). Dawn Jackson of the NGO You and Your Money emphasized the benefits of frank discussion, attributing these to the recent passing of the legislation:

> One of the positive things this act has done is that it has popularized conversations—for want of a better word—about managing your money, not managing your money, debt, etc. Every magazine, some targeting a cross section, has articles on this. Or at a more low-income, grass roots level . . . just switch the TV on and people are talking about it. It's the . . . flavor of the moment to be talking about these issues openly. In many ways this has actually helped. . . . We seem to be moving towards an open conversation.[11]

In similar vein, Vangile Makwakwa's message is that you need to come to terms with your own emotions, and to "own" your own feelings and your situation, before handling your financial problems. The ultimate purpose of such self-reflection is revealed by Phumelele Ndumo. "What has your budget revealed to you about yourself?" she asks. Implicit in this exercise is acknowledging the limitations of one's salary, not wasting one's money on "nice cars and other nice-to-haves," but rather investing in more meaningful and long-term assets, principally the education of one's children (Ndumo 2011, 147–50). She demonstrates by using the true-life case of a woman called Phindi. The aim, in sum, concerns honest recognition of what one is in the present, with the aim of becoming someone wealthier in the future. It is better to do this than to insist on becoming a rich person right now. The resulting "self," once realized, is thus certainly not devoid of a future orientation, but is enjoined to muster its resources toward an actualizable goal rather than an unrealistic one.

What is perhaps classically neoliberal about this and similar attempts to reshape subjectivities is the repudiation of the claims made by kinsmen. Reflecting the thorny question of how far those newly upwardly mobile feel more or less obliged to support less well-off family members, Ndumo points to how unwise it is to encourage too much dependency. There are "kind and well-meaning people" who have been "taken advantage of by those they love" (Ndumo 2011, 195–96). Some families, she says, become so dependent on a wage earner that they would do anything in their power to prevent the "cash cow" from marrying, since this would threaten their income. "Learn to put your needs first," she advises. The implicit corollary is that one ought to partner up in a stable nuclear family and focus on the future achievements and needs

of one's own children. In sum, one ought to learn to repudiate and ignore kinsmen and neighbors: not only their judgments as to what material items and
consumables define one's status but also their demands for redistribution.

Makwakwa makes a very similar point. "If people want to treat you like a
bank," she says during the phone-in show, "then let them go to a bank":

> The people who will love and respect you and respect the fact that you're honest
> about what is in your bank account, are the ones who will stand by you when
> times get hard. They may give you spiritual help, emotional help. There is noth-
> ing better in the world than not having to hide things constantly. You must be
> emotionally open with the people in your life, your wife, your girlfriend.[12]

In sum, the advice offered by these practitioners and other agencies draws
a clear line between "good" and "bad" debt, and the "good" and "bad" debtor.
Bad debtors, subject to the pain of ongoing inability to pay and no prospect of
securing a rosy future, and held back by the demands of strident relatives, have
been lured into self-deception by the promise of immediate prosperity, which
has mired them in obligations from which nothing can extract them. Their bid
for upward mobility is unsustainable. Good debtors, modestly moving upward
step by step, have invested in the future by eschewing frivolity and keeping an
eye on worthwhile values: measures achieved by pursuing self-realization.

Certain cases presented in the preceding chapters make it clear, however,
that there are limits to what can be achieved through sound financial behavior. Ignoring relatives' demands to avoid marriage, for example, is not enough.
Getting married and concentrating on the nuclear family will not, on its own,
ensure individual economic advancement. If we consider Ndumo's injunction
against being a "cash cow," and Makwakwa's against being seen as a "bank," in
light of the cases discussed in Chapter 1, we can see that the demands of in-
laws—for excessive bridewealth and showy displays of wealth—can be just as
onerous as those of one's own family. Those cases also demonstrate that it is
often spouses, as well as the wider group of prospective in-laws, who are seen
as nagging their partners to spend excessively. The tension between the claims
of the family of origin and those of one's affines or in-laws is a classic topic
in anthropology: it is a tension that Ndumo's book attempts to transcend by
recommending that the newly acknowledged "self," with its newly recognized
needs that are achievable rather than being unrealistic, position itself securely
within the nuclear family. This recommendation, however, fudges the fact that
many of the people in her target audience and those who are the topic of this

book, either avoid tying the conjugal knot or have short-lived marriages, and end up living their lives and planning their futures as single people.

There is a further important way in which these advice givers miss the mark. In the modest and incremental path laid out by Ndumo toward a bourgeois and ultimately neoliberal ideal, the role of private property is central. Alongside recommending that people buy their furniture for cash rather than on hire purchase, and that they cut up their store cards or leave them at home when going shopping, a key part of what she advises is to replace these expensive sources of credit by making use, instead, of the cheapest possible finance by taking out a mortgage bond to invest in property. In repudiation of the behavior often associated with "black diamonds," she advises people to do so in an affordable area, at least initially, rather than switching straight to "the suburbs." In one of the exemplary stories with which the book is dotted, Phindi and her husband—against the advice of friends who disparaged the fact that "they were buying a site in a low income area"—procured a site in Clermont, a township area near Durban, KwaZulu Natal, on which they built a "small starter home" (Ndumo 2011, 147). They later sold the house and moved to the "white suburb" of Pinetown. Ndumo's advice to get a home loan, buy a house, eventually move to a better house, and make this strategy serve as the basis of further investment in university education for one's children is well meant and sensible. But it is predicated on assumptions about secure tenure that many of the stories in Chapter 6 demonstrate to be unfounded, or at best unevenly achievable, in what remains a "dual economy" of property.

Irrespective of these areas of mismatch, the two advisers undoubtedly offer valuable counsel: some more practical, and others more spiritually focused. The case studies not only reveal much about how individual selves are being advised to reshape their habits; they also demonstrate that many are already following their injunctions and similar NGO-style advice expressed elsewhere. In many cases—the investment in children's education rather than in frivolous consumables by residents in Sunview, the judicious and differentiated use of bank accounts by Impalahoek residents, the avoidance of furniture store credit or vehicle finance by *stokvel* members, or the reliance on bank loans rather than moneylenders by Tembisa residents—these insights did not represent a sudden Damascene reorientation of the self to present-day realities. Instead, they involved a mustering of older habits and attitudes of frugality to tackle twenty-first-century goals. There is strong evidence, then, that while such advice may be needed to help reshape neoliberal subjectivities, its more important purpose is that of providing technical steps to be followed by those whose values already approximate the ones recommended.

Conclusion

In attempting to analyze the discourses—interrelated although somewhat discrete—on self-improvement and self-transformation that emanate from the world of the churches and the world of self-help and advice, it is difficult to avoid reverting to functionalist-sounding approaches that outline the uses they serve for those who take this advice. But if this can be done without sounding patronizing, perhaps it is no bad thing.

Both forms of transformative discourse alternately conceal and reveal aspects of individual and group identity, respectively. Both, in different ways, seem to spur transformation while providing individuals with the psychic means for self-reflection about it and its shortcomings. They enable the emergence of a new language in which participants can both articulate the aim for and the experience of success, on the one hand, and cope with difficulties in achieving it, on the other hand. In the case of neo-charismatic churches, there is a coexistence of aspired-for self-betterment and consolation for ongoing marginality, as various writers have shown (Comaroff 2012; Martin, cited by Bernstein and Rule 2011, 97–98). Going further, church membership can conceal the true grounds on which self-improvement actually occurred, as Kopano complained was the case with her fellow congregants. But—given the insight imparted by higher education, which many in this category have been acquiring—it can also enable the emergence of critical consciousness and the possibility to reflect upon the nature of socioeconomic causes and the extent of the social inequality that results.

In the case of the "rights"-oriented self-help discourse more pervasive in advice-giving agencies, there is an insistence on the benefits of honest self-disclosure, on insights into one's own values and the nature of one's financial problems, and on the need for self-revelation about the reasons for excessive indebtedness. But by forcing responsibility upon the individual, this discourse to some extent denies the broader socioeconomic context—beyond simply the "pressure from neighbors to compete"—which has led members of particular groups to become indebted in the first place or might in the future prevent them from taking such advice. Its individualizing thrust, somewhat like that of the churches, also seems to deny the role of the party-state in having enhanced the wealth of those in the new middle class who have "made it" without undertaking the stringent measures being advised. Indeed, Ndumo's and Makwakwa's advice might be seen as specifically addressed at the sizeable group, such as the entrepreneurs mentioned in Chapter 6, who have had to make their own way without "connections" to those in power.

Commentaries on the thorny and irresolvable question of increasing inequality that is so pervasive in South Africa are offered by both the charismatic church discourse and the secular, rights-oriented advice one. Both criticize the flashy consumption of commodities that is said to be practiced by the wealthy. For beneficiaries of the political developments that have made their newfound wealth possible, being a church member offers a more positive self-identity than the view, prevalent in the critical media and in some academic accounts, that this new wealth is the outcome of "rent-seeking, cronyism and corruption" (Southall 2012, 13). Church membership is a means for reflecting on, celebrating, and consolidating one's own new status, as Sello's account shows. It enables a certain distance from what would otherwise be an agonizing and daily confrontation with the realities faced by those who do not share that status. For these latter—the nonbeneficiaries—or for the pastors who minister to them without necessarily sharing their humbler position, a language is provided for disparaging the world of salaries, BMWs, and pay-TV subscriptions. The sermons apparently aim to help congregants transcend "this world's financial system" to bring abundance that will nonetheless be evident in the here and now. But they also provide a powerful "this-world" commentary on the paradoxical ambiguities of class. A similar critique of shallow consumerism exists in the advice given by businesswomen like Ndumo and Makwakwa, advice that is likewise aimed at recommending an end to flashy acquisitiveness in the interests of ultimate, more sustainable enrichment. Only by avoiding debt, by ceasing to want to "have it all now," and by buying appropriate insurance, Ndumo (2011) says, can one secure upward mobility that lasts. In her case, demystifying the apparently opaque world of finance and loans, this happens through the use of judiciously applied techniques that "the credit providers don't want you to know." In Makwakwa's case, it occurs through the use of spiritual techniques such as meditation, aimed at better coming to "know oneself" and developing "emotional intelligence." For the churches, a similar transcending and repudiation of the world of the here and now will at some point bring abundant reward; but in the meantime, members are enjoined to work hard and also to pay their tithes into funds that will enable some redistribution.

Haunting much of this debate has been the spirit of Weber ([1905] 2002). It will always be difficult to know whether the "Protestant ethic" precedes the practice of economic advancement and class mobility, or vice versa. Reading Weber's works in their fullest nuance suggests that the two coexist in a complex and nondeterminant corelationship, rather than one of causality in which one precedes the other (see Camic, Gorski, and Trubeck 2005). If interventionist counsel, aimed at reorienting values and changing the economic practices that accompany them, has been a long-standing feature of South African life, so too is the readiness to alter and modernize without explicit encouragement. In both pastors' charismatic preachings and congregants' self-reflections, as well as self-help advice, there is some evidence that the much-vaunted transformations of subjectivity simply lag behind changes that have already occurred.

Conclusion

THIS BOOK has explored the untold stories that lie behind one country's "credit crunch." Giving an account of the experiences of individuals and groups as they attempt to reclaim the rights and experience the prosperity they were previously denied, it has aimed to go beyond some of the usual platitudes—the moralistic criticisms of consumer excess, the despairing hand-wringing about the need for financial education—to establish the kind of broader ethos that explains these attitudes and what might underlie the practices so sternly criticized.

The reader might, however, be forgiven for feeling confused by the multiplicity of themes and the apparent contradictions that have emerged. Are South African borrowers extravagant or thrifty? Are they unsustainably overindebted, or do the items they invest in justify the means they use to do so? Do they have a view of the long term, like the ant in the fable, or only of the short term, like the grasshopper? Similar puzzles emerge when one looks at the behavior of lenders. If they operate by the logic of the self-regulating free market, as they claim, then why is state regulation required to restrain them from offering products that will lead borrowers into penury, thus ultimately killing the goose that laid the golden egg? And if the government seriously intended regulation of such recklessness, then why the later heeding of borrowers' calls for their credit records to be deleted, thus effectively enabling them to take on further debt?

In trying to answer these questions, it is necessary to sum up what makes South Africa different from other settings where the problem of indebtedness has been identified. Part of the answer to these questions lies in the rapidity of transition and the grand scale of the accompanying expectations: it was not only political liberation but also wealth, comfort, and well-being that were hoped for, as well as the restoration of all those benefits that had been previously withheld. Such benefits were unevenly experienced. The political elite's pursuing of its own advantage, combined with the pressures to liberalize at breakneck speed, resulted in a transition that has been decried for its "limited" character (Marais 2001), a liberation that has been described as "precarious" (Barchiesi 2011).[1] Another part of the answer, then, lies in the complex intersection of interests—those of politicians (and their constituents), trade unions (and their members), capitalist corporations, human rights activists—that have come into play. Finally, part of the answer lies in the contradictory forces that have shaped but also blurred the boundaries between classes and status groups. In response to this complex terrain, market forces have interacted with and fed into uneven forms of redistribution and regulation, often with state backing. On-the-ground realities demand compromises of various sorts, between forces deriving from and pushing toward opposite ends of a scale: labor and capital, rights and property, redistribution and the market.

Penetrating below the level of these political-economic issues and complementing official accounts and survey materials, this book gives a South African take on a wider global story by exploring how borrowers experience the situation. By looking at the small and incremental ways they save, invest, and husband resources; convert by choice between different registers of value; combine borrowing and lending in complex "portfolios" (Collins et al. 2010); or borrow from Peter to pay Paul, the book has aimed to complement the narrow view, through the lens of deferred payment with interest, that is often taken by economists, regulators, and policy makers. It has used informants' models to provide a more local, "house"-centered or "human" view (Gudeman 2001, 2010; Hart, Laville, and Cattani 2010) to yield a perspective on indebtedness that includes—as do other anthropologists' accounts (Graeber 2011; Guyer 2004; Peebles 2010; Shipton 2007)—entanglements in forms of social commitment and webs of long-term obligation.

In post-1994 South Africa, a long history of proletarianization and commodification has coexisted with a realm of social solidarity, often phrased in terms of custom. Embodying the former, the Afrikaans-derived *sekôlôtô* (debt) has negative connotations of perpetual enslavement that hark back to rural cultivators' experiences of owing money to trading stores and, more recently, refer to their sense of entrapment in hire-purchase arrangements. Embodying the latter, *lobola* captures—even epitomizes—the idea of long-term obligation and reciprocity between families (James 2012, 22–23; Kuper 1982). I explained in Chapter 1 how even though the classic Maussian system of reciprocities this practice implies is on the decline in some cases, and is much disputed in others, *lobola* is tenacious and resilient in the contemporary mind (Krige 2012b; White 2004, 2010). Combined with this, and having similar tenacity, a further aspect of local social solidarity centers on saving money in clubs. Members are motivated by the wish to remove money from circulation, prevent its everyday use, and invest it in particular goods. These two registers—commodification and solidarity—are forced into juxtaposition when slender means make it necessary to "borrow speculative resources . . . from [the] future" (Peebles 2010, 226). The resulting attitude is one of deep ambivalence. The negative experiences of financialized arrangements (alienation and enslavement) marry uneasily with the positive character of house-centered aspirations (long-term obligation and reciprocity) that necessitate these. To elaborate, let me briefly revisit some topics discussed in the introduction.

Class and Status

A complex layering has yielded South Africa's particular version of socioeconomic differentiation. A newly liberalized capitalism combined with pronounced state patronage was superimposed on top of what existed before: that is, apartheid's peculiar version of state capitalism in which discriminatory repressiveness played a key role. Whereas the official system of earlier classification used race as the means to categorize the population, this has been replaced by a market system emphasizing lifestyle, consumption, and consumer choice: the living standards measures, or LSMs. Folk categories partly converge with but partly contradict these schemas. During apartheid, a long period of struggle focused on the rights of organized labor generated a strongly Marxist view in which capital was counterposed to labor. This view—and the struggle from which it was born—continues, in modified form, in the current era. But an even longer history of status awareness within the black community emphasized features less commensurate with a Marxist perspective. Those considering themselves more modern and respectable distinguished themselves from those they viewed as more custom bound and less sophisticated. Overlaid on and intersecting with these earlier patterns, the new dispensation has generated further differentiation within black society. As depicted in this book, some have overtly benefited from the transition, rising to prominence in the new civil service as holders of important positions, gaining wealth by profiting from government tenders, or—more modestly—working as teachers or police officers, or employees of parastatals, and receiving the accompanying housing benefits and the like. Of these various beneficiaries, however, not all were newly elevated or advantaged by the transition. For some, it was their parents' earlier investment in education that led to their current advancement; others have simply remained in jobs they previously held. A further group, complaining of the fact that only those with "connections" can gain advancement, has nonetheless managed to become small-scale entrepreneurs—and in some cases eventually big-time ones (although there were and are considerable barriers to such an option, as I outlined in Chapter 6). The new middle class, if that is what we should call it, includes all of the above but remains fragmentary in terms of income. Positioned not far below it in the hierarchy are the remains of the industrial and mining proletariat (including some who are migrant workers, such as the miners of Marikana, and many whose status as "employed" does not lessen the precariousness of their situation, such as Richard Madihlaba, whose story is told in Chapter 5). Finally, a vast number have lost their jobs, especially those in industry, and have joined the ranks of those who have never worked. They are left to depend on one of various state welfare grants, on a relative who receives a grant, or on a relative who remains in employment.

Across all these strata, people have found themselves, to different degrees, exposed to new pressures to consume and have been readily offered the wherewithal to do so. Credit and debt are what make it possible for people to buy more than they can afford. Countering the apparent homogeneity—"everyone is now middle class"—one of the things that varies widely, as Chapter 5 shows, is whether individuals borrow, from whom, how much, what for, and what they do about repayment. In this sense, credit and debt and their usage serve further to differentiate those in these categories and status groups from one another. Credit and debt, under the current dispensation, have thus played a constitutive role in shaping such status groups and distinguishing them from one another. For some, although achieving upward mobility and modern-style comfort has been possible because of state patronage, access to credit has also been necessary to complete that picture. For others, the absence of such patronage has left credit to play an even larger role in promising (if not in fact delivering) such mobility. But for those with no income at all, credit is difficult or impossible to access.

Conversely, the avoidance of credit and debt has played its part in defining class and status. A self-image centered on propriety is an important ingredient in middle-class identity, and being thrifty and sensible with money is both a means and an end to such respectability. In tandem with this, but more ambiguously, diverse impulses push new achievers in two directions. One of these is avoiding undue demands from the parents and relatives who helped one to achieve success, setting one's mind against being a "cash cow," and "owning" one's own desires and acknowledging rather than denying the cost of these. The opposite impulse involves acknowledging the need to reciprocate to relatives for the sacrifices they have made to enable this position of privilege in the first place. In all these ways, engaging with (or avoiding) credit and debt plays a role in constituting people's sense of belonging within a distinctive social category or status group.

Countering the splintered character of the socioeconomic landscape and indicating an emerging homogeneity, one might follow Graeber (2011, 2013) by pointing out that involvement with the world of credit—and hence debt—is what everyone across this wide spectrum now has in common. As yet, however, this common experience has played little role in yielding a collective sense of identity in response.

The Household

Rather than establishing the grounds for solidarity, debt and credit serve to intensify differentiation along other, further fault lines. Profoundly fragmenting any solidarity, gender divisions within and between households play a particular role in crosscutting whatever hierarchical distinctions of status might exist. These divisions are often intensified by the tensions that arise in short-lived marriage or conjugal arrangements. The habits and propensities that might make people get into debt, seen through the prism of manhood or womanhood, respectively, appear as skewed in one or the other direction. Men, faced with the new climate of aspiration, may shoulder their responsibilities to provide housing in the suburbs and schooling but find these unsustainably onerous (Steinberg 2008, 105–6). Meanwhile, women often represent their male partners as spendthrift, often inaccurately so. They speak of their current or former spouses as "eating" resources rather than husbanding them, and of themselves, in contrast, as inclined toward saving and thrift. They seek to establish their own ownership over property and feel disadvantaged when the ownership of family houses, for example, effectively excludes them.

Yet if the house is the venue where resources are husbanded, it is also the site where consumption occurs: and it is that consumption that generates the need to borrow. If all mothers were inclined to instruct their children in the ways of deferred gratification, as Abigail Mlate and Thandi Thobela say they are (Chapter 1) and as Phumelelo Ndumo advises (Chapter 7), would there be no crisis of indebtedness? Or is it the case that, no matter how much abstemiousness is taught to children, the expenses are simply too great to avoid the inevitable: borrowing "speculative resources" from the future and transforming them "into concrete resources to be used in the present" (Peebles 2010, 226)? (Although women and men may both engage in self-justificatory discourses that mask that the "blame" perhaps lies with both, this denial is not the only way to respond to current circumstances, as we will be reminded further on.)

Restoring of Rights

In explaining the particularities of South Africa's debt situation, this book has shown the complex processes involved in restoring citizenship rights and in redistributing associated resources and entitlements to a population that keenly felt the pain of their earlier denial. Using "reversionary legislation" (Falk Moore 2011), these matters were more readily addressed in obvious areas such as land or by creating dramas of conciliation and forgiveness than they were in less apparently racially discriminatory arenas, such as that of credit provision.

Partly explaining the relatively low profile of credit and debt during the transition is the imprint left by the antiapartheid struggle itself. One result of South Africa's period of industrial growth and the widespread proletarianization of its populace was that resistance to apartheid was often articulated via workers' rights and trade unionism. Although other protests certainly took place, including widespread payment boycotts for rental and municipal services (von Schnitzler 2008), conceptualizations of consumer rights were—and so far have remained—relatively undeveloped. Or, where legislation has been passed, its enforcement has lagged. Worker and consumer struggles have certainly converged to some degree, as was seen, for example, with the repeated demands of COSATU—on behalf of its worker constituents and in defense of their "right to borrow"—for a credit information amnesty (Chapter 2). But such claims are profoundly ambiguous. Asking to be reinstated as a borrower might appear as less a form of robust consumer resistance against financialized capitalist corporations than as a clamoring against exclusion from, and a wish to be readmitted to, the charmed circle of those who are allowed to get into debt. If owing money represents some kind of enslavement—a situation of "working for" the lender—then trade unions petitioning to have their members' records expunged are effectively requesting to become perpetually debt bonded.

A second and associated area in which strident protests by consumers might, in another society, have occurred (Nader 2000) is that of information and privacy. Breckenridge (2005) has suggested that records captured during the apartheid regime for the purposes of "security" were readily transferred to the commercial sector for the purposes of "sales," with little attention to citizens' rights to privacy. In a similar but little explored vein, a further manifestation of this tendency has been the sheer weight of information about individuals captured by the credit bureaus themselves, and the readiness to sell this on to, for example, prospective employers.[2] A comparison with countries that have similar sharp inequalities of wealth and where poor rural populations cohabit with wealthy urban ones, such as India (Guérin 2014) and Mexico (Villarreal 2014), reveals similar stories of debt, but much less in the way of technologized information gathering. The extent of this information, together with the banking of "the unbanked" and the readiness of magistrates' courts' clerks to issue garnishee orders (Chapter 2), might be seen to have resulted in a situation of insidious surveillance akin to that famously discussed by Foucault (1991), after Bentham.

There is something that further complicates the situation. Worker organizations, fewer members of which in any case are blue collar than they were, are less likely than before to protest against the institutions that lend them money at interest. This owes something to the particular way that market forces combine with redistributive impulses in South Africa. The powers that be are attentive not only to their own interests and to those of other well-heeled elites who have benefited from involvement in financialized capitalism but also to those of various individuals who make a living in the interstices of the system. These include community moneylenders (*mashonisas*), small-scale sellers on credit, debt administrators, debt counselors, and a range of other agents who have been described in the pages of this book. The consumers whose rights as borrowers might otherwise be robustly defended are often lenders as well, or they live alongside them in an informal economy (Hart 1973, 2010) that mirrors and is inextricably interwoven with the formal one.

The Logic or Absurdity of Credit and Debt

Many features of the system described in this book might appear dysfunctional at best, absurd at worst. But are they?

It is now widely accepted that, leading up to the global credit crunch, high finance had become not only all-powerful but also unpredictable and uncontrollable.[3] Market forces, previously kept in some sort of check, were driven by a need for continual expansion and reinvestment that moved beyond the realm of logic. They ultimately spiraled out of control (Williams 2004), especially when those unable to afford repayment were included in the borrower client base and when the mortgage bonds in question were "securitized," thereby sparking the subprime crisis (Lanchester 2010; Tett 2010). The fact that the loans were also, in a more conventional way, "secured" by being tied to landed property was of little use in the frenzy of repossession that ensued.

In the South African version of this story, credit and debt extended to black people was not new, but its skewed form as "credit apartheid" meant it had earlier been available only in certain forms. As a result of discriminatory legislation after 1913, landed property was unavailable as collateral, and movable property—that is, furniture and appliances—was made to serve in its place. Even with postapartheid credit, the availability of land and housing was patchy and uneven, and much immovable property remained unavailable for sale, as shown in Chapter 6. But there was one significant change. The more streamlined, financialized version of lending that then emerged, especially for loans smaller than mortgage ones, came to rely on something other than the repossession of property to hedge against risk. The alternative took various forms. Credit bureaus, in a system used worldwide to "secure" lenders' enterprises and protect them against the risk of nonrepayment, were able to collect information on customers and then blacklist those in default. Informal lenders, or *mashonisas*, used borrowers' ATM cards to ensure that money was paid back. Offering what are now known as "payday" loans, microlenders charged high rates of interest to compensate themselves for the obvious risk: that some money lent would never be repaid. Meanwhile credit providers of all kinds were seemingly little concerned with monitoring their clients' other repayment commitments before granting them yet further loans. This was unnecessary given that there was always the option of deducting a borrower's owings directly from his or her salary with a readily granted garnishee order. Credit-extending savings clubs, in contrast, placed the responsibility to get the money back with interest on the shoulders of each individual member who had taken out the compulsory loan that month.

But these systems of guarding against risk—the local, simpler equivalent of "securitization," perhaps—seem contradictory when seen in the light of other trends. In the 1990s, South African credit providers of all kinds lent money to anyone, irrespective of his or her history of repayment. Albeit on a small scale, this certainly proved as unsustainable as equivalent global processes. Why during this period—and indeed until 2013, despite attempted regulation—have "unsecured lenders" continued to offer loans that continue to be borrowed? Why do they do so, seemingly oblivious to the various risk-calculating mechanisms described in this book? A possible answer lies in the sheer numbers of those at the bottom of the pyramid, as Prahalad calls it (2006). If lenders never run out of borrowers, and especially if many customers—like Richard Madihlaba in Chapter 5—attempt assiduously to repay their debts, then those lenders can presumably afford to make a few losses along the way. The word *pyramid* is here appropriate, but less in the sense of "bottom of the pyramid" finance and more in the sense of a pyramid scheme, whose would-be investors often illogically clamor for more and similar investment opportunities despite all indications that their investments have yielded nothing (see Krige 2012; Piot 2014).

But should people assiduously repay their debts—and do they? Parker Shipton (2011, 217) called for a questioning of the self-evident truth that "all loans and repayments should cancel each other out": a line of argument that Graeber (2011, 3–4) pursues even more robustly when, for example, he challenges the obligation of indebted nations to pay back interest-bearing loans to donor ones. What normally makes this truth rather less than self-evident, when anthropologists document the ideas and values that underpin relations of obligation, is that local "understandings about wealth, time, and the relation between them" (Shipton 2011, 215; see also Guyer 2004, 162–63, 165–69) are often incompatible with financiers' and bankers' views. Quite apart from culturally relativist revelations that obligations to repay may differ from one context to another, there is also a political consideration when it comes to black South African borrowers. This concerns the strong impulse, during the height of the antiapartheid struggle in the 1980s, against paying what was owed for municipal services, or rental: an impulse that became known to frustrated municipal authorities and others as "the culture of non-payment" (von Schnitzler 2008, 906). The move toward implementing "responsibilized citizenship" that was subsequently attempted (Chipkin 2003; von Schnitzler 2008) meant trying to change this culture. In a similar vein, various social enterprises aimed at uplifting poor and previously disadvantaged people, such as the Johannesburg Housing Company, described in Chapter 4, intended to nudge them toward sustainable self-sufficiency and "owning" their own expenses. It is possible that something of this culture of nonpayment, and indeed of entitlement, remains. But I never heard anyone express a willful intention not to honor his or her debts. On the contrary, cases of people with precarious means, like that of Richard Madihlaba, show that it was often the conscientious repayment of loans that led them into further trouble when their creditors offered them further loans.

We return to the government spokesperson who said, "I didn't join the revolution to be poor." How far do sentiments like this incline people to indulge consumerist impulses and desires, despite the strong emphasis on frugality and the need for forward-looking, family-oriented investments described in this book? The question throws a further ingredient into the mixing pot, thus complicating what is already a mismatch between obligations to others and the self-discipline needed to fulfill those obligations, as outlined earlier. As Chapter 5 shows, sources of credit have proliferated and become more diverse. "Portfolios" contain diverse bank accounts, store cards, and school fees; there are rentals and taxes owed, alongside informal loans (Collins et al. 2010). (At the same time, as Chapter 2 reveals, the technologies of collection have narrowed and become more streamlined.) As householders echo and buy into discourses of the "reasonable" terms that lenders offer on either side of the regulatory divide, it becomes clear that their thriftiness is being constantly chipped away as they come to collaborate in their own indebtedness.

Self-Responsibility or Paternalism

"Giving in is just not on," said one of my informants. Coming back to Foucauldian approaches via another route, the only alternative solution to "giving in" so far offered—despite the attempted regulation, array of legislation, and establishment of institutions such as the National Credit Regulator—involves self-discipline and the reshaping of subjectivities. Such self-policing regimes are remarkably similar, whether pursued by civil society organizations and social enterprises, by debt counselors, or through self-help books and advice. There is a suggestion that such a self-regulatory regime of responsibilization can work, but it will be better for those who start out with resources to husband than it will be for those who have none to begin with. For the former, education and upward mobility has enabled a degree of individualization and self-reflection (Chapter 7), also allowing some escape from the entangled sociability of long-term obligations.

Alternatively, with a greater group orientation but still entailing some internalized and individualized reflection, joining a neo-charismatic church has proved to be a supportive option. Interestingly, and perhaps counterintuitively, among of the list of self-help agents discussed here, the church stands out as offering—alongside the self-policing that is required by tithing—some critique of the current socioeconomic conjuncture. The sermon cited in Chapter 7, for example, railed against cronyism, corruption, affirmative action, and the blind pursuit of a university "degree" without a view to what lies beyond it. Church membership also furnished congregants with introspective awareness about their own class mobility. Members of the new or not-so-new middle class, by identifying with like-minded people at church, become able to distinguish themselves from those who are less upwardly mobile, thus further contributing to the new forms of differentiation outlined earlier. But in addition to this, the self-realization these churches offer—combined with the education their members have acquired—affords a critical insight into the sociopolitical circumstances that installed these members in their present positions.

Necessary as they may be, particularly if there is no alternative, there is a darker underside to these pervasively advocated disciplinary regimes. The paternalism for which South Africa has long been known also involved shaping the way the self was experienced, but it increased dependency rather than reducing it.[4] Based on the system laid out in the Magistrates' Court Act, the approach removed individual accountability while also being profoundly alienating and decreasing protection. Relieving indebted people of responsibility for their own actions, salaries, bank accounts, and debts, the system placed them instead under "external judicial control" (Haupt et al. 2008, 51). And that system continues to this day, despite attempted reforms. This handing over of control offers ultimate security to the lender, not the borrower: the principle of advantage to creditors that underpins existing insolvency law remains intact despite attempts to provide "debtor relief" (Boraine and Roestoff 2002, 4; Wiggins 1997, 510). The latter is left to the mercies of the former, whose ability to gather and store information about him or her represents an invasion of privacy, even a reshaping of subjective experience of the self, but without the alleged safeguards that might normally be assumed to exist when one is dependent on another for one's well-being.[5]

∗ ∗ ∗

Aspiration and indebtedness are intertwined. The South African context combines a clientelistic party state with opportunities for individualized self-advancement and the promise of enhanced social solidarity. Media reports at their most extreme suggest a somewhat monolithic narrative in which members of the new middle class confine their passions to the purchase of consumer items in a kind of mad potlatch, becoming increasingly self-absorbed. Meanwhile, those further down the ladder struggle simply to stay alive. Everything seems to be "for sale" in a setting where civil society is on the wane, replaced by churches that promote a new prosperity gospel for yuppies while offering some solace to the poor. While for the very few these upward trajectories may be enabled by financial formality, many others are blocked, with the promise of a prosperous lifestyle receding ever further into the distance as they grasp at the few possibilities offered by making "money from nothing."

The alternative account that I have provided here attempts to qualify this picture. It points to the social embeddedness of monetary exchange and the availability of choice—albeit a restricted choice, given the character of post-transition South African society—about how and where to convert between registers and scales of value. Local logics of conversion and investment drive people to rank monetized exchanges against moral or personal transactions, weighing them up against each other. This book has shown how these apparently divergent narratives are interrelated in complex and unexpected ways.

Reference Matter

Notes

Introduction

1. I use *black* to denote the members of Bantu-language groups, now often termed *indigenous*, who were at the bottom of the social ladder under apartheid. I do this is in contrast with older South African practice, which terms them *African* but misleadingly suggests that other inhabitants of the country are "non-African."

2. The meaning and history of the term *credit apartheid* is explored in detail in Chapter 3.

3. For the changed racial profile of South Africa's public service, see Schlemmer (2005) and Southall (2004). Parastatals are South Africa's equivalent of state-owned enterprises. For more on these, see Clark (1994) and Freund (2013), during the apartheid period; for the postapartheid period, see Southall (2007).

4. Shneiderman writes this in regard to South Asian circular migrants for whom indebtedness compels mobility, which in turn yields transformations in social and political consciousness. See also Shneiderman (2014, forthcoming).

5. I am grateful to Detlev Krige for encouraging me to pursue this line of investigation.

6. Sam Sole and Stefaans Brummer, "'Auditors' secret report reveals how millions flowed to President Zuma," *Mail and Guardian*, 7 December 2012; Gerald McKune, "Banks bent over backwards for Zuma," *Mail and Guardian*, 7 December 2012. At the time this book was going to press in 2014, the public protector Thuli Madonsela had recently released a report showing that the state had borne much of the financial burden for the overspend on President Zuma's private residence at Nkandla. Phillip de Wet and Sarah Evans, "Madonsela exposes the rot at the heart of Nkandla," *Mail and Guardian*, 20 March 2014.

7. Patrick McGroarty, "In South Africa, a consumer debt bubble forms," *Wall Street Journal*, 26 December 2012.

8. For a discussion of South Africa's financial "deepening," see Ardington et al. (2004); Daniels (2004); Porteous with Hazelhurst (2004); Schoombee (2004, 2009).

9. See Harvey (2005); Marais (2011, 134–35); see also Dieter Plehwe and Tom Mills, "Defending capitalism: The rise of the neoliberal thought collective (part 2)," 2012, http://www.newleftproject.org/index.php/site/article_comments/defending_capit alism_the_rise_of_the_neoliberal_thought_collective_part_2.

10. Given these considerations, I use the term *neoliberalism* sparingly in this book, aware of the many caveats. It does not serve as a single explanatory trope that accounts for everything in the modern world (Kipnis 2007; Sanders 2008). Furthermore, "neoliberal governmentality" is least useful when applied in African settings where attempts at instigating techniques of self-control, encouraging people to become self-motivated, and the like, have been "very limited" (Ferguson 2010a, 173); see also J. L. Comaroff (1998, 340); James (2013a).

11. For an account of these processes, see Barchiesi (2011); Marais (2011, 124–28, 132–39).

12. For an account of lending in the United States that similarly stresses the recklessness of creditors, see Margaret Atwood, "Our faith is fraying in the god of money," *Financial Times*, 13 April 2012.

13. The Zulu word *mashonisa* relates to the verb stems *-shona* (to sink, become poor, die) and *-shonisa* (to impoverish, cause to become poor) (Dent and Nyembezi 1969, 481). It may be translated as "one who impoverishes" or who "takes and continues to take indefinitely" (Krige 2011, 144). In popular parlance the plural is *mashonisas* (Krige 2011, 151; Siyongwana 2004, 851).

14. For criticisms of the elite and limited character of the transition, see Bond (2000); Marais (2001).

15. The history and social life of this village have been extensively documented by Isak Niehaus with his assistants (Niehaus, with Mohlala and Shokane 2011; Niehaus 2013).

16. I am grateful to Isabel Hofmeyr and Liz Gunner for introducing the two novels to me and for confirming that fiction can be valuable in capturing the spirit of a time and place, as these books do.

17. Patrick McGroarty, "In South Africa, a consumer debt bubble forms," *Wall Street Journal*, 26 December 2012.

18. Ibid.

19. This penetration occurred as the more established markets reached saturation point (Porteous with Hazelhurst 2004, 89).

20. In the first quarter of 2008, South Africans spent 82.3 percent of their disposable income on household debt, compared to 60.2 percent in 1998. Consumer Debt Report of 2008, compiled by National Debt Agency Credit Matters, cited in Lungi Mazibuko, Lindiwe Dlukulu, Dimakatso Qocha, Veli Mfetane, Desiree Thloaele, and Shokie

Bopape (Group Five), "An investigation into the indebtedness of consumers: A case study of the South African middle class," pp. 5, 23, http://atplay.biz/clients/iwfsa/wp-content/uploads/Indebtedness-of-Consumers-SA-Middle-Class.pdf. For a discussion of race categories, see note 1.

21. Kevin Davie, "Drowning in debt or rolling in riches," *Mail and Guardian*, 22 July 2011.

22. For the (former) importance of the public service in other African economies, see Anders (2009); Macgaffey and Bazenguissa-Ganga (2000). For more on the new black middle class in South Africa, see von Holdt (2010).

23. See also Mazibuko et al., "An investigation into the indebtedness of consumers."

24. Such attention to informants' subjective consciousness of class has recently been shown, equally, to be Durkheimian (Grusky with Galescu 2005). Seekings (2009) gives an interesting account of why the Weberian style of analysis that informed these accounts was squeezed out by more materialist or Marxist ones. See Olin Wright (2005), Breen (2005), and Grusky with Galescu (2005) for a nuanced account of how Marxist, Weberian, and Durkheimian approaches to class analysis differ and converge.

25. For an account of the way policies deliberately disadvantaged aspirant black businesspeople over the course of the twentieth century, see Crankshaw (2005, 361, 382); Cobley (1990, 48; 151–56); Kuper (1965, 76–77).

26. On the prevalence of blacks in civil service jobs performing "black administration," see Crankshaw (2005, 384), Cobley (1990, 40–43), Kuper (1965, xii).

27. For accounts of how the black middle class consolidated around the public sector in the 1990s, see Crankshaw (2005); Southall (2004, 533; 2012); Seekings and Nattrass (2005, 312), von Holdt (2010, 11).

28. The Gini coefficient is commonly used as a measure of inequality of income or wealth. A coefficient of zero expresses perfect equality, where everyone has an exactly equal income; a coefficient of one expresses maximal inequality. "In a global ranking by Gini coefficient, a measure of income inequality, South Africa comes off as one of the worst (of a generally bad bunch)." "South Africa. Cheerleaders and naysayers: Who is making the right call about Africa's future?" *The Economist*, 2 March 2013, http://www.economist.com/news/special-report/21572381-who-making-right-call-about-africas-future-cheerleaders-and-naysayers.

29. See note 1 herein, where I explain my preference for *black* over *African*. For discussion of the size and rise of this group, see Crankshaw, cited in Southall (2004, 529); Seekings and Nattrass (2005, 308), von Holdt (2010, 11, 21)

30. Carol Paton, "De Doorns—where dreams refuse to die," *Business Day*, 6 December 2012.

31. SAFM, *Talkshop*, 28 January 2013, discussion between Masechaba Mtolo and directors and members of various chambers of commerce.

32. It is notable that the microcredit miracle, much lauded by some and criticized by others, has not been part of South Africa's story. (Nonetheless, as this book will show, the borrowing and lending nexus, though focused on consumers, has enabled the generation of wealth and income earning, albeit in ways normally condemned as usurious.)

33. Attempting to answer why both academic analysts and policy makers proved "so wrong," Feinstein shows how "both groups clearly failed to recognize the extent to which the needs of manufacturing diverged from those of mining and farming, and ignored the difficulty of achieving high productivity in industry on the basis of a migrant labor force" (2005, 247).

34. This arrangement has been dubbed the "house-property complex" (Gluckman 1950; Oboler 1994).

35. For accounts of these gendered conflicts over expectations and resources, see Ainslie (2012); Hull (2010); Hunter (2006); Jensen (2012); Niehaus (2012); White (2012a, 2012b).

36. Khunou (2006) and Niehaus (2013) give accounts of multiple partnerships; Spiegel (1991) and Anita Heeren and colleagues (2011) outline how these are legitimized as polygyny.

37. Isak Niehaus, an anthropologist long acquainted with Impalahoek (see note 15), also conveyed these points to me in a personal communication.

38. Khulumani Support Group, "Khulumani looks back on a decade of legal activism," http://www.khulumani.net/reparations/corporate/item/706-khulumani-looks -back-on-a-decade-of-legal-activism.html. Some twelve years down the line, on 27 February 2012, in what was hailed as a "symbolic victory" against multinationals, a US court finalized a $1.5 million settlement between General Motors Liquidation Company, formerly known as General Motors Corporation, and the apartheid lawsuit claimants represented by Khulumani and those represented by Lungisile Ntsebeza (http://www .khulumani.net/reparations/).

39. The points in this paragraph are drawn from my book on land reform (James 2007).

Chapter 1

1. The Luo of Kenya were entangled in endless claims and obligations, often enduring over generations. A native commissioner was puzzled at the way they were thus "in a state of chronic indebtedness," yet this is not necessarily problematic: such webs can be what sustains life (Shipton 2007).

2. Rose Setshege, "Local soaps overrating black diamonds," *Business Day*, 27 March 2007.

3. Sophie Chevalier's translation.

4. Mager (2010) shows that advertising strategy targeted at black people frequently has made use of the allure of "otherness" by associating products with white society. For

a comparable argument in the case of lower castes in India, see Guérin (2014, 47): "Dalit women, who have long been excluded from . . . expenditure reserved for upper castes, give these expenses a considerable symbolic value." The social meanings of consumption can be as telling in regard to the internal differences within rapidly differentiating communities compared to those between the races. For example, Krige (2011) describes a group of male friends who get together to drink a "yuppie" brand of beer. While drinking in the suburbs distances them from their origins in Soweto and marks off their new and altered status, drinking in Soweto reconnects them to those roots. Consumption thus mediates their social relationships to former neighbors and kin, rather than simply marking them off as distinct from them. It is not my intention here to review the vast literature on consumption. For a useful summary of how consumption can both distinguish consumers from others and serve more inclusive purposes, see Ross (2008, 8).

5. Jabu Mabuza, "No-carat diamonds," *Financial Mail*, 13 July 2007, cited in Krige (2009, 23). See also Tonny Mafu, "Black middle class defies easy definition," *Business Report*, 24 June 2007.

6. Bongani Madondo, "Jub Jub: The life and trial of a South African child star," *Mail and Guardian*, 21 December 2012.

7. Bernard Dubbeld, "Quick analysis of black greed isn't legitimate," *Mail and Guardian*, 11 January 2013.

8. Echoing the truism in the proverb "act in haste, repent at leisure," these perceptions endorse Keith Hart's point about the time dimension of credit (1999, 200). What distinguishes debt from exchange is a lapse in time between the moment of acquisition and the moment of repayment. It is during the delay, the time after the purchase has been made, that one might regret one's action of buying the longed-for item.

9. There is disagreement on whether or not such "tall poppies" meet with the approval of the ruling African National Congress, although many in its ranks could be reckoned as belonging in the upper ranks of the ruling elite. See Sandile Memela, "Why historically unANChored young black professionals are coping very well," *Mail and Guardian*, 15 December 2008, http://www.thoughtleader.co.za/sandilememela/2008/12/15/why-historically-unanchored-young-black-professionals-are-coping-very-well/.

10. On the complex tension between individualistic and communitarian values that emerged in 1950s township settings, see Wilson and Mafeje (1963) and Pauw (1963).

11. "Credit creating a 'time bomb,'" *Financial Mail*, 27 December 2006.

12. In a self-help book, Phumelele Ndumo explicitly warns against this practice (2011, 89) (see Chapter 7). For an account of the sudden popularity of clothes as commodities in a global context, see Ross (2008).

13. Had she read the self-help book by Phumelele Ndumo (2011, 37), she would have realized that the debt had "prescribed." See Chapter 7.

14. See also Margaret Atwood, "Our faith is fraying in the god of money," *Financial Times*, 13 April 2012.

15. "Today's 'go-getter generation' is more confident," *Business Day*, 17 June 2008.

16. For an account of how conversions occur between monetary and moral spheres, see Parry and Bloch (1989).

17. The term *lobola* has become ungrammatical in its transformation into general slang or township lingo. The strictly correct form in isiZulu would be *ilobolo*.

18. She uses the grammatically proper isiXhosa form *ilobolo* rather than the slang *lobola*.

19. See the case of Richard Madihlaba in Chapter 5.

20. Phone-in show on *ilobolo*, SAFM, 29 March 2010.

21. For a discussion of the wellsprings of respectability in South Africa, and of its expression through the purchase of commodities, see Ross (1999, 2008). The ramifications of short-term versus medium- and long-term horizons are interesting and require further investigation. It is unclear whether prospective in-laws have simply "given in" to instant gratification or whether something else is at play, such as lack of trust in long-term commitments and old-fashioned relations between families. It is also unclear whether, in the case of marriage dissolution, the debt disappears.

22. Phone-in show on household finances, SAFM, 15 April 2010.

Chapter 2

1. The organization, having been started by a group of white women in the 1950s, was referred to by Mandela on his release as "the conscience of white South Africa." It later moved away from being a member-driven organization made up mainly of white women volunteers. By the end of 1995, the Black Sash had evolved into its current structure of a professionally staffed nongovernmental organization, led by a national director and accountable to a board of trustees. See "Our History," The Black Sash, http://www.blacksash.org.za/index.php/our-legacy/our-history.

2. This and all other quoted sections in the next few paragraphs are from a conversation I had with Xolela May, Knysna, 8 October 2008.

3. "If a debtor is insolvent but he or she cannot put up the funds to apply for the proper relief in terms of the Insolvency Act or cannot proof [*sic*] advantage to creditors, a sequestration order that would eventually lead to a discharge of debt, would be out of reach of such a debtor" (Boraine and Roestoff 2002, 4). For further detail, see Smit (2008, 2, 5–6); Schraten (forthcoming)

4. Lynley Donnelly, "NCR raises alarm at unsecured lending in Marikana," *Mail and Guardian*, 11 October 2012; Chantelle Benjamin, "Ghastly garnishee abuse exposed," *Mail and Guardian*, 30 November 2012; "Editorial: Grapple garnishee ghoul," *Mail and Guardian*, 30 November 2012; Keith Breckenridge, "Revenge of the commons: The crisis in the South African mining industry," *History Workshop Online*, 5 November 2012, http://www.historyworkshop.org.uk/revenge-of-the-commons-the-crisis-in-the-south-african-mining-industry/. For a similar situation in Malawi, where up to

two-thirds of civil servants' salaries were being deducted to pay back loans, see Anders (2009, 76). Some of the material in this chapter was published online in James (2013b).

5. Lynley Donnelly, "NCR raises alarm at unsecured lending in Marikana," *Mail and Guardian*, 11 October 2012.

6. The same had been done in the United States in 1980 (Graeber 2011, 376).

7. Mark Seymour, Pretoria, 2 September 2008.

8. For a retrospective analysis in an interview with African Bank's chief executive officer Leon Kirkinis, see Chris Barron, "African Bank CEO takes on the watchdogs" *Business Day*, 17 February 2013. He "decided in the late 1980s that good money could be made granting loans to poor people whom no bank would help because they did not have collateral. . . . His hunch that there was money to be made out of granting unsecured loans to the poor and then charging them exorbitant interest was so spectacularly borne out by African Bank's stellar returns that Capitec joined in, followed by the same banks which weren't interested until belatedly realising they'd missed a very profitable trick. . . . African Bank . . . has 40% of the unsecured lending market."

9. See the website of Finmark Trust (http://www.finmark.org.za/). Its mission is "Making financial markets work for the poor, by promoting financial inclusion and regional financial integration."

10. COSATU submission on the National Credit Bill B18-2005, presented to the Portfolio Committee for Trade and Industry, 31 August 2005, p. 11. These and the following citations are from representations made on the final draft of the bill. I am grateful to Elroy Paulus of the Black Sash for bringing these to my attention and letting me have copies of them.

11. Gabriel Davel, Department of Trade and Industry, 14 June 2005, submission on the National Credit Bill, presented to the portfolio committee for Trade and Industry.

12. The Black Sash submission on the final draft of the National Credit Bill, 2005, presented to the Portfolio Committee for Trade and Industry.

13. The National Credit Bill 2005 and related changes to the National Payment System Act: implications for ABIL, Johan de Ridder, August 2005, presented to the Portfolio Committee for Trade and Industry.

14. Submission on the National Credit Bill 2005 by the Clothing Retailer Members of the Consumer Credit Association, presented to the Portfolio Committee for Trade and Industry.

15. COSATU submission on the National Credit Bill B18-2005, presented to the Portfolio Committee for Trade and Industry, 31 August 2005, p. 10. The submission cites a seminal study by Penelope Hawkins: "Possible reasons why registered micro-lenders were charging annual interest rates of between 80–140% per annum included the acknowledgement that they had a 'captive audience and no competition'; were pricing interest rates 'to what the market will bear'; and practiced 'poor disclosure to a vulnerable consumer segment.'"

16. "Blacklisted and Unemployed," Carte Blanche, MNet, 21 October 2010, http://beta.mnet.co.za/carteblanche/Article.aspx?Id=4170&ShowId=1. COSATU claimed that this was unacceptable and unconstitutional, since it threatened to increase unemployment and relegate "jobseekers to further economic hardship."

17. Balboa submission on the National Credit Bill, 28 July 2005, presented to the Portfolio Committee for Trade and Industry.

18. Chantelle Benjamin, "New credit amnesty raises alarm," *Mail and Guardian*, 22 March 2013; Stuart Theobald, "Credit information amnesty makes things worse for borrowers, lenders," *Business Day*, 17 September 2012.

19. The phrase "on tick" is said to have come from the practice of keeping a book to record the purchases of people who had no money until payday. As payments were made, the shopkeeper put a tick mark (or checkmark) in the book.

20. "We have 1.2 million to 1.3 million public servants at the national and provincial level. We found that 210,000 public servants are now affected by garnishee orders," "Low savings a concern says Minister Gordhan," *Engineering News*, 23 July 2009. For a detailed breakdown, see Haupt and colleagues (2008, 47–70).

21. Frans Haupt, Pretoria, 3 September 2008. See also Haupt and colleagues (2008, 60–67). Showing that not much had changed in the interim, emoluments attachment orders were later discussed in a series of newspaper articles in 2012, in which members of the legal profession voiced similar concerns. For the Magistrates' Court Act of 1944, section 65J, see http://www.justice.gov.za/legislation/acts/1944-032.pdf.

22. Smit cites the interim research report on the review of administration orders in terms of section 74 of the Magistrates' Courts Act 32 of 1944 during May 2002, volume 1 document 30, by Marilyn Budow. To be "struck off" means to be removed from the register and no longer permitted to practice as a lawyer.

23. The Black Sash submission on the final draft of the National Credit Bill, 2005, presented to the Portfolio Committee for Trade and Industry; see also du Plessis (2007, 79).

24. Preamble to National Credit Act (http://www.thenct.org.za/NCTDocs/founding-legislation/9a669fbc-ef58-4bd2-8a5e-d12f37d018bf.pdf).

25. The Black Sash submission on the final draft of the National Credit Bill, 2005, presented to the Portfolio Committee for Trade and Industry; Furniture Traders' Association submission, 2005, presented to the Portfolio Committee for Trade and Industry.

26. Commentary by Vincent Van Der Merwe, J. C. Grobler & Burger Inc., 5 August 2005, presented to the Portfolio Committee for Trade and Industry.

27. Dr. M. Sefularo (ANC), statement to Portfolio Committee on Trade and Industry, 24 March 2006.

28. Frans Haupt, Pretoria, 3 September 2008.

29. Ibid.

30. Rethabile Tlou and Richard Mutshekwane, Midrand, 1 August 2008.

31. Mareesa Erasmus, Pretoria, 3 September 2008.

32. Dawn Jackson, You and Your Money, Cape Town, 13 August 2008. This often threw up problems of jurisdiction: a matter that became a particular bugbear for lawyers, paralegals and debt counselors attempting to tackle the problem of garnishee orders.

33. Rethabile Tlou, Midrand, Gauteng, 15 April 2009.

34. For more on the South African credit crunch, see Chapter 5.

35. Marlene Heymans, Pretoria, 15 April 2009.

36. "Absa guilty of reckless lending," *Fin24.com*, 30 April 2010, http://www.fin24 .com/Money/Money-Clinic/Absa-guilty-of-reckless-lending-20100430.

37. Barron, "African Bank CEO."

38. Thekiso Anthony Lefifi, "African Bank faces rap over its lending," *Business Day*, 10 February 2013; Barron, "African Bank CEO."

39. Rethabile Tlou, Midrand, 15 April 2009.

40. Barron, "African Bank CEO."

Chapter 3

1. John Comaroff and Jean Comaroff have argued that the emerging contrast between local and imported concepts was not "a confrontation between a primordial folk tradition and the modern world"; rather, tradition came to be formulated through its complementary opposition to "the ways of the European" (1987, 194–95).

2. Lerato Mohale, Impalahoek, 18 August 2008. On the origins of the term *mashonisa*, see the Introduction.

3. Solomon Mahlaba, Impalahoek, 26 March 2009.

4. For an earlier period, see Ross (1986, 68–70). For the slavery period, see Dooling (2008).

5. For an earlier period, see Beinart (1979); Cobley (1990, 43); Krige (2011, 137); Roth (2004, 62); Whelan (2011).

6. For similar arrangements on a white-owned farm, see Bolt (2012).

7. Barchiesi (2011, 216, 227) is critical of the account by Collins and colleagues (2010) that emphasizes choice by describing these kinds of arrangements as "portfolios."

8. In the period from 1900 to the late 1940s, certain members of the black elite or "petty bourgeoisie" had been able to access mortgages from building societies and buy property in particular areas, but this was later legislated against (Cobley 1990, 33–35; Crankshaw 2005; Phillips 1938, 42). For accounts of the decorating of council houses, see Bank (2011); Ginsberg (1996).

9. For similar additions of "charges" in the case of small-scale borrowers in Fiji, see Gregory (2012).

10. Muzila Nkosi, Impalahoek, 26 March 2008. See also "The JD Group," Carte Blanche, MNet, 25 March 2007, http://beta.mnet.co.za/carteblanche/Article .aspx?Id=3279&ShowId=1.

11. Muzila Nkosi, Impalahoek, 26 March 2008. See Chapter 2 for a discussion of garnishee orders.

12. Xolela May, Knysna, 8 April 2010.

13. Rosalind Morris, anthropologist, Columbia University, who has researched mining communities in Carletonville, personal communication. Catherine Burns, a historian at Wits University, told me that similar monthly rounds of repossession were common in white working-class communities, for example, at the mines, in an earlier period (Catherine Burns, personal communication). The relentless social pressures to be upwardly mobile and the shame of repossession are described for nineteenth-century England by George Eliot in her novel *Middlemarch*.

14. Ace Ubisi, Impalahoek, 23 August 2008.

15. In South Africa and the United Kingdom the term is *store card*; in the United States, it is *store credit card*.

16. Bridget Lamont, Johannesburg, 21 April 2008.

17. I am grateful to Ruben Andersson for pointing this out.

18. See Chapter 2 for an account of the collapse of this bank.

19. Maarten Mittner, "Mzansi accounts flop," *Sake24.com*, 9 June 2010.

20. Samuel Kgore, Impalahoek, 22 August 2008. For insights into the relationship of gambling to lending and to other income sources in another South African setting, see van Wyk (2012).

21. Solomon Mahlaba, Impalahoek, 26 March 2009.

22. Ace Ubisi, Impalahoek, 16 August 2008.

Chapter 4

1. The name originates from the phrase "stock fairs," rotating cattle auctions held by English settlers in the Eastern Cape during the early nineteenth century.

2. This and the previous quote are from a meeting with officers of the Johannesburg Housing Company, Johannesburg, 10 September 2008.

3. Showing that such problems with tenancy were endemic in a setting of inequality, the JHC in 2012 sought a court order to evict nonpaying tenants. Ernest Mabuza, "No order by judge to find homes for evictees," *Business Day*, 19 November 2012. One of JHC's buildings was "hijacked" by a freeloading "landlord" in 2012. David Gleason, "Whipping the ass of evictions law," *Business Day*, 21 November 2012.

4. For the text of the act, see the *Government Gazette*, http://www.thenct.org.za/ NCTDocs/founding-legislation/9a669fbc-ef58-4bd2-8a5e-d12f37d018bf.pdf. See also Sanchia Temkin, "New Act to throttle unfair credit deals," *Business Day*, 5 April 2007. Despite the fact that the act did not require savings clubs to register, since they were excluded from its remit, many members I spoke to, and many in other provinces (personal communication from Elizabeth Hull, member of the Popular Economies research team)

were unclear on this point and anxious about their savings clubs, and especially their lending with interest, coming to the attention of the authorities.

5. "Award-winning *Stokvel* returns," *News24.com*, 27 March 2008. In 2004 the soap opera with that title became the only South African television show to date to make the finals of the International Emmy Awards, and it was a nominee for the Rose d'Or Awards for entertainment excellence.

6. "More blacks must build SA," *Fin24.com*, 19 April 2007; "Post office faces huge claim from *stokvel* body," *Business Day*, 13 April 2007.

7. Address by SACP's Blade Nzimande to the Workers' First International Conference in KwaZulu-Natal, 24 February 2009.

8. Sophie Mahlaba, Impalahoek, 19 August 2008.

9. Mary Chiloane, Impalahoek, 23 August 2008.

10. Mary Chiloane, Impalahoek, 28 March 2009.

11. *Bangane* is a xiTsonga word, but the other vernacular terms here are seSotho sa Leboa (Northern Sotho). The area is one of linguistic and cultural hybridity, where xiTsonga and seSotho language and customs interlock. "From the head to the legs" signifies that each person must contribute fully, as her membership stipulates. The metaphor used is a bovine one, reminding participants that although they are giving cash, their contributions are nonetheless framed as relating to that more ceremonially appropriate unit of exchange: cattle.

12. Meeting of Kwanang Bana Basehlare, Impalahoek, 23 August 2008.

13. Ibid.

14. Michael Hibidu, Soweto, 9 September 2008.

15. Sophie Mahlaba, Impalahoek, 19 August 2008.

16. Thomas Thale, Johannesburg, 31 July 2008.

17. Dinah Zulu, Sunview, 16 April 2009.

18. For similar club memberships among informal entrepreneurs in the Western and Eastern Cape, see Neves and du Toit (2012, 140).

19. Modiegi Nong, Leondale, 6 September 2008.

20. Lerato Mohale, Impalahoek, 18 August 2008.

21. On the relationship between banks and *stokvels*, Ndumo (2011, 98) acknowledges that banks offer very low rates of saving but she erroneously states that *stokvels* offer no interest (see Chapter 7): she advises consumers to save with Capitec Bank.

22. For a broader discussion of financialization, see the Introduction. A similar phrase, the "financialization of everyday life," is discussed by Graeber (2011, 376).

23. The term *mashonisa*, besides its other uses documented in the Introduction, can be used—as Elizabeth Hull found in KwaZulu-Natal—to describe the activities of these credit-granting clubs (personal communication).

24. Elizabeth Hull, personal communication.

25. Muzila Nkosi, Impalahoek, 26 March 2009.

Chapter 5

1. See also Liezl Maclean, "South Africa weathers the financial storm," *South African*, 25 November 2008; Miles Donohoe, "What the credit crunch means for South Africa." *Trade Invest South Africa*, 22 October 2008, http://www.tradeinvestsa.co.za/feature_articles/843629.htm.

2. Gordon Bell, "South African economy strong, no recession risk," *Mail and Guardian*, 9 July 2008. For a summary of the debate between those convinced South Africa would weather the storm and those who took a more pessimistic view, see Cramer, Johnston, and Oya (2009, 646). The authors argue that "South Africa's large economy, which since the end of apartheid has pinned its flag to international openness and the benefits of foreign investment, is exposed to the crisis in highly particular ways, especially via the flight of portfolio investment and a fall in foreign direct investment. The *Economist* suggested in February 2009 that South Africa was the most vulnerable of emerging economies, on an index reflecting expected current account deficits, short-term debt as a percentage of foreign exchange reserves, and the ratio of banks' loans to deposits" (Cramer, Johnston, and Oya 2009, 648).

3. "Business confidence plunges further," *Mail and Guardian*, 10 September 2008.

4. "Six million can't pay their debts," *The Times*, 22 August 2008.

5. Mariam Isa, "Household debt falls for first time in five years," *Business Day*, 5 September 2008.

6. Leon Louw, "Reasons for financial crisis are nonsense," *Business Times*, 9 November 2008.

7. Eamonn Ryan, "NCA hits mid-market," *Mail and Guardian*, 11 March 2008; see also Maya Fisher-French, "Credit gets picky," *Mail and Guardian*, 25 July 2008.

8. Sikonathi Mantshantsha, "7.3m in SA behind on bills," *Fin24.com*, 24 May 2009.

9. Isaac Moledi, "Monitor your finances," *Sowetan*, 9 September 2008. These were the microlenders whose rapid rise was documented in Chapter 2.

10. "R1.1 trillion in debt a 'shocking' burden for SA," *Business Report*, 4 June 2008.

11. "The debt abyss lures more SA consumers," *Business Day*, 26 February 2008. For an explanation of the LSM categorization, see Chapter 1.

12. David Williams, "Overindebted? Interview of Consumer Assist's Andre Snyman," 18 August 2008, http://www.summit.co.za. The newspaper used pseudonyms in this report. Kuisie fit the profile of the "overindebted" provided by those in advice organizations like Consumer Assist: a person between twenty-five and thirty-five years old, earning between R8,000 and R12,000 monthly. Kay was representative in her own way: she belongs to "the largest group of debtors identified in National Credit Regulator data" at the time. "People earning between R3,500 and R7,500 a month account for 44,6% of SA's 16,9-million credit consumers": Michael Bleby, "Credit consumer's slippery slope into debt," *Business Day*, 28 February 2008.

13. Bleby, "Credit consumer's slippery slope." Many, but not all, South African salary earners receive a birthday bonus or "thirteenth check"; the annual calculations here do not include that check. See Lavery Modise, "South Africa: It is not compulsory for an employer to pay a 13th cheque to its employees," *Sunday Times*, 7 December 2011.

14. Bleby, "Credit consumer's slippery slope." For difficulties experienced by debt counselors in instigating and arriving at such agreements, see Chapter 2.

15. "The debt abyss lures more SA consumers," *Business Day*, 26 February 2008. Alongside vehicle repossession, what was noted was that the "middle-income market," with a household income of between R100,000 and R400,000 a year, was the "worst hit group for house repossession over the past six months."

16. Sibongile Khumalo, "Black diamonds feel the credit crunch," *Sunday Independent*, 10 August 2008.

17. Thabiso Thakali, "Warning on abuse of debt review," *Weekend Argus*, 11 October 2008.

18. "Business confidence plunges further," *Mail and Guardian*, 10 September 2008.

19. "Schools get tough on cash-strapped parents," *Sunday Times*, 31 August 2008.

20. Mary Ubisi, Impalahoek. 29 March 2009.

21. "Lobola affected by high interest rates," *Women24.com*, 31 December 2008.

22. Woolworths, distinct from and unrelated to the United Kingdom's defunct retail chain of the same name, sells both clothes and groceries.

23. "Verbatim: how the credit crunch is affecting South Africans," *Saturday Star*, 19 July 2008.

24. Mareesa Erasmus, Pretoria, 3 September 2008; see also Chapter 2.

25. Richard Madihlaba and Mareesa Erasmus, Pretoria, 3 September 2008.

26. See the website of Retail Credit Solutions, at http://www.retailcreditsolutions.com/retail-credit-product.html.

27. "The JD Group," Carte Blanche, MNet, 25 March 2007, http://beta.mnet.co.za/carteblanche/Article.aspx?Id=3279&ShowId=1.

28. Richard Madihlaba and Mareesa Erasmus, Pretoria, 3 September 2008.

29. For an account of garnishee or emoluments attachment orders, see Chapter 2.

30. "R1.1 trillion in debt a 'shocking' burden for SA," *Business Report*, 4 June 2008.

Chapter 6

1. "SA 24th on property rights index," *Business Report*, 24 February 2010.

2. For the extent of such movement and its tendency to center in these areas, see Crankshaw (2008, 2012); for its fragile character, see Steinberg (2008); for the psychic dissonance it can entail, see Matlwa (2007) and Madondo (2007); for a comic take on the phenomenon, see Mda (2009).

3. As discussed later, these "township" houses were originally built by the township municipal authorities and are known locally as "family houses." Occupants tended to be cautious about selling them, viewing them as inalienable homes for the whole family. In a related situation in Malawi, Anders (2009, 55–59) gives the historical background on how housing was set apart from market forces, skewing supply and demand, and discusses the later pressure to "reform" by privatizing this housing.

4. In these additions, the "garage" normally does not house a car but is used as a room by a family member or let out to a tenant.

5. Frank Pule, Soweto, 3 August 2008.

6. Section 26(1) of the Constitution of South Africa Act 108 of 1996.

7. "About Finmark Trust," http://www.finmark.org.za/about/overview-and-facts/.

8. These debates over housing can be found in reports on commissioned research (e.g., Payne et al. 2008, 39; SDMS 2003). Forde's (2011) biography of Julius Malema contains an example of the way family homes are seen in terms of "use" rather than "exchange value." Having enriched himself, Malema wanted to demolish and rebuild his natal home, but his grandmother would not allow it, having struggled to keep it for years previously when her ex-husband had tried to sell it off following their marital breakdown. He built the new elaborate structure around the original house instead, only later getting his way and demolishing the original house.

9. *Jaftha v. Schoeman and Others; van Rooyen v. Stoltz and Others*, 2005(2) SA 140 (CCT 74/03), http://www.saflii.org/za/cases/ZACC/2004/25.html. I am grateful to Glenda Webster for bringing this and the following two cases to my attention.

10. Yolandi Groenewald, "RDP homes 'dead capital' of R50 billion," *City Press*, 9 February 2012; Sandiso Phaliso, "Department finds up to a third of RDP houses illegally occupied," *West Cape News*, 25 November 2010, http://westcapenews.com/?p=2518.

11. *Standard Bank of SA v. Saunderson and Others*, 2006, JOL 16559 (SCA), Case 358/05.

12. *First Rand Bank v. B. L. Smith*, 31 10 2008, High Court of South Africa (Witwatersrand Local Division), Case 24205/08.

13. Material in this chapter comes from Frank Pule, Soweto, 3 August 2008; Sara Leroke, Soweto, 23 April 2009; Dora Usinga, Soweto, 17 April 2009; Joanna Chiloane, Impalahoek, 20 August 2008; Alice Mokgope, Impalahoek, 29 March 2009. The following two cases come from Sara Leroke, Soweto, 23 April 2009, and Dora Usinga, 17 April 2009.

14. See Niehaus (2012, 337–38) for an account of a man from the same area who borrowed from a loan shark to pay for his children's higher education but his son misused the money. Realizing he would never be able to pay the loan shark back, the man committed suicide.

15. Beinart (2012) suggests that communal tenure and cheap access to plots account for these areas having steady and growing populations. Thus—in line with the

way economic activity is driven by consumption rather than production—it is to some extent property rather than employment that has come to influence population movement and migration.

16. Southall (2012, 14–15) categorizes entrepreneurs such as Frank as part of a "black business and trading bourgeoisie" that "combines a mix of owners and managers of medium and small sized businesses, the diversity of this grouping indicated by the fact that at the lower levels, black operators merge into the lower regions of the informal sector of the economy."

17. For accounts of the new elites, see Adam, van Zyl Slabbert, and Moodley (1998); Atkinson (2007); Johnson (2009); Southall (2012).

18. On a 30 November 2012 SAFM phone-in radio show, a caller complained about how the Health Department had been failing to pay people who had successfully tendered to do work, citing the case of a woman who with her husband ran a building contracting business that employed fifteen people. They were owed several million rand but had not been paid. This had severe repercussions on their health and well-being, and she had suffered depression as a result. They had narrowly averted having their house repossessed, and she owed substantial amounts of money to various loan sharks.

19. Michael Bleby, "Black and in business no thanks to empowerment," *Business Day*, 2 June 2008.

20. One of the most famous examples is that of Richard Maponya, owner and founder of Soweto's first supermarket, who disparages how BEE has undermined entrepreneurs' self-reliance. Chris Barron, "BEE killed self-reliance, says Richard Maponya," *Business Day*, 9 December 2012.

21. "Property queen feathers nest on high-end rental," *Business Day*, 23 June 2008.

22. Ibid.

23. Barchiesi (2011, 204) notes a similar tendency for workers with financial problems to cash in their retirement benefits, even seeking redundancy to do so.

24. Rethabile Tlou, Midrand, 15 April 2009.

Chapter 7

1. Since missionaries first arrived at the Cape and later penetrated the heartland, efforts were made to alter people's faith and to change and modernize their habits and practices. Often the latter was more effective than the former: the Tswana were originally more interested in the behavioral attributes of modernity than in the deeper aspects of faith (Comaroff and Comaroff 1991, 1997), but the reshaping of both faith and habit soon followed for many.

2. Many philanthropic and humanitarian NGOs are explicitly church based, and even those with a more secular remit often have a vaguely Christian underpinning (Bornstein 2002, 2003).

3. Rethabile Matome, Soweto, 31 August 2008.

4. On *sekôlôtô*, see Chapter 3.

5. Pastor Mohau Rammile, "God's standing orders," *Financial Seminar*, Global Reconciliation Church, 2009, CD.

6. Pastor C. Matome, "Two financial systems," *Living Word International*, 15 March 2009, CD.

7. Rammile, "God's standing orders."

8. Other biblical episodes, such as the raising of Lazarus from the dead, have been evoked by Pentecostals in support of "the virtues of assertiveness and the evils of giving up" (Barchiesi 2011, 203).

9. The points on this and subsequent pages are from Kopano Twala, Pretoria, 21 April 2009, and Sello Morake, Pretoria, 19 April 2009.

10. Phone-in show on finance, Radio 2000, 9 January 2013.

11. Dawn Jackson, Cape Town, 13 August 2008.

12. Phone-in show on finance, Radio 2000, 9 January 2013.

Conclusion

1. The contradictory juncture of political liberation and economic liberalization has been analyzed by Comaroff and Comaroff (2001).

2. See Chapter 2, especially note 16. I am grateful to Keith Breckenridge for this suggestion.

3. Margaret Atwood, "Our faith is fraying in the god of money," *Financial Times*, 13 April 2012.

4. For an illuminating account of discourses of dependency in southern Africa, see Ferguson (2013).

5. As this book was going to press, one of the unsecured lenders whose rise was detailed in Chapter 2, African Bank Investments Limited (Abil), was placed under curatorship. On 19 August 2014, as a result of the government's having been forced to bail out this troubled lender, Moody's downgraded South Africa's "big four" banks by one notch to Baa1. The financial strength rating of Capitec, the largest unsecured lender left standing after African Bank's collapse, was also slashed by two notches. Agency Staff, "Moody's downgrades Standard Bank, Absa, FNB and Nedbank," *Business Day*, 19 August 2014. In seeming disregard, one of its executives, Tami Sokutu, estimated to have made more than R50 million in share options alone during more than a decade at the bank, indicated that he cared little about those blacklisted because of their inability to repay, or investors whose savings in the sector overall would now be affected. Thekiso Anthony Lefifi, "'F*** the poor!' is the message from a top executive at African Bank," *Times Live*, 17 August 2014. The former CEO, Leon Kirkinis, defended the industry, saying "that the unsecured lending market had grown from about R30bn in 2006 to over R159bn by 2012" (see page 247, note 8). However, Tim Cohen of the *Financial Mail* pointed out that "we now know . . . that this level of microlending is unsustainable." Tim Cohen, "Editor's note: Un-Abil to unwind," *Financial Mail*, 14 August 2014.

Bibliography

Adam, Heribert, Frederick van Zyl Slabbert, and Kagila Moodley. 1998. *Comrades in Business: Post-Liberation Politics in South Africa*. Utrecht, The Netherlands: International Books.

Ainslie, Andrew. 2012. Harnessing the ancestors: Uncertainty and ritual practice in the Eastern Cape Province. Paper presented at European Association of Social Anthropologists conference, 10–13 July, Nanterre.

Anders, Gerhard. 2009. *In the Shadow of Good Governance: An Ethnography of Civil Service Reform in Africa*. Leiden, The Netherlands: Brill.

Anderson, Allan. 2004. *An Introduction to Pentecostalism: Global Charismatic Christianity*. Cambridge: Cambridge University Press.

Anita Heeren, G., John B. Jemmott III, Joanne C. Tyler, Sonwabo Tshabe, and Zolani Ngwane. 2011. Cattle for wives and extramarital trysts for husbands? Lobola, men, and HIV/STD risk behavior in southern Africa. *Journal of Human Behavior in the Social Environment*. 21(1): 73–81.

Ardener, Shirley. 2010. Microcredit, money transfers, women, and the Cameroon diaspora. *Afrika Focus* 23(2): 11–24.

Ardington, Cally, David Lam, Murray Leibbrandt, and James Levinsohn. 2004. Savings, insurance and debt over the post-apartheid period: A review of recent research. *South African Journal of Economics* 72(3): 604–40.

Atkinson, Doreen. 2007. Taking to the streets: Has developmental local government failed in South Africa? In *State of the Nation: South Africa 2007*, eds. Sakhela Buhlungu, John Daniel, and Roger Southall, 53–77. Pretoria: HSRC Press.

Bähre, Erik. 2007. *Money and Violence: Financial Self-Help Groups in a South African Township*. Leiden, The Netherlands: Brill.

———. 2011. Liberation and redistribution: Social grants, commercial insurance, and religious riches in South Africa. *Comparative Studies in Society and History* 53(2): 371–92.

———. 2012. The Janus face of insurances in South Africa: From costs to risk, from networks to bureaucracies. *Africa* 82(1): 147–64.

Bahri, Girum. 2008. Ensuring personal financial wellness: A range of intervention measures and the role of voluntary approaches. In *Employee Financial Wellness: A Corporate Social Responsibility*, ed. Elsa Crous, 7–17. Pretoria: GTZ (Deutsche Gesellschaft für Technische).

Bank, Leslie J. 2011. *Home Spaces, Street Styles: Contesting Power and Identity in a South African City.* London: Pluto.

Barchiesi, Franco. 2011. *Precarious Liberation: Workers, the State, and Contested Social Citizenship in Postapartheid South Africa.* Albany: State University of New York Press.

Beinart, William. 1979. European traders and the Mpondo paramountcy, 1878–1886. *Journal of African History* 20(4): 471–86.

———. 1986. Settler accumulation in East Griqualand from the demise of the Griqua to the Natives Land Act. In *Putting a Plough to the Ground: Accumulation and Dispossession in Rural South Africa, 1850–1930*, eds. William Beinart, Peter Delius, and Stanley Trapido, 259–310. Johannesburg: Ravan Press.

———. 2012. Beyond "homelands": Some ideas about the history of African rural areas in South Africa. *South African Historical Journal* 64(1): 5–21.

Beinart, William, and Peter Delius. 1986. Introduction to *Putting a Plough to the Ground: Accumulation and Dispossession in Rural South Africa, 1850–1930*, eds. William Beinart, Peter Delius, and Stanley Trapido, 1–55. Johannesburg: Ravan Press.

Bernstein, Ann. 2008. *Under the radar? Pentecostalism in South Africa and its potential social and economic role.* CDE Indepth No. 7. Johannesburg: Centre for Development Enterprise. http://www.cde.org.za/publications/jobs-growth/83-jobs-and-growth/180-under-the-radar-pentecostalism-in-south-africa-and-its-potential-social-and-economic-role.

Bernstein, Ann, and Stephen Rule. 2011. Flying under South Africa's radar: The growth and impact of Pentecostals in a developing country. In *The Hidden Form of Capital: Spiritual Influences in Societal Progress*, eds. Peter L Berger and Gordon Redding, 91–130. London: Anthem Press.

Bernstein, Henry. 1996. South Africa's agrarian question: Extreme and exceptional? *Journal of Peasant Studies* 23(2–3): 1–52.

Berry, Sara. 1985. *Fathers Work for Their Sons: Accumulation, Mobility, and Class Formation in an Extended Yorùbá Community.* Los Angeles: University of California Press.

Besley, Tim, Stephen Coate, and Glenn Loury. 1993. The Economics of Rotating Savings and Credit Associations. *American Economic Review* 83(4): 792–810.

———. 1994. Rotating savings and credit associations, credit markets and efficiency. *Review of Economic Studies* 61(4): 701–19.

Besnier, Nico. 2011. *On the Edge of the Global: Modern Anxieties in a Pacific Island Nation.* Contemporary Issues in Asia and the Pacific, an East–West Center Series. Stanford, CA: Stanford University Press.

Bolt, Maxim. 2012. Waged entrepreneurs, policed informality: Work, the regulation of space and the economy of the Zimbabwean–South African border. *Africa* 82(1): 109–28.

Bond, Patrick. 2000. *Elite Transition: From Apartheid to Neoliberalism in South Africa.* London: Pluto Press.

Boraine, André, and Melanie Roestoff. 2002. Fresh start procedures for consumer debtors in South African bankruptcy law. *International Insolvency Review* 11(1): 1–11.

Bornstein, Erica. 2002. Developing faith: Theologies of economic development in Zimbabwe. *Journal of Religion in Africa* 32(1): 4–31.

———. 2003. *The Spirit of Development: Protestant NGOs, Morality, and Economics in Zimbabwe.* New York: Routledge.

Bozzoli, Belinda. 1983. Marxism, feminism and South African studies. *Journal of Southern African Studies* 9(2): 139–71.

Bozzoli, Belinda, with M. Nkotsoe. 1991. *Women of Phokeng: Consciousness, Life Strategy and Migrancy in South Africa 1900–1983.* Johannesburg: Ravan Press.

Brandel, Mia. 1958. Urban lobolo attitudes: A preliminary report. *African Studies* 17: 34–51.

Brandel-Syrier, Mia. 1978. *"Coming Through": The Search for a New Cultural Identity.* New York: McGraw-Hill.

Breckenridge, Keith. 2005. The biometric state: The promise and peril of digital government in the New South Africa. *Journal of Southern African Studies* 31(2): 267–82.

———. 2010. The world's first biometric money: Ghana's E-Zwich and the contemporary influence of South African biometrics. *Africa* 80(4): 642–62.

Breen, Richard. 2005. Foundations of a neo-Weberian class analysis. In *Approaches to Class Analysis*, ed. Erik Olin Wright, 31–50. Cambridge: Cambridge University Press.

Cameron, Jenny, and Katherine Gibson. 2005. Building community economies in marginalised areas. In *Community and Local Governance in Australia*, eds. P. Smyth, T. Reddel, and A. Jones, 149–66. Sydney: University of New South Wales Press.

Camic, Charles, Philip S. Gorski, and David M. Trubek. 2005. Introduction to *Max Weber's "Economy and Society,"* eds. Charles Camic, Philip S. Gorski, and David M. Trubek, 1–28. Stanford, CA: Stanford University Press.

Carton, Benedict. 2000. *Blood from Your Children: The Colonial Origins of Generational Conflict.* Charlottesville: University of Virginia Press.

Chevalier, Sophie. 2010. Les black diamonds existent-ils? Médias, consommation et classe moyenne noire en Afrique du Sud. *Sociologies Pratiques* 20: 75–86.

Chipkin, I. 2003 "'Functional" and "dysfunctional" communities: The making of national citizens. *Journal of Southern African Studies* 29(1): 63–82.

Clark, Nancy. 1994. *Manufacturing Apartheid: State Corporations in South Africa*. New Haven, CT: Yale University Press.

Cobley, Alan Gregor. 1990. *Class and Consciousness: The Black Petty Bourgeoisie in South Africa, 1924 to 1950*. New York: Greenwood Press.

Cohen, David. 2004. *People Who Have Stolen from Me: Rough Justice in the New South Africa*. London: St. Martin's Press.

Cohen, Shana. 2004. *Searching for a Different Future: The Rise of a Global Middle Class in Morocco*. Durham, NC: Duke University Press.

Collins, Darryl. 2008. Debt and household finance: Evidence from the financial diaries. *Development Southern Africa* 25(4): 469–79.

Collins, Darryl, Jonathan Morduch, Stuart Rutherford, and Orlanda Ruthven. 2010. *Portfolios of the Poor: How the World's Poor Live on $2 a Day*. Princeton, NJ: Princeton University Press.

Comaroff, Jean. 2012. Pentecostalism, populism and the new politics of affect. In *Pentecostalism and Development: Churches, NGOs and Social Change in Africa*, ed. Dena Freeman, 41–66. London: Palgrave Macmillan.

Comaroff, Jean, and John L. Comaroff. 1987. The madman and the migrant: Work and labour in the historical consciousness of a South African people. *American Ethnologist* 14(2): 191–209.

———. 1991. *Of Revelation and Revolution: Christianity, Colonialism and Consciousness in South Africa*. Vol. 1. Chicago: University of Chicago Press.

———. 1997. *Of Revelation and Revolution: The Dialectics of Modernity on a South African Frontier*. Vol. 2. Chicago: University of Chicago Press.

———. 2000. Millennial capitalism: First thoughts on a second coming. *Public Culture* 12(2): 291–343.

———. 2001. *Millennial Capitalism and the Culture of Neoliberalism*. Durham, NC: Duke University Press.

Comaroff, John L. 1998. Reflections on the colonial state, in South Africa and elsewhere: Factions, fragments, facts and fictions. *Social Identities* 4(3): 321–61.

Cooper, Frederick. 2002. *Africa Since 1940: The Past of the Present*. Cambridge: Cambridge University Press.

Cramer, Christopher, Deborah Johnston, and Carlos Oya. 2009. Africa and the credit crunch: From crisis to opportunity? *African Affairs* 108(433): 643–54.

Crankshaw, Owen. 2005. Class, race and residence in black Johannesburg, 1923–1970. *Journal of Historical Sociology* 18(4): 353–93.

———. 2008. Race, space and the post-Fordist spatial order of Johannesburg. *Urban Studies* 45(8): 1692–1711.

————. 2012. Deindustrialization and racial inequality in Cape Town. *Urban Affairs Review* 48(6): 836–62.

Crous, E., ed. 2008. *Employee Financial Wellness: A Corporate Social Responsibility.* Pretoria: GTZ (Deutsche Gesellschaft für Technische Zusammenarbeit).

Daniels, Reza. 2004. Financial intermediation, regulation and the formal microcredit sector in South Africa. *Development Southern Africa* 21(5): 831–49.

de Haas, M. 1987. Is there anything more to say about lobolo? *African Studies.* 46(1): 33–55.

Dent, G. R., and C. L. S. Nyembezi. 1969. *Scholars' Zulu Dictionary.* Cape Town: Shuter and Shooter.

Department of Trade and Industry, with Reality Research Africa. 2002. *Credit Contract Disclosure and Associated Factors.* Pretoria: Department of Trade and Industry.

Department of Trade and Industry. 2004. *Consumer Credit Law Reform: Policy Framework for Consumer Credit.* Pretoria: Department of Trade and Industry.

de Soto, Hernando. 2002. *The Mystery of Capital: Why Capitalism Triumphs in the West and Fails Everywhere Else.* London: Black Swan.

de Wet, Chris. 2013. Land administration, resettlement and local socio-economic change, against the background of the Land Acts of 1913 and 1936: An Eastern Cape case study. Paper presented at Land Divided conference, 24–27 March, Cape Town.

Dooling, Wayne. 2008. *Slavery, Emancipation and Colonial Rule in South Africa.* Athens: Ohio University Press.

Du Plessis, M. A. 2007. The National Credit Act: Debt counselling may prove to be a risky enterprise. *Journal for Juridical Science* 32(2): 76–94.

Edwards, Jeanette, Gillian Evans, and Katherine Smith. 2012. Introduction: The middle classification of Britain. *Focaal—Journal of Global and Historical Anthropology* 62: 3–16.

Evens, T. M. S., and D. Handelman. 2006. *The Manchester School: Practice and Ethnographic Praxis in Anthropology.* New York: Berghahn Books.

Fakier, Khayaat, and Jacklyn Cock. 2009. A gendered analysis of the crisis of social reproduction in contemporary South Africa, *International Feminist Journal of Politics* 11(3): 353–71.

Falk Moore, Sally. 1973. Law and social change: The semi-autonomous social field as an appropriate field of study. *Law and Society Review* 7(4): 719–46.

————. 2011. The legislative dismantling of a colonial and an apartheid state. *Annual Review of Law and Social Science* 7: 1–15.

Feinstein, Charles H. 2005. *An Economic History of South Africa: Conquest, Discrimination, and Development.* Cambridge: Cambridge University Press.

Ferguson, James. 1992. The cultural topography of wealth: Commodity paths and the structure of property in rural Lesotho. *American Anthropologist* 94(1): 55–73.

————. 1999. *Expectations of Modernity*. Berkeley: University of California Press.

————. 2010a. The uses of neoliberalism. *Antipode* 41(suppl. 1): 166–84.

————. 2010b. What comes after the social? Historicizing the future of social assistance in Africa. Mimeo.

————. 2013. Declarations of dependence: Labour, personhood, and welfare in southern Africa. *Journal of the Royal Anthropological Institute* 19: 223–42.

First, Ruth. 1983. *Black Gold: The Mozambican Miner, Proletarian and Peasant*. New York: St. Martin's Press.

Fisher, William. 1997. Doing good? The politics and anti-politics of NGO practices. *Annual Review of Anthropology* 26: 439–64.

Forde, Fiona. 2011. *An Inconvenient Youth: Julius Malema and the "New" ANC*. Johannesburg: Picador Africa.

Foucault, Michel. 1991. Governmentality. In *The Foucault Effect: Studies in Governmentality*, eds. G. Burchell, C. Gordon, and P. Miller, 87–104. Chicago: University of Chicago Press.

Freeman, Dena. 2012. The Pentecostal ethic and the spirit of development. In *Pentecostalism and Development: Churches, NGOs and Social Change in Africa*, ed. Dena Freeman, 1–40. London: Palgrave Macmillan.

Freund, W. 2013. A ghost from the past: The South African developmental state of the 1940s. Paper presented at the conference "The Human Economy: Economy and Democracy," University of Pretoria.

Fuller, C. J., and Haripriya Narasimhan. 2014. *Tamil Brahmans: The Making of a Middle-Class Caste*. Chicago: University of Chicago Press.

Geertz, Clifford. 1962. The rotating credit association: A "middle rung" in development. *Economic Development and Cultural Change* 10(3): 241–63.

Genovese, Eugene. 1976. *Roll Jordan Roll: The World the Slaves Made*. New York: Vintage.

Ginsberg, R. 1996. "Now I stay in a house": Renovating the matchbox in apartheid-era Soweto. *African Studies* 55(2): 127–39.

Gluckman, Max. 1950. Kinship and marriage among the Lozi of Northern Rhodesia and the Zulu of Natal. In *African Systems of Kinship and Marriage*, eds. A. R. Radcliffe Brown and D. Forde, 166–206. London: Oxford University Press.

Goody, Jack. 1971. Class and marriage in Africa and Eurasia. *American Journal of Sociology* 76(4): 585–603.

————. 1976. *Production and Reproduction: A Comparative Study of the Domestic Domain*. Cambridge: Cambridge University Press.

Graeber, David. 2011. *Debt: The First 5,000 Years*. New York: Melville House.

————. 2013. *The Democracy Project: A History, a Crisis, a Movement*. New York: Spiegel & Grau.

Gregory, Chris A. 2012. On money debt and morality: Some reflections on the contribution of economic anthropology. *Social Anthropology* 20(4): 380–96.

Grusky, David, with Gabriela Galescu. 2005. Foundations of a neo-Durkheimian class analysis. In *Approaches to Class Analysis*, ed. Erik Olin Wright, 51–81. Cambridge: Cambridge University Press.

Gudeman, Stephen. 2001. *The Anthropology of Economy*. Oxford, UK: Blackwell.

———. 2008. *Economy's Tension: The Dialectics of Market and Economy*. New York: Berghahn Books.

———. 2010. A cosmopolitan anthropology? In *Culture Wars: Context, Models, and Anthropologists' Accounts*, eds. Deborah James, Christina Toren, and Evelyn Plaice, 136–51. New York: Berghahn Books.

Guérin, Isabelle. 2014. Juggling with debt, social ties, and values: The everyday use of microcredit in rural south India. *Current Anthropology* 55, Supplement 9: S40–S50.

Guérin, Isabelle, Solène Morvant-Roux, and Magdalena Villarreal, eds. 2013. *Microfinance, Debt and Over-Indebtedness: Juggling with Money*. London: Routledge.

Guyer, J. 1993. Wealth in people and self-realization in equatorial Africa. *Man* 28(2): 243–65.

———, ed. 1995. *Money Matters: Instability, Values and Social Payments in the Modern History of West African Communities*. London: Heinemann.

———. 2004. *Marginal Gains: Monetary Transactions in Atlantic Africa*. Chicago: University of Chicago Press.

Guyer, Jane, and Endre Stiansen, eds. 1999. *Credit, Currencies and Culture: African Financial Institutions in Historical Perspective*. Uppsala, Sweden: Nordiska Afrikainstitutet.

Hann, Chris, and Keith Hart. 2011. *Economic Anthropology: History, Ethnography, Critique*. Cambridge, UK: Polity.

Hart, Keith. 1973. Informal income opportunities and urban employment in Ghana. *Journal of Modern African Studies* 11(1): 61–89.

———. 1999. *The Memory Bank: Money in an Unequal World*. London: Profile Books.

———. 2010. Informal economy. In *The Human Economy: A Citizen's Guide*, eds. Keith Hart, Jean-Louis Laville, and Antonio David Cattani, 142–54. Cambridge, UK: Polity.

Hart, Keith, Jean-Louis Laville, and Antonio David Cattani. 2010. Building the human economy together. In *The Human Economy: A Citizen's Guide*, eds. Keith Hart, Jean-Louis Laville, and Antonio David Cattani, 1–20. Cambridge, UK: Polity.

Hart, Keith, and Vishnu Padayachee. 2000. Indian business in South Africa after apartheid: New and old trajectories. *Comparative Studies in Society and History* 42(4): 683–712.

Harvey, David. 2005. *A Brief History of Neoliberalism*. Oxford: Oxford University Press.

Haupt, Frans, and Hermie Coetzee. 2008. The emoluments attachment order and the employer. In *Employee Financial Wellness: A Corporate Social Responsibility*, ed.

E. Crous, 81–92. Pretoria: GTZ (Deutsche Gesellschaft für Technische Zusammen-arbeit).

Haupt, Frans, Hermie Coetzee, Dawid de Villiers, and Jeanne-Mari Fouché. 2008. *The Incidence of and the Undesirable Practices Relating to Garnishee Orders in South Africa.* Pretoria: GTZ (Deutsche Gesellschaft für Technische Zusammenarbeit).

Houghton, Hobart. 1976. *The South African Economy.* Cape Town: Oxford University Press.

Hull, Elizabeth. 2010. International migration, "domestic struggles" and status aspiration among nurses in South Africa. *Journal of Southern African Studies* 36(4): 851–67.

———. 2012. Banking in the bush: Waiting for credit in South Africa's rural economy. *Africa* 82(1): 165–83.

Hull, Elizabeth, and Deborah James. 2012. Introduction: Local economies and citizen expectations in South Africa. *Africa* 82(1): 1–19.

Hunter, Mark. 2006. Fathers without amandla: Zulu-speaking men and fatherhood. In *Baba? Men and Fatherhood in South Africa,* eds. Linda Richter and Robert Morrell, 99–107. Cape Town: HSRC Press.

Hurwitz, Ingrid, and John Luis. 2007. Urban working class credit usage and over-indebtedness in South Africa. *Journal of Southern African Studies* 33(1): 107–31.

James, Deborah. 2002. "To take the information down to the people": Life skills and HIV/AIDS peer-educators in the Durban area. *African Studies* 61(1): 169–91.

———. 2007. *Gaining Ground? "Rights" and "Property" in South African Land Reform.* London: Routledge.

———. 2009. Making money from nothing. Paper presented at first "Popular Economies" workshop, London School of Economics.

———. 2011. The return of the broker: Consensus, hierarchy and choice in South African land reform. *Journal of the Royal Anthropological Institute* 17: 318–38.

———. 2012. Money-go-round: Personal economies of wealth, aspiration and indebtedness in South Africa. *Africa* 82(1): 20–40.

———. 2013a. Citizenship and land in South Africa: From rights to responsibilities. *Critique of Anthropology* 33(1): 26–46.

———. 2013b. Regulating credit: Tackling the redistributiveness of neoliberalism. *Anthropology of This Century* 6. http://aotcpress.com/articles/regulating-credit -tackling-redistributiveness-neoliberalism/.

James, Deborah, with Geoffrey Mphahle Nkadimeng. 2003a. The land and the word: Missions, African Christians, and the claiming of land in South Africa. In *Orality, Literacy and Colonialism in Southern Africa,* ed. Jonathan Draper, 111–33. Leiden, The Netherlands: Brill Press.

———. 2003b. "A sentimental attachment to the neighbourhood": African Christians and land claims in South Africa. *Itinerario: European Journal of Overseas History* 27(3–4): 243–62.

Jensen, Steffen. 2012. This house is not my own: On tradition and history in former KaNgwane. Paper presented at European Association of Social Anthropologists conference, 10–13 July, Nanterre.

Johnson, R. W. 2009. *South Africa's Brave New World: The Beloved Country Since the End of Apartheid.* Harmondsworth, UK: Penguin.

Kaplan, Mendel. 1986. *Jewish Roots in the South African Economy.* Cape Town: C. Struik.

Khunou, Grace. 2006. Maintenance and changing masculinities as sources of gender conflict in contemporary Johannesburg. Unpublished D.Phil. diss., University of the Witwatersrand, Johannesburg. http://wiredspace.wits.ac.za/bitstream/handle/10539/4651/khunougracethesis.pdf?sequence=2.

———. 2012. Money and gender relations in the South African maintenance system. *South African Review of Sociology* 43(1): 4–22.

Kibuuka, L. E. 2006. Informal finance for the middle and high income individuals in South Africa: A case study of high budget "stokvels" in Pretoria. MSc diss., University of Pretoria.

Kiernan, J. P. 1988. The other side of the coin: The conversion of money to religious purposes in Zulu Zionist churches. *Man* 23(3): 453–68.

Kipnis, Andrew. 2007. Neoliberalism reified: *Suzhi* discourse and tropes of neoliberalism in the People's Republic of China. *Journal of the Royal Anthropological Institute* 13: 383–400.

Krige, D. 2009. Black diamonds are not forever: Neo-liberal explanations of social change and the South African "black middle class." Paper delivered at 3rd European Conference on African Studies, 4–7 June, Leipzig, Germany.

———. 2011. Power, identity and agency at work in the popular economies of Soweto and Black Johannesburg. D.Phil. diss., University of the Witwatersrand, Johannesburg. http://wiredspace.wits.ac.za/handle/10539/10143.

———. 2012. Fields of dreams, fields of schemes: Ponzi finance and multilevel marketing in South Africa. *Africa* 82(1): 68–90.

———. Forthcoming. Letting money work for us: Self-organization and financialisation from below in an all-male savings club in Soweto. In *People, Money and Power in the Economic Crisis*, eds. Keith Hart and John Sharp. New York: Berghahn Books.

Krige, E. J., and J. D. Krige. 1943. *The Realm of a Rain Queen.* London: International African Institute.

Kuper, Adam. 1982. *Wives for Cattle: Bridewealth and Marriage in Southern Africa.* London: Routledge and Kegan Paul.

Kuper, Hilda, and Selma Kaplan. 1944. Voluntary associations in an urban township. *African Studies* 3(4): 178–86.

Kuper, Leo. 1965. *An African Bourgeoisie: Race, Class, and Politics in South Africa.* Cambridge: Cambridge University Press.

Lanchester, John. 2010. *Whoops! Why Everyone Owes Everyone and No One Can Pay.* Harmondsworth, UK: Penguin.

Little, K. 1957. The role of voluntary associations in West African urbanization. *American Anthropologist* 59(4): 579–96.

MacGaffey, Janet, and Rémy Bazenguissa-Ganga. 2000. *Congo-Paris: Transnational Traders on the Margins of the Law.* Oxford, UK: James Currey.

Madondo, Bongani. 2007. *Hot Type: Icons, Artists and God-Figurines.* Johannesburg: Pan Mac Picador.

Mager, Anne Kelk. 2010. *Beer, Sociability, and Masculinity in South Africa.* Bloomington: Indiana University Press.

Makwakwa, Vangile. 2013. *Heart, Mind and Money: Using Emotional Intelligence for Financial Success.* Cape Town: Jacana.

Marais, Hein. 2001. *South Africa: Limits to Change—The Political Economy of Transition.* 2nd ed. London: Zed Books.

———. 2011. *South Africa Pushed to the Limit: The Political Economy of Change.* London: Zed Books.

Martin, Nicholas. 2010. Class, patronage and coercion in the Pakistani Punjab and in Swat. In *Beyond Swat: History, Society and Economy along the Afghanistan-Pakistan Frontier*, eds. Benjamin Hopkins and Magnus Marsden, 107–18. London: Hurst.

Matlwa, Kopano. 2007. *Coconut.* Johannesburg: Jacana Media.

Maurer, Bill. 2012. Mobile money: Communication, consumption and change in the payments space. *Journal of Development Studies* 48(5): 589–604.

Mbembe, Achille. 2004. Aesthetics of superfluity. *Public Culture* 16(3): 373–406.

McAllister, Patrick. 1980. Work, homestead and the shades: The ritual interpretation of labour migration among the Gcaleka. In *Black Villagers in an Industrial Society*, ed. Philip Mayer, 205–53. Oxford: Oxford University Press.

McNeill, Fraser G. 2011. *AIDS, Politics and Music in South Africa.* Cambridge: International African Library, Cambridge University Press.

———. 2012. Making music, making money: Informal musical production and performance in Venda, South Africa. *Africa* 82(1): 91–108.

Mda, Zakes. 2009. *Black Diamond.* Harmondsworth, UK: Penguin.

Meintjes, Helen. 2001. "Washing machines make lazy women": Domestic appliances and the negotiation of women's propriety in Soweto. *Journal of Material Culture* 6(3): 345–63.

Morrell, Robert. 1986. Competition and cooperation in Middelburg 1900–1930. In *Putting a Plough to the Ground: Accumulation and Dispossession in Rural South Africa, 1850–1930*, eds. William Beinart, Peter Delius, and Stanley Trapido. Johannesburg: Ravan Press.

Mosotho, Mehlaleng. 1998. *The Tikieline Yuppie.* Florida, South Africa: Vivlia.

Mosse, David. 2004. *Cultivating Development: An Ethnography of Aid Policy and Practice.* London: Pluto Press.

Murray, Colin. 1992. *Black Mountain: Land, Class and Power in the Eastern Orange Free State 1880s–1980s.* Johannesburg: Witwatersrand University Press.

Murray Li, Tania. 2010. Indigeneity, capitalism, and the management of dispossession. *Current Anthropology* 51(3): 385–414.

Nader, Ralph. 2000. *The Ralph Nader Reader.* New York: Seven Stories Press.

Ndumo, Phumelelo. 2011. *From Debt to Riches: Steps to Financial Success.* Johannesburg: Jacana.

Neves, D., M. Samson, I. Van Niekerk, S. Hlatshwayo, and A. du Toit. 2010. The use and effectiveness of social grants in South Africa. Research Report No. 8. Johannesburg: Finmark Trust.

Neves, David, and Andries du Toit. 2012. Money and sociality in South Africa's informal economy. *Africa* 82(1): 129–46.

Niehaus, Isak. 2012. Gendered endings: Narratives of male and female suicides in the South African Lowveld. *Culture, Medicine and Psychiatry* 36: 327–47.

———. 2013. *Witchcraft and a Life in the New South Africa.* Cambridge: Cambridge University Press.

Niehaus, Isak, with Eliazaar Mohlala and Kally Shokane. 2001. *Witchcraft, Power and Politics: Exploring the Occult in the South African Lowveld.* London: Pluto Press.

Nuttall, Sarah. 2004. Stylizing the self: The Y generation in Rosebank, Johannesburg. *Public Culture* 16(3): 430–52.

Oboler, Regina Smith. 1994. The house-property complex and African social organisation. *Africa* 64(3): 342–58.

Olin Wright, Erik. 1997. *Class Counts: Comparative Studies in Class Analysis,* Cambridge: Cambridge University Press.

———. 2005. Foundations of a neo-Marxist class analysis. In *Approaches to Class Analysis,* ed. Erik Olin Wright, 4–30. Cambridge: Cambridge University Press.

Parry, Jonathan. 2012. Suicide in a central Indian steel town. *Contributions to Indian Sociology.* 46(1–2): 145–80.

Parry, Jonathan, and Maurice Bloch. 1989. Introduction: Money and the morality of exchange. In *Money and the Morality of Exchange,* eds. Jonathan Parry and Maurice Bloch, 1–32. Cambridge: Cambridge University Press.

Pauw, B. A. 1963. *The Second Generation.* Cape Town: Oxford University Press.

Payne, Geoffrey, Alain Durand-Laserve, Carole Rakodi, with Colin Marx, Margot Rubin, and Selle Ndiaye. 2008. Social and economic impacts of land titling programmes in urban and peri-urban areas: International experience and case studies of Senegal and South Africa. Report submitted to Ministry of Foreign Affairs, Government of Norway; Swedish International Development Agency; and Global Land Tools Network, UN-Habitat.

Peebles, Gustav. 2010. The anthropology of credit and debt. *Annual Review of Anthropology* 39: 225–40.

Phadi, Mosa, and Claire Ceruti. 2011. Multiple meanings of the middle class in Soweto, South Africa. *African Sociological Review* 15(1): 88–108.

Phillips, Ray E. 1938. *The Bantu in the City: A Study of Cultural Adjustment on the Witwatersrand.* Alice, South Africa: Lovedale Press.

Piot, Charles. 2014. Hedging the future. Paper presented at a Wits Institute of Social and Economic Research seminar, University of the Witwatersrand, Johannesburg, 26 March.

Porteous, David, with Ethel Hazelhurst. 2004. *Banking on Change: Democratizing Finance in South Africa, 1994–2004 and Beyond.* Cape Town: Double Storey Books.

Posel, Deborah. 2010. Races to consume: Revisiting South Africa's history of race, consumption and the struggle for freedom. *Ethnic and Racial Studies* 23(2) 157–75.

Prahalad, C. K. 2006. *The Fortune at the Bottom of the Pyramid: Eradicating Poverty through Profits.* Upper Saddle River, NJ: Prentice Hall.

Rajak, Dinah. 2011. *In Good Company: An Anatomy of Corporate Social Responsibility.* Palo Alto, CA: Stanford University Press.

Reinke, Jens. 1998. How to lend like mad and make a profit: A micro-credit paradigm versus the start-up fund South Africa. *Journal of Development Studies* 34(3): 44–61.

Robins, Steven. 2002. Planning "suburban bliss" in Joe Slovo Park, Cape Town. *Africa* 72(4): 511–48.

Ross, Robert. 1986. The origins of capitalist agriculture in the Cape Colony: A survey. In *Putting a Plough to the Ground: Accumulation and Dispossession in Rural South Africa, 1850–1930*, eds. William Beinart, Peter Delius, and Stanley Trapido, 57–100. Johannesburg: Ravan Press.

———. 1999. *Status and Respectability at the Cape of Good Hope: A Tragedy of Manners.* Cambridge: Cambridge University Press.

———. 2008. *Clothing: A Global History; or, The Imperialists' New Clothes.* Cambridge, UK: Polity.

Roth, James. 2004. Spoilt for choice: Financial services in an African township. PhD diss., University of Cambridge.

Sanders, Todd. 2008. Buses in Bongoland: Seductive analytics and the occult. *Journal of Anthropological Theory* 8(2): 107–32.

Schama, Simon. 1987. *The Embarrassment of Riches: An Interpretation of Dutch Culture in the Golden Age.* New York: Alfred A. Knopf.

Schapera, Isaac. 1947. *Migrant Labour and Tribal Life.* London: Oxford University Press.

Schlemmer, Laurence. 2005. Lost in transformation? South Africa's emerging African middle class. Occasional Paper 8. Johannesburg: Centre for Development and Enterprise.

———. 2008. Pentecostal power in South Africa. Speech to the conference "Media & Religion," Johannesburg, 11–12 November 2008. http://themediaproject.org/article/pentecostal-power-south-africa-full-text-speech?page=0,0.

Schoombee, Andrie. 2004. South African banks and the unbanked: Progress and prospects. *South African Journal of Economics* 72(3): 581–603.

———. 2009. Access to formal financial services for South Africa's poor: Developments since 1990. *South African Journal of Economic History* 24(2): 131–56.

Schraten, Jürgen. Forthcoming. Habits of austerity: Monetarism and new ways of dealing with money. In *Economy for and Against Democracy*, eds. Keith Hart and John Sharp. New York: Berghahn Books.

Schreiner, Mark, Douglas H. Graham, Manuel Cortes Font-Cuberta, Gerhard Coetzee, and Nick Vink. 1997. Racial discrimination in hire/purchase lending in apartheid South Africa. paper presented at meeting of the American Agricultural Economics Association, 27–30 July, Toronto, ON.

Scorgie, F. 2004. Mobilising tradition in the post-apartheid era: *Amasiko*, AIDS and cultural rights in KwaZulu Natal, South Africa. PhD diss., Cambridge University.

Seekings, Jeremy. 2009. The rise and fall of the Weberian analysis of class in South Africa between 1949 and the early 1970s. *Journal of Southern African Studies* 35(4): 855–61.

Seekings, Jeremy, and Nicoli Nattrass. 2005. *Class, Race, and Inequality in South Africa*. New Haven, CT: Yale University Press.

Servet, Jean-Michel, and Hadrien Saiag. 2013. Household over-indebtedness in contemporary societies: A macro-perspective. In *Microfinance, Debt and Over-Indebtedness: Juggling with Money*, eds. Isabelle Guérin, Solène Morvant-Roux, and Magdalena Villarreal, 45–66. London: Routledge.

Shah, Alpa. 2010. *In the Shadows of the State: Indigenous Politics, Environmentalism, and Insurgency in Jharkhand, India*. Durham, NC: Duke University Press.

Shipton, Parker. 2007. *The Nature of Entrustment: Intimacy, Exchange and the Sacred in Africa*. New Haven, CT: Yale University Press.

———. 2009. *Mortgaging the Ancestors: Ideologies of Attachment in Africa*. New Haven, CT: Yale University Press.

———. 2011. *Credit Between Cultures: Farmers, Financiers, and Misunderstanding in Africa*. New Haven, CT: Yale University Press.

Shisaka Development Management Services. 2003. Workings of township residential property markets. A research project sponsored by the Finmark Trust, Ford Foundation, Micro Finance Regulatory Council, USAID, South African National Treasury, and the National Housing Finance Corporation.

Shneiderman, Sara. 2011. Debt as a condition of mobility: Preliminary reflections from South Asia. Paper presented at the conference "Debt: Interdisciplinary considerations of an enduring human passion," Centre for Research in the Arts, Social Sciences and Humanities, Cambridge University.

———. 2014. Circular lives: Histories and economies of belonging in the transnational Thangmi Village. In *Facing Globalisation: Belonging in the Himalayas*, eds. Joanna Pfaff-Czarnecka and Gérard Toffin, 63–94. Delhi: Sage Publications.

———. Forthcoming. *Rituals of Ethnicity: Thangmi Identities Between Nepal and India*. Philadelphia: University of Pennsylvania Press.

Siyongwana, Paqama Q. 2004. Informal moneylenders in the Limpopo, Gauteng and Eastern Cape provinces of South Africa. *Development Southern Africa* 21(5): 861–66.

Skhosana, Nokuthula. 2012. The political economy of teenage sexuality in the time of HIV/AIDS: The case of Soweto, South Africa. PhD diss., Witwatersrand University, Johannesburg.

Smit, Anneke. 2008. Administration orders versus debt counselling. LLM diss., University of South Africa.

Southall, Roger. 2004. Political change and the black middle class in democratic South Africa. *Canadian Journal of African Studies* 38(3): 521–42.

———. 2007. The ANC, black economic empowerment and state-owned enterprises: A recycling of history? In *State of the Nation: South Africa 2007*, eds. Sakhela Buhlungu, John Daniel, and Roger Southall, 201–25. Pretoria: HSRC Press.

———. 2012. The ANC: Party vanguard of the black middle class? In *One Hundred Years of the ANC: Debating Liberation Histories Today*, eds. Arianna Lissoni, Jon Soske, Natasha Erlank, Noor Nieftagodien, and Omar Badsha, 325–46. Johannesburg: Wits University Press.

Spiegel, A. D. 1991. Polygyny as myth: Towards understanding extramarital relations in Lesotho. *African Studies* 50(1–2): 145–66.

Stauffer, Carolyn. 2010. Patterns of social reciprocity in the new South Africa. DPhil diss., University of the Witwatersrand, Johannesburg. http://wiredspace.wits.ac.za/bit stream/handle/10539/8583/Official%20WITS%20PhD%20Submission%20-%20June %202010.pdf?sequence=2.

Steinberg, Jonny. 2001. *Crime Wave: The South African Underworld and Its Foes*. Johannesburg: Wits University Press.

———. 2008. *Thin Blue: The Unwritten Rules of Policing South Africa*. Johannesburg: Jonathan Ball.

Tett, Gillian. 2010. *Fool's Gold: How Unrestrained Greed Corrupted a Dream, Shattered Global Markets and Unleashed a Catastrophe*. London: Abacus.

Thomson, Robert J., and Deborah Posel. 2002. The management of risk by burial societies in South Africa. *South African Actuarial Journal* 2: 83–128.

Tlali, Miriam. 1979. *Muriel at Metropolitan*. London: Longman.

Trapido, Stanley. 1978. Landlord and tenant in a colonial economy: The Transvaal 1880–1910. *Journal of Southern African Studies* 5(1): 26–58.

Vally, Natasha. 2013. The social life of grants in South Africa: A case study of Bushbuckridge. Paper presented at the conference "Crossroads in African Studies," 4–6 September, Birmingham, UK.

van Onselen, Charles. 1996. *The Seed Is Mine: The Life of Kas Maine, a South African Sharecropper, 1894–1985*. New York: Hill & Wang.

van Wyk, Ilana. 2012. "Tata Ma Chance": On contingency and the lottery in post-apartheid South Africa. *Africa* 82(1): 68–90.

———. 2014. *A Church of Strangers: Sociality, Ritual and the Success of the Universal Church of the Kingdom of God in South Africa*. Cambridge: International African Library and Cambridge University Press.

Verhoef, Grietjie. 2001. Informal financial service institutions for survival: African women and stokvels in urban South Africa, 1930–1998. *Enterprise and Society* 2(2): 259–96.

———. 2009. Concentration and competition: The changing landscape of the banking sector in South Africa, 1970–2007. *South African Journal of Economic History* 24(2): 157–97.

Villarreal, Magdalena. 2014. Regimes of value in Mexican household financial practices. *Current Anthropology* 55, Supplement 9: S30–S39.

Von Holdt, Karl. 2010. Nationalism, bureaucracy and the developmental state: The South African case. *South African Review of Sociology* 41(1): 4–27.

von Schnitzler, Antina. 2008. Citizenship prepaid: Water, calculability and techno-politics in South Africa. *Journal of Southern African Studies* 34(4): 899–917.

Weber, Max. (1905) 2002. *The Protestant Ethic and the Spirit of Capitalism*. Harmondsworth, UK: Penguin.

Whelan, Deborah. 2011. Trading lives: The commercial, social and political communities of the Zululand trading store. PhD diss., University of London.

White, Hylton. 2004. Ritual haunts: The timing of estrangement in a post-apartheid countryside. In *Producing African Futures*, ed. Brad Weiss, 141–66. Leiden, The Netherlands: Brill.

———. 2010. Outside the dwelling of culture: Estrangement and difference in postcolonial Zululand. *Anthropological Quarterly* 83(3): 497–518.

———. 2011. Youth unemployment and intergenerational ties. Paper presented to workshop "Making Youth Development Policies Work," Centre for Development Enterprise, Johannesburg.

———. 2012a. A post-Fordist ethnicity: Insecurity, authority and identity in South Africa. *Anthropological Quarterly* 85(2): 397–427.

———. 2012b. Value, solidarity, and life course in South Africa. Paper presented at European Association of Social Anthropologists conference, 10–13 July, Nanterre.

Wiggins, Mary Jo Newborn. 1997. Rethinking the structure of insolvency law in South Africa. *New York Law School Journal of International and Comparative Law* 17: 509–13.

Williams, Brett. 2004. *Debt for Sale: A Social History of the Credit Trap.* Philadelphia: University of Pennsylvania Press.

Wilson, Monica, and Archie Mafeje. 1963. *Langa: A Study of Social Groups in an African Township.* Cape Town: Oxford University Press.

Wilson, Richard A. 2001. *The Politics of Truth and Reconciliation in South Africa: Legitimizing the Post-Apartheid State.* Cambridge: Cambridge University Press.

Wolpe, Harold. 1972. Capitalism and cheap labour power in South Africa: From Segregation to Apartheid. *Economy and Society* 1(4): 425–56.

Zelizer, Viviana. 1995. *The Social Meaning of Money: Pin Money, Paychecks, Poor Relief, and Other Currencies.* New York: Basic Books.

Zhang, Li. 2008. Private homes, distinct lifestyles: Performing a new middle class. In *Privatizing China: Socialism from Afar*, eds. Li Zhang and Aihwa Ong, 23–40. Ithaca, NY: Cornell University Press.

Index